How to
Master
the UKCAT

How to
Master
the UKCAT

700+ Practice Questions

Mike Bryon, Dr Chris Tyreman,
Jim Clayden, Dr Christopher See

5th edition

KoganPage

LONDON PHILADELPHIA NEW DELHI

First published in Great Britain and the United States in 2009 by Kogan Page Limited as *How to Pass the UKCAT* Second edition published as *How to Master the UKCAT*, 2010
Third edition 2011
Fourth edition 2013
Fifth edition 2015
Reprinted 2015

2nd Floor, 45 Gee Street	1518 Walnut Street, Suite 1100	4737/23 Ansari Road
London EC1V 3RS	Philadelphia PA 19102	Daryaganj
United Kingdom	USA	New Delhi 110002
www.koganpage.com		India

© Mike Bryon and Jim Clayden, 2009
© Mike Bryon, Chris Tyreman and Jim Clayden 2010, 2011, 2013
© Mike Bryon, Chris Tyreman, Jim Clayden and Christopher See, 2015

The right of Mike Bryon, Chris Tyreman, Jim Clayden and Christopher See to be identified as the authors of this work have been asserted by them in accordance with the Copyright, Designs and Patents Act 1988.

ISBN   978 0 7494 7374 7
E-ISBN 978 0 7494 7375 4

British Library Cataloguing-in-Publication Data

A CIP record for this book is available from the British Library.

Library of Congress Cataloging-in-Publication Data

Bryon, Mike, author.
    How to master the UKCAT : 700+ practice questions / Mike Bryon, Chris John Tyreman, Jim Clayden, Christopher See. – Fifth edition.
        pages cm
    ISBN 978-0-7494-7374-7 (paperback) – ISBN 978-0-7494-7375-4 (ebk)   1. UK Clinical Aptitude Test–Study guides.   I. Tyreman, C. J., author.   II. Clayden, Jim, author.   III. See, Christopher, author. IV. Title.
    R838.5.B79 2015
    610.76–dc23

                                                                            2015000571

Typeset by Graphicraft Limited, Hong Kong
Print production managed by Jellyfish
Printed and bound by Ashford Colour Press Ltd

Contents

Introduction

The UKCAT (United Kingdom Clinical Aptitude Test) is a compulsory test for all applicants to Medical and Dentistry schools. The test is split into five sections and lasts for two hours. It is entirely on-screen and multiple choice. Verbal Reasoning (VR) is taken first, followed by Quantitative Reasoning (QR), Abstract Reasoning (AR), Decision Analysis (DA) and finally Situational Judgement (SJ). There is no pass mark. Instead, only the higher-scoring candidates are invited to an interview. Please visit the UKCAT website at www.ukcat.ac.uk to find all the information you need about the UKCAT. You can also visit www.pearsonvue.co.uk to learn more about UKCAT test centres.

UKCAT test format (may vary)

Section	Number of Questions	Time allowed
VR	44	22 min
QR	36	25 min
AR	55	14 min
DA	28	32 min
SJ	67	27 min
Totals	230	120 min

Verbal reasoning tips

The verbal reasoning section is the lowest scoring section for the majority of candidates. There are 11 texts and 44 questions. Do not spend time reading the passages carefully from start to finish. Instead, read each question first noting the key words (eg names, numbers and verbs) or phrases. Read the passage quickly by placing your finger on the screen, starting at the centre of the top line. Scan the text quickly as you move your finger down, looking for the relevant information without reading every word. Do not expect a simple lead-in question to begin with. A solid start is important so skip any long passage (eg 350+ words), flagging it for review. Return to the question at the end of the test and if you are unable to make a decision then choose the 'Can't tell' option or make a guess. You have a one in three chance of choosing the correct answer in the verbal reasoning section.

Quantitative reasoning tips

In this section you have to extract and analyse data from graphs, charts, tables, diagrams and text. You can gain marks quickly by skipping the more challenging questions in favour of those that are more obvious or need fewer steps. Make sure that you know how to use the on-screen calculator and how to minimize it without losing the information displayed. The calculator is a basic one that performs a single arithmetic process, so write down partial answers in the laminated booklet provided; do not try to hold too much information in your head.

Make sure that the marker pen you are given is working. Raise your hand to attract the attention of the test centre staff if you need a new pen or a second booklet.

The number work is only of GCSE standard but conceptualizing the problem can be difficult. You need to read the question carefully, identify the relevant data and then decide what to do with it. Take a look at the answer choices before making any calculations. You have a one in five chance of choosing the right answer, so try to eliminate any wrong answers.

Revise fractions, decimals, percentages, percentage change, ratios, graphs, charts (eg bar, line and pie), areas and volumes, and speed, distance and time (SDT) calculations. Refresh your mental arithmetic skills so that you can add, subtract, multiply and divide numbers without always having to use the calculator or write things down. Arithmetic techniques such as 'adding back' and 'place value' should be familiar to you, for example:

Adding back: $2350 - 185 = 2350 - 200 + 15 = 2165$

Place values: $860 \div 4 = (800 \div 4) + (60 \div 4) = 200 + 15 = 215$

Abstract reasoning tips

In this section the candidate has to identify the relationships between various shapes in two sets (A and B) and then match shapes with the correct set. There are six boxes of shapes per set and the boxes have something in common. The best tip for this section is to practice as many questions as possible because it is impossible to say exactly what patterns will appear. You have less than 15 seconds per question but this is enough time once you have established the relationship between the boxes. Do not look at the five questions initially, only the sets. Study set A and find the common relationship between the shapes in each of the six boxes, then study set B to find a different relationship; and finally, classify each of the five question shapes as belonging to either set A, set B or neither set. You have a one in three chance of choosing the correct answer.

Decision analysis tips

You are presented with a table of codes in the form of letters, numbers and symbols matched to a word, typically a noun or verb. Some of the codes may be described as operators and others as basic or specialist codes but the type of code plays no part in its deciphering. Translate the code literally in English and write the more complex elements on the whiteboard. Compare the translated code with its five possible interpretations to find the closest match. The answer is found by eliminating the incorrect translations; for example, those that lack components that appear in the code or those that add words not coded for. Skip the questions that ask you to choose the best code for a given message or to choose additional code words that are helpful in translating a message, because these questions take longer; mark them up for review. You have a one in five chance of choosing the correct answer.

Situational Judgement tips

This final section of the test can be the most disconcerting because it can be difficult to select the best answer with a high degree of confidence. However, your first step is to decide whether a response is broadly right (A, B) or broadly wrong (C, D) because a partial mark is awarded if your answer is close to the correct answer. Some of the responses may appear very different to each other though they could be equally appropriate. You might find yourself selecting four A's or four D's for example. Be aware that the response may not be the one that you would have made in similar circumstances but it could still be very appropriate. Always choose the best response even if what it says appears untimely, for example it could have waited until later or would have been better done sooner. You have a one in four chance of choosing the best answer and a one in two chance of at least a partial mark.

Ten top tips for UKCAT

1 Book a test early in the year to allow you to re-book if you have to cancel though illness on the day of the test. Even a headache or a cold will blunt your performance especially if you are dosed with medication. Make sure that you are properly hydrated.

2 Locate the test centre in advance so that you know exactly where it is and how long it takes to get there. Arrive 15 to 30 minutes early. Do not rush to the venue, looking for the entrance or where to park the car.

3 Take your UKCAT registration document to the test centre and make sure that your photo ID and the personal details match those that you registered with.

4 Check that the marker pen will write on the double-sided whiteboard. Do not use the board excessively, but if you fill it you can request another one by raising it above your head.

5 Ask for headphones or earplugs if you find the room too noisy; otherwise headphones are not required for the UKCAT.

6 There is no negative marking of incorrect answers in the UKCAT, so never leave any questions unanswered.

7 Flag questions for review later if they appear too challenging. If in doubt, trust your intuition and stick with your first answer.

8 Practice your mental arithmetic skills because overuse of the calculator in the QR section wastes precious time.

9 A good score is required in all sections of the test so identify your weakest section and keep practising.

10 Devote plenty of time to UKCAT preparation so that you feel confident about taking the test.

CHAPTER 1

Verbal reasoning

For a sizable minority of candidates, tests of verbal reasoning are their worst nightmare. Often these individuals are accomplished in, for example, science or mathematics but they can do little better than realize the norm rating in these common verbal tests. If you are the sort of candidate who will shine in the quantitative reasoning and abstract reasoning tests but fear that you will struggle with the verbal reasoning paper of the UKCAT, now is the time to get down to some serious score-improving practice.

The verbal reasoning sub-test comprises a series of passages followed by questions. Each question is a statement, and your task is to decide whether, according to the passage, the statement is true or false or whether you cannot tell if it is true or false. Typically these questions require you to comprehend meaning and significance, assess logical strength, identify valid inference, distinguish between a main idea and a subordinate one, recognize the writer's intention and identify a valid summary, interpretation or conclusion.

The subjects of the passages are drawn from a great many fields, such as current affairs, business, science, the environment, economics, history, meteorology, health and education. In fact, expect almost any subject. If you know something of the area, take care not to use your own knowledge. Be especially careful if you know a great deal about the subject or if you believe the passage to be factually incorrect or controversial. You are expected to answer the questions using only the information the passage contains. It is not a test of your general knowledge, your knowledge of the latest findings in the discipline or your political views. So feel completely at ease about answering true to a statement that is true in the very limited context of the passage even if you know that it is false given what you have learnt at university or read in a newspaper that morning.

When publishers of real tests develop an advanced verbal reasoning test they rely on fine distinctions between the suggested answers in order to distinguish between the scores of the large numbers of candidates. These distinctions are much finer than those we draw on a day-to-day basis. As a result, it is common for candidates to feel irritation and complain that these tests are to a large extent arbitrary. And in a way they are, for after all this is not how we use language at work or anywhere else but in the surreal world of tests. This is something you just have to accept and get used to, and with practice you will get to recognize the subtle distinctions being drawn.

Take care not to err too much towards the 'can't tell' suggested answer by making the mistake of applying too strict or too inflexible a test of proof. Be sure to read the questions as carefully as you read the passage and learn to pick up the many clues provided in the wording of it. For example, if the passage refers to 'a valid argument, inference or premise' or asks 'Is it necessarily the case that...?', apply a strict criterion of proof. However, if the question asks 'Is it reasonable...?', 'On the balance of prob- ability...?', 'Might the author...?', then apply a less strict criterion. You will soon master these subtle differences and gain the necessary confidence to make the correct judgements.

If, when taking lots of time in the relaxed conditions of your home, you find these questions easy, take care that you do not slip into a false sense of security. In the real test you will be pressed for time and may well be suffering from some anxiety. You should aim at undertaking just one careful read of the passage before referring back to it in order to answer the question. Some people find it helps to read the questions before the passage.

There are 156 practice questions in this chapter. They are organized as 60 warm- up questions, six mini-tests and a full-length practice test. You will find hundreds more verbal reasoning questions and full-length verbal reasoning practice tests ideal for practice for the UKCAT verbal reasoning sub-test in *The Verbal Reasoning Test Workbook*; *How to Pass Advanced Verbal Reasoning Tests*; *The Graduate Psycho- metric Test Workbook*; and *How to Pass Graduate Psychometric Tests*, 3rd edition, all published by Kogan Page.

Warm-up questions

Your studies to date should mean that you are perfectly able to comprehend the pas- sages in the UKCAT verbal reasoning sub-test. But, as we have already noted, verbal reasoning questions are not simply a test of comprehension they are also about making judgements and drawing inference and this you may be less well practised in. These warm-up questions will help you learn to draw accurate interpretations and make correct decisions based on the given information. Look at this warm-up section as practice for this aspect of the verbal reasoning paper which candidates find most challenging. Then, practise more against time with the mini tests and full-length timed test that follow.

The aim of this practice is to make you feel more confident when answering verbal reasoning questions of the type found in the UKCAT. Practise these questions without a time limit and in an informal relaxed situation. This section includes some deliberately hard material, so don't expect to get all the questions right. Refer to the answers and explanations as often as you like, and take time thinking about the question and passage before selecting your answer. Feel free to check the precise meanings of the words you are unsure of in a dictionary or thesaurus. However, remember to use the information in the passage to answer the questions, so if you use a dictionary to check the meaning of a word and a question asks, for example, about the author's intended meaning or how a term or phrase is used then be sure to refer only to the passage in deciding your answer and leave the dictionary aside.

Passage 1

Towns that have become popular with commuters and second-home owners are valued for their housing stock, schools and unspoilt civic centres. It is now possible for working families to relocate away from cities without affecting their earning power. Commuting three days a week and working from home the rest has meant that many more people are willing to give up the city life and move to more rural areas to fulfil their dream of homes with gardens and cricket on the green. So many metropolitan dwellers have made the move that property prices in the more popular locations have become amongst the most expensive in the country.

However, commuting comes with disadvantages too, and the question is whether these are compensated by the benefits so that personal well-being is enhanced overall. Compared to those who work from home, surveys have shown that commuters are less satisfied with their lives, less happy and have higher anxiety. The situation will vary for each individual and one factor is the length of time people commute for. Each minute of travel time affects the sense that one's activities are worthwhile, and after the first 15 minutes emotions are adversely affected, with anxiety rising. After half an hour activities seem less worthwhile and life less satisfying. However, people still continue to commute, even when the burdens are very high.

Q1 New technology is the reason why it is possible for working families to relocate without affecting their earning power.

True ☐   False ☐   Can't tell ☐

Q2 These locations have only become popular because it is possible to commute to work from them even if it is only for just part of the week.

True ☐   False ☐   Can't tell ☐

Q3   An idea of an unspoilt civic centre could include, along with cricket on the green, a traditional high street with local shops.

   True ☐   False ☐   Can't tell ☐

Q4   Although there are downsides to commuting, commuters find that the benefits outweigh the disadvantages.

   True ☐   False ☐   Can't tell ☐

Passage 2

Asparagus is a perennial and wild asparagus is found growing in light, well-drained soil across Europe, northern Africa and central Asia. People from all over the world enjoy eating it. The most sought-after domesticated varieties are from Canada and they prefer a soil with a ph of around 6.5. The domesticated varieties grow best in a humus-rich medium and will then each produce around half a kilo of crop. In the spring the plant sends up the spears that if left will open to form new foliage but for the first six weeks of each season these are cut when they are around 10 centimetres tall. After the cutting season the spears are allowed to mature so that the plants can re-establish themselves. The spears of the cultivated varieties are far thicker than those that grow in the wild and the crown (the shallow root ball) much larger, but the flavour of wild asparagus is superior. In the autumn the female plants fruit to produce small inedible berries.

A variety of problems can affect the cultivation of asparagus. Pests include slugs, snails and asparagus beetle. The winged asparagus beetle is 6–8mm long, black with a red thorax and yellow blotches. Its larger (10mm) larvae are grey in colour. Both larvae and mature beetle feed on the plant, stripping bark and leaves from the stem and leaving it desiccated and yellow-brown. Removal by hand or use of insecticides can minimize their damage, and during the winter, beetles may be eradicated by burning the old stems.

Q5   There are three kinds of pest that affect asparagus.

   True ☐   False ☐   Can't tell ☐

Q6   All asparagus plants like a soil with a ph of 6.5.

   True ☐   False ☐   Can't tell ☐

Q7   It can be inferred from the passage that when the author describes the fruit as inedible he means that it is unpalatable.

   True ☐   False ☐   Can't tell ☐

Q8   Asparagus only grows in Europe, northern Africa and central Asia.

True ☐   False ☐   Can't tell ☐

Passage 3

A declining population can lead to economic problems such as lower overall tax receipts, a falling industrial output and difficulty paying off national debt. Ensuing fiscal crises can lead to social and political instability. It can be argued that when assessing a nation's overall strength, more populous countries tend to be more powerful and those with smaller populations less so. However, immigrants can also be seen as a drain on resources, particularly healthcare and education.

When each year an average of 500,000 immigrants entered the UK, the Home Office calculated that the fiscal benefit of this level of inward migration was £2.5 billion a year. This calculation was used extensively by the government of the day to support their immigration policies. The findings of the Home Office stood out against the findings of other Western nations which found the benefits of large-scale inward migration to be so small as to be close to zero. The difference in the findings arose because the Home Office figure was based only on the effect of inward migration on the country's total Gross Domestic Product (GDP), while the other studies measured the effect on GDP per head. However, the Home Office calculation was obviously flawed, and they have since stopped using it, because immigration manifestly increases both the total GDP and the population. While the overall effect of inward migration may be negligible nationally in fiscal terms, the indigenous low paid and low skilled stand to lose out because as a consequence of the inward migration they face greater competition for work. Some employers have much to gain from the improved supply of labour and savings made from not having to train young people.

Q9   It can be inferred from the passage that without immigration a country's population will decline, causing economic problems.

True ☐   False ☐   Can't tell ☐

Q10   It is no longer the case that half a million immigrants enter the country.

True ☐   False ☐   Can't tell ☐

Q11   While nationally in fiscal terms the overall effect of inward migration may be negligible, at least no one loses out if inward migration occurs.

True ☐   False ☐   Can't tell ☐

Q12   There are no clear winners in an economy experiencing large-scale inward migration.

True ☐   False ☐   Can't tell ☐

Passage 4

Jupiter orbits the sun every 12 years and is five times the distance of Earth from the sun. It is a huge gaseous planet with a rocky core twice the size of Earth and has four principal moons, Io, Europa, Ganymede and Callisto. These moons were first recorded by Galileo in 1609. The Italian astronomer and philosopher Galileo was a controversial figure. His account of Jupiter's moons confounded the astronomical principles of the day, in particular the belief that all heavenly bodies should circle the earth. He played a major role in shaping modern science, recognized by the fact that the satellites of Jupiter were named 'The Galilean moons'. The outer reaches of our solar system contain three giant gaseous planets, the others being Uranus and Neptune which both lie beyond Jupiter. Uranus takes 84 years to orbit while Neptune takes 165 years. These planets were visited by Voyager space probes between 1979 and 1989 and all were found to have distinctive rings, satellites (or moons) and experience enormous storms in their upper atmospheres identifiable as large white or coloured rotating spots, some of which last for months or even years. Voyager missions 1 and 2 were part of a US space programme that took place in the late 1970s in order to exploit the favourable alignment of the planets. Both took photographic images that far exceeded anything previously captured. 19,000 pictures were taken by Voyager 1, and 33,000 by Voyager 2. Scientists were surprised by many of the findings, particularly the discovery of active volcanoes on the satellite Io.

Q13   Photographs from Voyagers 1 and 2 proved the existence of active volcanoes.

True ☐   False ☐   Can't tell ☐

Q14   The huge gaseous planets of the outer reaches of our solar system have rocky cores.

True ☐   False ☐   Can't tell ☐

Q15   A telescope will bring into view some of the detail of Jupiter's rings.

True ☐   False ☐   Can't tell ☐

Q16   Of the three gaseous planets, Neptune is the furthest from the sun.

True ☐   False ☐   Can't tell ☐

Passage 5

If anyone was surprised when the US dollar eventually weakened it was only because it did not happen sooner. People can live beyond their means for quite some time before they run out of credit and so they must start to address the accumulated debt. An enormous economy like that of the United States can live beyond its means for years and accumulate an enormous amount of debt before the inevitable happens. The correction to the exchange rate of the US dollar occurred when too many of the dollars held by the United States' creditors were sold. The American central bank responded to the crisis by lowering interest rates, which triggered further selling as investors sought higher returns in alternative currencies. The emergent Chinese and Indian economies have also contributed to the weakness of the dollar. Rising living standards in those countries have led to their currencies strengthening. The dollar is trading against the currencies of these fast-developing nations at a much lower historic rate and this is a trend that is bound to continue.

China's economy expanded 7.0 per cent last year. It is projected to grow 6.4 per cent this year and 6.2 per cent next year (2016); this compares with 6.9 per cent and 6.8 per cent forecast three months ago. While the figures suggest China's projected slowdown will be more dramatic than previously thought, banking chiefs believe it is unlikely to have a major global impact.

Q17 China's economy expanded 7.0 per cent in 2014.

True ☐   False ☐   Can't tell ☐

Q18 Even if the US economy was free of debt, the dollar would have weakened and remained trading at below the historic rate at least against some of the world's currencies.

True ☐   False ☐   Can't tell ☐

Q19 The passage is about the possibility or otherwise of a US recession.

True ☐   False ☐   Can't tell ☐

Q20 For years people had predicted that the dollar would weaken.

True ☐   False ☐   Can't tell ☐

Passage 6

The giant wind turbines on the nearby hill supply the community with 8 million kilowatt hours of electricity each year. Several hundred homeowners have erected solar panels on their roofs to provide most of their summer-time hot water needs. Bio-waste is collected for fermentation to produce methane gas, which drives a local generator to augment the town's electricity needs when there is insufficient wind to fully power the turbines. Better insulation has cut the fuel requirements of many homes. Local generation in this isolated, rural community has led to saving on the investment cost of additional transmission lines in the national network. Further efficiencies are gained because the local production of power avoids losses to electrical resistance in the long-distance transmission of power.

Key to it all was a governmental energy-saving programme funded by the big six energy suppliers and electricity generators. The programme sought to significantly reduce the fuel bills of rural communities and improve the energy efficiency of rural housing stock. These objectives were achieved through the strategies community partnership working, targeting rural areas with concentrations of low income households and intensive action in clearly defined, specific areas.

A number of residents had refused to participate in the programme and did so for reasons which included the anticipated distress and disruption the works might cause and a desire not to change their current heating and insulation systems. Some who initially refused later changed their minds.

Q21   The passage describes two objectives and three strategies to the government's energy-saving programme.

True ☐   False ☐   Can't tell ☐

Q22   The motives for this community's investment in the local generation of its energy needs are rising fuel costs and climate worries.

True ☐   False ☐   Can't tell ☐

Q23   When the wind is blowing and the sun is shining, locally generated power accounts for most of this community's energy needs.

True ☐   False ☐   Can't tell ☐

Q24   This isolated rural community is located in a part of the world where there is no national power network.

True ☐   False ☐   Can't tell ☐

Passage 7

Outsourcing involves the contracting out of a business activity and began in the United States in an effort to find cost-savings. An example would be to outsource book-keeping to an independent accounting firm when it is cheaper than retaining an in-house accounting clerk. In the last few decades it has gained a multinational dimension whereby businesses outsourced activities, and the jobs associated with those activities, across national borders and even continents.

The outsourcing of jobs to India from Europe and the United States has evolved from giving them relatively low-skilled work to passing on highly skilled roles. Multinationals have decreased the number of employees in Europe and the United States that undertake engineering design, science and software writing and instead now employ tens of thousands of skilled Indian workers in these challenging roles. Some are establishing second headquarters in the country because they have so many senior executives working on key projects there. The shift is in part due to it being easier in India to fill highly skilled, English-speaking positions and because, for the time being anyway, the wages for these roles are notably lower than wages in Europe and the United States. But it is also because companies want to position their businesses where they believe the future lies. India is one of the world's three biggest pools of highly skilled English-speaking labour and some commentators believe that as many as 30 million European and US skilled jobs are at risk of being moved.

Q25   If highly skilled Indian workers did not speak English, outsourcing these business activities to India would remain just as attractive.

True ☐   False ☐   Can't tell ☐

Q26   If more than 30 million European and US jobs were at risk of being moved to India then they would be skilled jobs.

True ☐   False ☐   Can't tell ☐

Q27   Three rationales for the outsourcing to India are portrayed.

True ☐   False ☐   Can't tell ☐

Q28   The claim that US and European jobs are being lost to India because Indian workers are prepared to work harder than their US and European counterparts is rebutted in the passage.

True ☐   False ☐   Can't tell ☐

Passage 8

All too often organizations jump onto the real-food bandwagon to cynically exploit the public's appetite to know more about where their food comes from and by whom and how it is grown. An example might be a pack of processed meat with a picture on the packaging of a farmhouse, a kind-looking farmer and country scene, even though its content is processed in a factory and made from meat that has been taken from countless farms and transported from all over the world. The inclusion of the names of animal breeds such as 'Andalusian' or 'Rhode Island' chicken compounds this deception, giving the impression that they are from a specific locale, whereas in reality they are merely the breed of chicken which could be grown in any battery farm. The same is sadly true with respect to the rise of responsible tourism. Tourists want a guilt-free holiday and so they prefer to use the services of a tour operator who is contributing to the local community and contributes to, rather than distracts, from the ecosystem they visit. An example might be a holiday resort that provides the land and building for a community school and employs local people in the resort. Visitors to the resort are encouraged to contribute to the running costs of the school and to fund the provision of a meal each day for the children.

Q29 The holiday resort is portrayed as an example of a tour operator who is cynically exploiting our appetite for responsible tourism.

True ☐   False ☐   Can't tell ☐

Q30 Tourists who don't want a guilt-free holiday enjoy themselves more.

True ☐   False ☐   Can't tell ☐

Q31 Tourists do not want to use the services of a tour operator who is contributing to the local community and ecosystem only because they want a guilt-free holiday.

True ☐   False ☐   Can't tell ☐

Q32 The example of deceptive labelling of animal breeds in food products cannot be similarly abused by responsible tourism companies because promoting the local community is a feature of what they advertise.

True ☐   False ☐   Can't tell ☐

Passage 9

A thing of beauty can completely lack physical form. We find some experiences beautiful despite their lack of physical appearance and we find some theories beautiful despite them being ideas that lack any physical structure. Perfume is the only beauty product that just plays on the emotions. We cannot see a scent and despite its complete lack of visual structure it can have an immediate and intimate effect. We can love or hate a smell for the image it elicits. A smell can evoke memories of an unhappy episode while someone else will identify it as warm and pleasing. We can be moved to describe a scent as beautiful because of the delicate impression or because of its zesty, exciting chemistry. Interestingly, a scent can smell different on different people. We can love a scent for the way it smells on others but hate the way it smells on us. The interplay of that individual's own unique blend of odours, from their own body processes, clothing and even the composition of the sweat on their skin can be wonderful or terrible in the final result, and each is never quite the same. The perfume we are provoked into calling beautiful is not something we can objectively decide. Freewill and personal choice play no part in the process.

Q33   Beauty is literally in the eye of the beholder.

True ☐   False ☐   Can't tell ☐

Q34   In the opening sentence of the passage, when it is said that '*a thing of beauty can completely lack physical form*' it means that it lacks physical structure.

True ☐   False ☐   Can't tell ☐

Q35   There are other beauty products that we cannot see.

True ☐   False ☐   Can't tell ☐

Q36   It is fair to say that two different people wearing the same perfume will certainly smell at least slightly different.

True ☐   False ☐   Can't tell ☐

Passage 10

Over $50 billion was spent shopping online last year and it is hardly surprising that criminals want a share of the action. No businessman or woman in his or her right mind would leave a shop unattended, unlocked and without an alarm and most take precautions to protect their virtual shops too, but not to the same degree of security. Many businesses do little more than install a firewall and antivirus and anti-spyware software and they believe this is all the security that is required. But the more recent developments in online threats are no longer guaranteed to be excluded by the most commonly available security software. The incentives for cyber-criminals are not only the monetary rewards, but the fact that digital fingerprints are far harder to trace than physical ones. By hiding behind virtual locations, involving launching their attacks from one area but routing it through servers in different countries, it can be very complex for anyone to trace the source of cyber-crime, whether or not the attempt at theft was successful. Retailers should take professional advice on the system and consider redirecting all of their inbound and outbound traffic to web security specialists who scan all traffic and block threats. Extra special care needs to be taken with the management of systems involved in the handling of payments by credit cards.

Q37 Online shopping offers the criminal the promise of rich pickings.

   True ☐   False ☐   Can't tell ☐

Q38 Firewalls and antivirus and anti-spyware software are the virtual equivalents of shop assistants, locks and alarms.

   True ☐   False ☐   Can't tell ☐

Q39 The antivirus and anti-spyware software updates automatically and so the business owner is led to believe that their security will remain up-to-date too.

   True ☐   False ☐   Can't tell ☐

Q40 The use of 'virtual locations' by criminals increases the chances of a theft being rewarded.

   True ☐   False ☐   Can't tell ☐

Passage 11

As an institution the British public house, usually called a pub, has a very long tradition of selling alcoholic drinks, in particular beer, which people consume on the premises. In recent years, however, profits of British pubs have fallen by 20 per cent and many have reported a further worsening of their financial state since the introduction of a new law and a series of tax increases. The new law involved the banning of smoking in public places, which has had a strong effect on reducing the number of new smokers in the general population and decreasing the numbers of current smokers, and was seen by the government, public health physicians and the public in general to be a good thing. However, one of the lesser publicized effects is that this has led to a marked decrease in pub custom. The increase in taxes involves a series of above-inflation rises in the duty charged on alcohol sold both in pubs and off-licences (the name of licensed premises allowed to sell alcohol for home consumption) that has markedly increased the cost of drinking alcohol. The combined effect of the smoking ban and increase in the alcohol duty are reported to have led to the loss of many jobs in the pub trade.

Q41 The author is opposed to the new laws and the effects they are having on the pub trade.

True ☐   False ☐   Can't tell ☐

Q42 It is reasonable to infer that some pubs are operating at a loss or at no profit.

True ☐   False ☐   Can't tell ☐

Q43 The smoking ban has encouraged traditional pub customers to drink and smoke less.

True ☐   False ☐   Can't tell ☐

Q44 The largest effect of the smoking ban was to decrease the number of current smokers rather than decreasing the number of new smokers.

True ☐   False ☐   Can't tell ☐

Passage 12

Taking recreational drugs in the privacy of your own home should be no one else's business but your own and yet the government has made it illegal. Millions of law-abiding citizens have used recreational drugs. Studies suggest that some 10 million people have used recreational drugs at some stage of their lives and 2 million use them on a regular and long-term basis. The studies suggest that it's not just young people who are recreational drug users either; most studies find that close to half the long-term users are over 24 years of age. Recreational drugs are classified into three categories according to the level of harm they cause. Penalties for possession of class C drugs, the lowest classification, include imprisonment for up to two years and an unlimited fine. Dealing in these drugs can result in imprisonment for up to 14 years. Possession of class A drugs can result in seven years' imprisonment. Cannabis, perhaps the most commonly used recreational drug, is soon to be reclassified as class B from its current classification of class C. This move has been supported by parent associations and NGOs which deem that so-called gateway drugs such as cannabis are one of the routes by which youths start on their path of drug use, moving on to higher classes of drugs over time.

Q45   It is not True to say that people who use recreational drugs are law-abiding citizens.

True ☐   False ☐   Can't tell ☐

Q46   The author of the passage does not agree that it should be illegal to use recreational drugs in the privacy of your own home.

True ☐   False ☐   Can't tell ☐

Q47   Dealing in all classes of these drugs can result in imprisonment for up to 14 years.

True ☐   False ☐   Can't tell ☐

Q48   Cannabis is called a gateway drug because it is cheaper than higher class drugs, and youths starting on it move on to other drugs after a while.

True ☐   False ☐   Can't tell ☐

Passage 13

In 1997 a previously long-dormant volcano on the Caribbean island of Montserrat erupted. This was triggered by subtle movements of tectonic plates which make up the Earth's crust, which are constantly in grinding motion against one another. Montserrat's location at the edge of two of these plates makes it susceptible to such movements, which caused a build-up of pressure within its liquid core sufficient to cause molten rock (lava) to breach the surface of the volcano. In just a few minutes a fast-moving lava flow surged down the mountain covering a great swathe, including the capital Plymouth. The lava was followed by mud slides and almost the whole of the south of the island was buried in a choking layer of ash. The residents of the capital and the affected parts of the island had been evacuated prior to the eruption. A great many lives were undoubtedly saved but 19 lives were still lost and everyone knew that life there would never be the same again. Thirteen years after the eruption only 4,000 of the original population of 12,000 remain.

Q49 Twenty years after the eruption only 4,000 people lived on the island.

True ☐   False ☐   Can't tell ☐

Q50 The evacuation prior to the eruption averted a disaster.

True ☐   False ☐   Can't tell ☐

Q51 It was 2010 when it was found that 4,000 of the original population remain.

True ☐   False ☐   Can't tell ☐

Q52 This volcano required a high pressure at its core in order to erupt.

True ☐   False ☐   Can't tell ☐

Passage 14

Ever since the dawn of space flight, mankind's nearest physical target was always the moon, and this became the finishing line of the early space-races between national space agencies from various countries. The early manned missions visited lowlands and plains while the later missions explored highlands. Selecting a suitable site was never going to be easy as even the apparently flattest of locations were found to be on closer inspection potholed from meteorite strikes and plastered with small boulders. The moon is rugged and very mountainous and in the 1960s a number of lunar probes had photographed the moon's surface during close orbit passes and even performed soft landings in the search for suitable sites for the manned missions that were to follow. In 1969 Neil Armstrong and Edwin Aldrin in Apollo 11 made the first ever manned lunar landing. The last manned landing was made in 1972 with Apollo 17. Since then, more distant goals have become the new target, with Mars being the next physical landmark. In addition to the considerable additional duration of time it would take to land there, endeavours to Mars have also been put off by considerations of cost, and importantly environmental considerations which cite the waste of energy in construction and fuel consumption which would be incurred in any manned mission to Mars.

Q53 The first lunar landing was made in the 1960s.

True ☐   False ☐   Can't tell ☐

Q54 Apollo 17 visited a mountainous region of the moon.

True ☐   False ☐   Can't tell ☐

Q55 When referring to a 'suitable site' in the second sentence it means suitable sites for the landing of manned missions.

True ☐   False ☐   Can't tell ☐

Q56 It is fair to say that the environmental concerns regarding fuel consumption are flawed, because the fuel is consumed mostly in space and not in Earth's atmosphere.

True ☐   False ☐   Can't tell ☐

Passage 15

We suffer a suspension of judgement when we hand over a card to purchase something and spend funds that we intended to use for something essential or unintentionally create an unauthorized overdraft. These spur-of-the-moment lapses are more likely to occur when we pay for something electronically or with credit than with hard cash. This is because of a widely held perception that electronic money and credit are somehow not as real or valuable as notes and coins. Retailers play on this emotional weakness with offers of in-store cards and 'buy now pay later' deals. In particular, 'buy now pay later' deals which offer interest-free credit adds another layer of attraction, giving the perception of 'free money' to the purchaser. This makes a prospective product more appealing and customers more likely to buy, thereby offsetting any potential loss to the seller in offering seemingly consumer-friendly terms. But, nowhere is our Achilles' heel exploited more than on the internet where it is impossible to pay with ready money and perhaps the sites that have perfected this form of exploitation are those that offer gambling. The sites regulated by the Gaming Commission have safeguards but the unregulated sites set out to encourage people to stake more to recover their losses and do not provide facilities to allow the gambler to set limits on how much they will fritter.

Q57   We suffer a suspension of judgement whenever we hand over a card to purchase something.

   True ☐   False ☐   Can't tell ☐

Q58   Electronic money and credit have a lower psychological value than cash in your hand.

   True ☐   False ☐   Can't tell ☐

Q59   Sites unregulated by the Gaming Commission are unlicensed.

   True ☐   False ☐   Can't tell ☐

Q60   The use of interest-free credit periods incurs minimal losses to sellers.

   True ☐   False ☐   Can't tell ☐

Six mini-tests

The next 48 questions of this chapter are organized as six mini-tests. It is far better to practise little and often when preparing for a test and most people can find a few minutes without distraction to undertake one of these mini-tests. Each contains eight multiple-choice questions and you are allowed four minutes in which to attempt them. The first question is of average difficulty and they become progressively harder. This is what you can expect to happen in the real UKCAT. Use these questions to get down to some really serious score-improving practice and be sure of the very best start in your real UKCAT verbal reasoning paper.

Read the first passage and answer the questions that relate to it and, when you have very briefly rechecked your choice, enter your answer in the answer box and move on to the next question. Try to avoid going back to reconsider a previous answer because you will risk wasting precious time, so practise getting the answer right first time and move confidently on to the next question. You will find that each mini-test comprises two passages and each is followed by four questions (always making a total of eight).

Put away the dictionary and thesaurus and treat these mini-tests like a real test. Get the most out of this practice by setting yourself the personal challenge of trying to beat or, if you get all eight right, match your last score each time you take a mini-test. That way you will create a realistic, real-test feel. You will need to try very hard and take the challenge seriously if you are to really succeed in beating your previous best score or getting eight out of eight every time. Time management will be critical, so be sure to stick to the four-minute time limit and not spend too long on any one question, and practise making one careful detailed read of the passage to save on time going back to check detail. Keep practising until you consistently get all eight questions right. Achieve this and you can take strength from the fact that you are likely to make a very good start in your real UKCAT verbal reasoning paper. The only thing then left to do is to keep up that rate of success through to the end of the real tests!

Mini-test 1

Passage 1

The world's population is expected to increase to more than 10 billion by 2050. Having a child in the developed world has a greater environmental impact than having a child in the developing world. Likewise having a large family in the developed world has a far greater environmental impact than having a large family in the developing world. This is because a child born into the developed world is much more likely to go on to have a high carbon dioxide emission lifestyle given that they are more likely to take regular flights, drive cars, live in a large energy-hungry home and so on. This has led some campaigners to argue that families in the developed world should think far more seriously about the environmental consequences of having children and should elect or be encouraged to have fewer. Some have argued that supporting children in the developing world is predominantly reliant on subsistence agriculture, and the expansion of farming lands is often achieved by cutting down large amounts of rainforest. This could have a serious effect on carbon absorption by these rainforests, and also have a knock-on effect by disturbing the local ecosystem. However, others highlight the fact that rainforest is also removed to provide grazing for cattle destined for fast-food consumption in developed nations.

Q61 If it were the case that all of the world's future population growth was projected to occur in the developing world and that the population of most developed countries would have fallen if it wasn't for immigration, then the case made for smaller families in the developed world would be weakened.

True ☐   False ☐   Can't tell ☐

Q62 If families living in the developing world were to have fewer children then they too would make a major cut in their families' future carbon dioxide output.

True ☐   False ☐   Can't tell ☐

Q63   Transport is a greater contributor to negative environmental effects in developed countries compared to developed ones.

True ☐   False ☐   Can't tell ☐

Q64   Farming in developing countries is primarily driven by consumption in developed countries.

True ☐   False ☐   Can't tell ☐

Passage 2

To enjoy a comfortable retirement, many retired people recommend retiring on two-thirds of final salary and around 4 million workers have paid into pension schemes for the bulk of their working lives in order to realize this goal. Those who have contributed to a final salary pension scheme will reach that standard and in fact exceed it when the person's state pension is added to the equation. Those workers who have contributed to a pension scheme that lacks the final salary guarantee and instead depend on the investment value of their total contributions to purchase their pension on retirement are less fortunate. Even when their state pension is included the bulk of these people will retire on an income of around 40 per cent of their final salary. As for the remaining 11 million workers who have made little or no contribution to any other pension scheme than the compulsory state scheme, it is feared that they will find themselves dependent on means-tested benefits. One must consider the potential outcomes of living on a pension which is significantly below that which you are used to before deciding a pension strategy. Not only is physical comfort a factor, but social and psychological health have also been shown to make a direct impact as people on low pensions cannot afford to undertake the same social activities as they have before, which can lead to severe depression and withdrawal from society.

Q65   Four million workers will reach or exceed the standard where they retire on two-thirds of the final salary.

True ☐   False ☐   Can't tell ☐

Q66 Workers with pension schemes without the final salary guarantee will have to manage on a lot less than the amount thought to be needed for a secure retirement.

True ☐   False ☐   Can't tell ☐

Q67 The country to which the passage refers has a total population of 15 million.

True ☐   False ☐   Can't tell ☐

Q68 Comfortable retirement depends more on social and psychological health than physical wellbeing.

True ☐   False ☐   Can't tell ☐

End of test

Mini-test 2

Passage 1

Twice as many people live till they are 100 in France as in Britain. Yet the two countries have similar sized populations and have diets with similar amounts of fat. In fact life expectancy is considerably better in France from the age of 65 onwards and it seems that lifestyle and diet may have a lot to do with it. Leaving aside the fact that the French probably have the best national health service in the world, statistics suggest that the French remain active longer and consume more units of fruit and vegetables. They also enjoy considerably more glasses of red wine and it seems these differences give rise to far lower levels of death caused by heart disease and this allows significant numbers of people to live until their centenary. In contrast, drinking in Britain often seems to be associated with lower life expectancy, if it is treated simply as 'drinker' versus 'non-drinker'. However, a more sophisticated analysis reveals that drinking patterns at an early age can affect the life-expectancy of the average person. Binge drinking was defined as consuming 24 or more units in one session for males, or 21 units per session for females. Even as little as 15 episodes per year, over the course of four years, reduces the life expectancy by an average of five years. Binge patterns are far more prevalent in Britain than France, and the data seems consistent regardless of the type of alcohol consumed, even if it is similar to the French taste for red wine.

Q69   Four differences are attributed to the reason the French have a far lower level of death caused by heart disease: the best national health service, remaining active, consuming more fruit and vegetables and enjoying more red wine.

True ☐   False ☐   Can't tell ☐

Q70   Even if twice as many people in France see their centenary it may be that very few people live to see their 100th birthday in either country.

True ☐   False ☐   Can't tell ☐

Q71   If a female drank 315 units in a year for four years, one would expect a five-year reduction in life expectancy on average.

True ☐   False ☐   Can't tell ☐

Q72   It is fair to say that drinking culture in France and Britain have an impact on life expectancy, independent of the positive effects of red wine.

True ☐   False ☐   Can't tell ☐

Passage 2

Last year's summer was noteworthy for being very wet and very windy and yet neither of these qualities featured in the meteorological service's long-term forecast. We were advised that we could expect a typical summer with above-average temperatures and average or slightly above-average levels of rainfall. There was no mention whatsoever of the widespread flooding that occurred. This raises the question of whether the forecast was wrong and they in principle could have but did not forecast the exceptional weather or whether it is in principle impossible to forecast specific long-term exceptional events. Long-term forecasts are based on baseline averages over an extended period and trends in that baseline are used to build the forecast and predict, for example, if that trend is to continue. If extreme weather is occurring more frequently then it is feasible that the forecast might include the prediction that the frequency of these events will continue to be higher than the historic average. Short-term forecasts are far more focused on immediate and dynamic factors, which can be directly measured. Barometric pressure in particular can be used to give fairly accurate weather predictions 4–8 hours in advance of an event; however, the location of the measure-ments is very important, and it seems that short-term forecasts are most accurate in areas of high measurement such as the South East of England, whereas rural areas fall significantly below this level in the majority of cases.

Q73   It is a mistake to believe that the exceptional can be forecast over the long term.

True ☐   False ☐   Can't tell ☐

Q74   The summer of 2007 was noteworthy for being very wet and windy.

True ☐   False ☐   Can't tell ☐

Q75   It is not possible to predict long-term specific weather events such as the flooding last summer.

True ☐   False ☐   Can't tell ☐

Q76   Rural short-term weather forecasts are generally inaccurate.

True ☐   False ☐   Can't tell ☐

End of test

Mini-test 3

Passage 1

In almost zero gravity and no wind very large droplets of water can form. In normal atmospheric conditions and no wind droplets of around 2 millimetres diameter commonly occur. In normal conditions with wind smaller droplets form and the diameter of those found in a typical summer gale might measure less than one millimetre. In every situation droplets do collide and these combine to form larger droplets that may well survive but air resistance and the relatively weak surface tension of water mean that droplets with a diameter larger than 5 millimetres very quickly break up. Lightning is also a result of these collisions, and involves the transfer of electrons between drops in a manner similar to other static electricity phenomenon. The asymmetry of static charge builds up to a point where a discharge is inevitable, and this discharge is directly to the ground in the form of lightning. The rate of charge building up is dependent on the number of collisions of rain drops, and in turn the rate of collisions is inversely proportional to the size of the rain drops.

Q77 The claim that giant globules of water cannot form is rebutted by the passage.

True ☐   False ☐   Can't tell ☐

Q78 Droplets of between 2–5mm only occur in windless conditions.

True ☐   False ☐   Can't tell ☐

Q79 Static charge builds up more rapidly in wind than in a gale.

True ☐   False ☐   Can't tell ☐

Q80 In normal wind conditions, when droplets larger than 5 millimetres break up, the very small drops produced give rise to high levels of collisions, more rapid than those in a gale.

True ☐   False ☐   Can't tell ☐

Passage 2

So what is it that decides if a language is to endure or to be threatened with extinction? The number of languages spoken in the world is expected to continue to decrease dramatically but what decides the winners and the losers? Surprisingly some commentators argue that along with languages spoken by very small communities the really 'big' languages like English also face extinction. The case against the small linguistic community is obvious; if there is no one left to speak a language then that language dies. An example of this is Chimariko, which officially became extinct in 1922 after an outbreak of smallpox killed the last remaining enclave of speakers in Central America. With their strong oral traditions, so little written material was left that scholars were unable to fully 'revive' the language even if there was a population which wished to do so. The case against a dominant, apparently all-conquering, language like English is less apparent and is therefore so much more interesting. As more and more of the world speaks English it is inevitable, the argument runs, that it will break up first into dialects and then distinct languages linked only by their common linguistic heritage. This is a controversial point because it goes against the view that dialects need isolation before they can form (without isolation, speech is standardized by the dominant language promulgated through international science, engineering, medicine and business and worldwide printed and digital media and this squeezes out dialects).

Q81 The case made for the extinction of English derives from its worldwide dominance.

True ☐   False ☐   Can't tell ☐

Q82 Revival of a language which has gone extinct requires a sufficient quantity of written material.

True ☐   False ☐   Can't tell ☐

Q83 The passage does not answer the question asking what decides if a language is to endure or become extinct.

True ☐   False ☐   Can't tell ☐

Q84 The passage is ambivalent in respect to whether or not English will become extinct.

True ☐   False ☐   Can't tell ☐

End of test

Mini-test 4

Passage 1

At a university campus in 1971, 23 male volunteers spent two weeks role playing prisoners and guards. The volunteers were upright ordinary 'good' students, with no criminal or disciplinary records, and indeed no overt psychological evidence of a propensity towards cruelty. The exercise sought to explore the extent to which the external environment influences human behaviour and in particular our potential for evil. Early on in the experiment the guards started subjecting the prisoners to psychological and physical punishments. As the experiment proceeded the punishments got worse. Philip Zimbardo, the originator of the experiment, identified that conformity and anonymity were two of a number of factors that can bring about callous behaviour in otherwise caring people. Anonymity was important because it led the perpetrators to believe that they would not have to answer for their actions. Conformity was significant because it pressurized the more humane guards to adopt the behaviour of their less humane peers. Another of Zimbardo's factors was boredom.

Q85   In this experiment in social psychology there were more prisoners than guards.

   True ☐   False ☐   Can't tell ☐

Q86   The selection criteria for the volunteers was comprehensive in filtering out those with a predisposition towards punishment.

   True ☐   False ☐   Can't tell ☐

Q87   It would be wrong to deduce from the passage that women volunteers in the same circumstances would not act callously.

   True ☐   False ☐   Can't tell ☐

Q88   Two of Philip Zimbardo's factors that can bring about callous behaviour in otherwise caring people are identified.

   True ☐   False ☐   Can't tell ☐

Passage 2

Japan's population is projected to fall from the current almost 130 million to around 90 million by the middle of the next century and this smaller population will be faced with the added challenge that it will be disproportionately elderly. By then Japan's total GDP will be half that of India's and one-fifth the size of China's and Japan will have slipped to being the fifth largest super power in terms of the size of its GDP. Japan's answer to the challenge to its competitiveness is to seek out even greater innovation. It is currently very innovative if you measure it in terms of the number of patents registered and the amount spent on research and development. But in other measures of innovation it does not score so well. When compared to the European Union and the United States (currently the economic zones with the largest GDPs) its working practices are considered inflexible and it shuns foreign investment and cultural influences. The latter two are considered important because unless Japan engages in new ways of thinking and changes in worldwide values it is hard to see how it will remain the pioneer of bestselling products to future generations.

Q89 The big question for Japan is how it is to remain competitive.

True ☐   False ☐   Can't tell ☐

Q90 The tone of the passage suggests that the ability to engage in new ways of thinking can be attributed to India and China.

True ☐   False ☐   Can't tell ☐

Q91 The amount spent on research and development will decrease as Japan's overall GDP declines, reducing its current measure of innovativeness.

True ☐   False ☐   Can't tell ☐

Q92 If we count the EU as a single economic zone, if it is the fourth largest GDP by the middle of next century, and the United States retains its current relationship to all other countries, we can state that the order of countries by GDP size is the United States, China, India, EU and Japan.

True ☐   False ☐   Can't tell ☐

End of test

Mini-test 5

Passage 1

A general dictionary seeks to encompass an entire language and include entries for all the words of that language. Specialized dictionaries list the words specific to a career field or the vocabulary particular to a distinct part of a language (for example a legal dictionary or a dictionary of slang). A translation dictionary provides words in one language and its corresponding words from another while an encyclopedic dictionary offers greatly expanded definitions compared to general and translation dictionaries.

English is spoken as a first language by 400 million people and one in four of the world's population claims to speak elementary English. In an English dictionary the C section contains the second largest number of entries and is the second longest. The S section contains the largest number and the P section is the third largest in terms of entries. One of the shortest sections lists the words beginning with Q but the section with the fewest entries is the W. Italian is spoken by around 60 million people and in an Italian dictionary the sections J, K, Y and W are very short and contain only foreign words used in Italian while the U and Q sections contain the least number of Italian entries. The longest section in the Italian dictionary and the section that contains the most entries is the S section and the next longest is the C section.

Q93 You can deduce from the passage that 1.6 billion people claim to speak elementary English.

   True ☐   False ☐   Can't tell ☐

Q94 The S section of the Italian and English dictionaries both contain the largest number of entries.

   True ☐   False ☐   Can't tell ☐

Q95 In the English dictionary the S section is the longest.

   True ☐   False ☐   Can't tell ☐

Q96 The Q sections of both English and Italian dictionaries contain close to the fewest number of entries.

   True ☐   False ☐   Can't tell ☐

Passage 2

Andy, Betty, Charles, Diana, Edward, Fay, George, Hope. In an average hurricane season meteorologists in the Atlantic expect to name nine tropical storms. The christening of storms began when weather forecasts were broadcast over shortwave radio and naming them helped mariners to keep track of the weather system. The tradition evolved so that each successive storm was given a name beginning with successive letters of the alphabet. Initially only girls' names were used but later this was changed so that the names alternated from boy to girl names. If a named storm turns out to be particularly savage then the name may be dropped and not used in future years. The same system of naming storms is adopted in the north and south Pacific forecast regions.

They are called tropical because they form over tropical seas; in fact, NASA says that water temperatures must be 82 degrees Fahrenheit or warmer before one can form, however they don't form close to or at the equator. They are cyclonic and in the northern hemisphere their winds blow anti-clockwise while in the southern hemisphere their winds circulate in the opposite, clockwise, direction. Hurricane Andrew made landfall in the southern part of Florida and the Bahamas, with peak winds of 175mph while typhoon Haigan, with winds over 175mph, made landfall in the Philippines. As well as strong winds tropical storms bring large amounts of rain and high waves.

Q97 You can infer from the passage that the water close to or at the equator does not reach 82 degrees Fahrenheit or warmer.

True ☐   False ☐   Can't tell ☐

Q98 Andrew must have been the first named storm to occur that season.

True ☐   False ☐   Can't tell ☐

Q99 The list of names at the beginning of the passage could be the list of names used in a year that experienced an average hurricane season.

True ☐   False ☐   Can't tell ☐

Q100 When weather forecasts were broadcast over shortwave radio the storms were only given girls' names.

True ☐   False ☐   Can't tell ☐

End of test

Mini-test 6

Passage 1

Except for Nepal's, which is the shape of two connected triangles, all modern national flags are rectangular and their colours hark back to the days when flags were extensively used for identification and communication. They began as military standards and field signs, allowing combatants to identify their commander and mark out friends from foes. Such field signs included coloured tabards, a sash around the waist or over the shoulder. A ribbon or cockade pinned to the lapel or hat could be worn to show political allegiance, and some women wore this on their hat or in their hair. Outside the context of war, maritime flags were introduced in the early 17th century. By the late 18th century, nationalist sentiment in places such as the United States and the French Republic led to the displaying of flags in civilian context. Many countries adopted a national flag during the 19th and early 20th centuries, sometimes following independence.

Nowadays the colour red is intimately associated with the flags of nations born from left-wing political movements but at the time of the French revolution the tri-colour (blue, white and red) was the symbol of the fight for freedom and inspired the design of many national flags including, for example, those of the United States and the Republic of Ireland. In many instances green stands for Islam (along with the crescent moon) while the cross shape usually signifies a Christian nation. The pan-African movement adopted the colours of the Ethiopian national flag (green, yellow and red), the oldest independent African nation, and many African states when they emerged from colonialism adopted these colours.

Q101 The current Ethiopian national flag is coloured green, yellow and red and is rectangular.

True ☐   False ☐   Can't tell ☐

Q102 The reason given for most flags being rectangular is that in the past they were extensively used for identification and communication.

True ☐   False ☐   Can't tell ☐

Q103 Despite the fact that it is not, you can infer from the passage that the flag of the Republic of Ireland should be blue, white and red.

True ☐   False ☐   Can't tell ☐

Q104 Today symbolic designs as well as colours are used to convey meaning and identity on national flags.

True ☐   False ☐   Can't tell ☐

Passage 2

You can find out so much about people on the internet these days that civil liberty campaigners are arguing for new laws so that people can get back some vestige of control over their personal data. The 1998 Data Protection Act gives us the right to know the personal information companies are holding. But the new threat to personal liberty is quite the opposite – it is the threat of complete strangers finding out our personal details. Undertake an internet search on someone you know with any of the main search engines and you are likely to obtain thousands of results which if trawled through can provide particulars of employment, a work phone number and e-mail address. Find a CV belonging to that person and you will get hold of their home address, date of birth, home telephone number, personal e-mail address and a listing of their educational history and interests. If the person for whom you are searching is active on a social network site or an internet specialist-interest forum then you may well be able to identify a database of friends and contacts and by reading recent postings obtain a flavour of their views and preferences. Search the database of a genealogy site and you may well be able to identify generations of family members.

In 2014 the EU Court of Justice ruled that people have a right to be forgotten from internet search results and this was heralded as a victory for privacy. However, the ruling gave rise to a host of new sites which set about re-publishing the results which have been removed under the new ruling.

Q105 The Data Protection Act and the EU endorsed right to be forgotten from internet search results are the two main protections of personal privacy that exist.

True ☐   False ☐   Can't tell ☐

Q106 Sites which re-publish the results removed under the EU Court of Justice's ruling are infringing someone's rights.

True ☐   False ☐   Can't tell ☐

Q107 The threat to personal liberty is no longer one of secrecy and finding out what organizations know about us.

True ☐   False ☐   Can't tell ☐

Q108 The penultimate sentence of the passage illustrates the sort of things that people post on the internet.

True ☐   False ☐   Can't tell ☐

End of test

More UKCAT-style verbal reasoning

Hints and tips

As previously stated, this section of the aptitude test is based on English comprehension exercises. It requires a response to text, ie reading a passage of prose and then eliciting facts from it.

The material used for comprehension questions can be quite varied and the candidate is advised to read widely and to try to evaluate, particularly when reading a newspaper or textbook, what has actually been said. Another hint for preparation is to try and improve your reading speed without detracting from the understanding. The faster you can read the more time you have for answers.

In the UKCAT you are given passages of prose followed by a statement. You have to decide whether the statement is true, false, or impossible to say (can't say), based solely on the facts in the passage. The passages can vary in length, with most ranging between approximately 250 and 350 words.

When answering this type of question it is normal practice to read the passage through first, followed by the statement, before scanning back through the passage to find *key words or phrases* that relate to those of the statement. However, there is insufficient time in the UKCAT to read through the entire passage first so read the question and then scan through the passage for key words or phrases that fit with the statement. You have three choices:

True: the statement is clearly true, implied or a reasonable conclusion to draw.

False: the statement is clearly untrue, a distortion of the facts or an unreasonable conclusion to draw.

Can't tell: the statement lacks sufficient information to say whether it is true or false with any certainty.

Candidates are sometimes unsure when to use the answer 'can't tell' as opposed to true or false. The following example provides guidelines.

Example: conservative colours

Most people choose a conservative colour for their new car. According to one motoring organization, six out of ten people prefer silver, blue or red. In contrast, only one in ten people opt for white or green and only one in a hundred choose turquoise, yellow or pink. Car manufacturers have no desire to buck this trend and offer up to four shades of silver per model. If you order a silver car it can be ready in a week whereas a pink one can take up to three months to arrive.

With respect to the colour of new cars:

1	Most are silver, blue or red.	= True
2	Silver is one of the least popular.	= False
3	Silver is not as popular as blue.	= Can't tell
4	Silver is the most popular.	= Can't tell
5	Silver might be the most popular.	= True
6	Over half are silver, blue or red.	= True
7	Pink is one of the most popular.	= False
8	Pink is not as popular as yellow.	= Can't tell
9	Pink is the least popular.	= Can't tell
10	Pink might be the least popular.	= True
11	A silver car cannot be ready in a week.	= False
12	A pink car will be ready in a week.	= Can't tell
13	A pink car might be ready in a week.	= True
14	A pink car cannot be ready in a week.	= False

As a general principle, the answer is 'can't tell' (C) if there is uncertainty arising from the paragraph, ie it is impossible to indicate either true or false. Can't tell is also used when the question introduces new material that is not covered in the paragraph. The answer is likely to be true (T) or false (F) rather than 'can't tell' if the uncertainty arises in the question.

Read the following comprehension passage carefully then choose whether the statements are true, false or can't tell.

Passage 1

Modern society is increasingly less tolerant of racism in almost any setting. Racism can be defined in two slightly different ways, each of which manifests itself in complicated settings. Firstly and perhaps more simply, racism can be defined as acting in a manner which is discriminatory against certain racial groups. For example, activities which perpetuate unequal access to education or health for racial groups is racist, as is legislation which favours one group over another in terms of business or property ownership. The other form of racism is holding views that some racial groups have intrinsically better characteristics than others, and therefore are actually superior. Again, this has happened historically in Nazi Germany, but the belief that people from certain ethnic backgrounds are worse at some things than other races still continues today.

There are many steps which can be taken to try and tackle the problems that arise from racism. Affirmative action in the form of quota systems address the problem of inequality by fixing an amount of certain ethnic groups which must be admitted to certain jobs or institutions. Under such circumstances, regardless of the preferences of the admitting staff or ability of a candidate, the person of the nominated racial group is selected in favour of others until the quota is filled. Obviously, within each racial group that has a quota, the top candidates are selected as normal.

However, it becomes much more of a problem when people hold discriminatory views which are positive. One recent stand-up comedian has got into a lot of trouble over his routine which features many comments about how Oriental students are cleverer and more hardworking than others. He states that 'when I've got something good to say, I say it, and people laugh'. Some of the lead complainants to the TV station which carried material were Oriental persons themselves. The stand-up comedy community is divided in its support for this individual.

1   Acting in a manner which creates inequalities in access to universities, hospitals or general practice consultations is classified as racism.

   True ☐   False ☐   Can't tell ☐

2   Affirmative action, such as requiring a university to have a fixed quota for certain ethnic groups which are underrepresented, is racist.

   True ☐   False ☐   Can't tell ☐

3   Holding views which are positive about certain races are nevertheless racist.

   True ☐   False ☐   Can't tell ☐

4   There are many people who still hold racist views in various areas of society.

   True ☐   False ☐   Can't tell ☐

Passage 2

When medical students embark on their journey into undergraduate training, they often face a host of problems. These can often be to do with the workload, pressure to perform in exams, being away from their familiar home environment for the first time and so on. However, recently a few students have had problems regarding their conduct, particularly when it comes to online behaviour. One such story included a student missing a lecture and posting the following 'status' online:

Way too hungover to remain upright and listen at the same time! Someone pick me up a set of notes for Biochem 1 please.

This was brought to the attention of the tutor of this student, who then called him in to have a serious discussion. Clearly, as a medical professional of the future, this type of behaviour demonstrated a level of irresponsibility which is unsuitable, but even more problematic was his flagrant willingness to publicize this to others. Several studies have shown that so called 'Group Think' can emerge when one person 'gets away with' doing something negative, others immediately see that behaviour as being less negative.

The following rules were issued by the GMC for doctors and students with regards to social networking websites:

- You must never reveal confidential patient information.

- You should strive to maintain a professional impression in any online profile.

- Lying in order to miss classes or lectures is totally unacceptable and subject to disciplinary measures.

- Ensure you change your password regularly.

5   A doctor or medical student can be found to be in breach of the GMC rules if he or she presents an unprofessional impression on their Facebook profile.

True ☐   False ☐   Can't tell ☐

6   The main problems faced by medical students are being overworked, pressure to score highly in exams and being outside of a familiar environment.

True ☐   False ☐   Can't tell ☐

7   You should never reveal patient information of any kind online.

True ☐   False ☐   Can't tell ☐

8   In order to avoid disciplinary problems with such online networks, you should not 'add' your tutor as a friend, even if he has sent you a request.

True ☐   False ☐   Can't tell ☐

Passage 3

The Euro crisis is a problem borne of the greed of people. The Greek government is a democratically elected government, and since they represent the people through a two-thirds majority in the last election, its conduct represents those very same people. And the government has acted very greedily indeed.

In order to stay in elected office, a government needs to ensure votes, and this is usually achieved by enacting policies which are popular with the public. These include increasing wages, decreasing retirement and pension age and so on. They do not include austerity, sensible budgeting with diligent tax collection and high taxation. Sure, they might see the need to reduce a country's overall deficit, but realistically it is not a priority. The bottom line is that of leaving the Euro by default-ing on its debts and not being able to borrow money on the open markets. Even taking into account other considerations, this fact alone means that economic growth will continue to be at rock bottom for a very long period of time.

And its interaction with the rest of the Eurozone is relatively complex. There are those who think that over-inflated public sector wages are the main cause of the current crisis, and others who say that a lack of tax collection has a substantial contribution.

Tourism in Greece is one of the major trades, and we expect that if it converts over to the Drachma, then holiday-makers will benefit from low prices for everything from, accommodation to food, and flock there in droves. This input of extra spending will help the Greek economy in its efforts to rebuild itself in the years immediately after its exit from the Euro.

9   There are many who believe that over-inflated public sector wages and lack of tax collection are main problems.

   True ☐   False ☐   Can't tell ☐

10   The majority of Greek people are greedy.

   True ☐   False ☐   Can't tell ☐

11   Things such as the improvement in tourism will allow the Greek economy to recover in the years after an exit from the Euro.

   True ☐   False ☐   Can't tell ☐

12   In order to achieve popularity, governments must enact policies which are popular.

   True ☐   False ☐   Can't tell ☐

Passage 4. Weighty problem

The World Health Organisation (WHO) reports that obesity has reached epidemic proportions worldwide with three times as many overweight adults as there were 20 years ago. Almost one-quarter of the adult population of the UK are now classed as obese and they are over-represented in their use of NHS services.

The most widely used tool to assess obesity is Body Mass Index (BMI), which divides weight in kilograms by height in metres squared to give the units kg/m^2. A BMI of 25 or above is defined as overweight or pre-obese and a BMI of 30 or more is defined as obese. People with a BMI of 40 or above are morbidly obese; they are at severe risk of developing co-morbidities like cardiovascular disease and type 2 diabetes which reduce life expectancy and increase hospital stay. Patients weighing more than 20 stone are described as bariatric – the word originated from the Greek word *baros* meaning heavy and *iatrics* meaning medical treatment. The large size of bariatric patients often leads to poor mobility with implications for manual handling, equipment, beds, chairs and space.

Most bariatric patients will have a BMI in excess of 40 though not all bariatric people will be morbidly obese nor will every person with a BMI over 30 be obese. For example, a six-foot-five rugby player weighing 21 stone (BMI = 35) with a muscular build and a good weight distribution might be athletic. In these larger people the waist to hip ratio can serve as a more reliable indictor of a weight problem. A ratio of 1.0 or more is consistent with an excess of fat around the waist and the need to lose weight. From a health perspective, maximum safe waist measurements are reported as 40 inches (102 cm) for men and 35 inches (89 cm) for women irrespective of fat distribution.

13   At least one-quarter of obese adults use NHS services.

    True ☐   False ☐   Can't tell ☐

14   A patient with a BMI of between 25.0 and 29.9 is pre-obese.

    True ☐   False ☐   Can't tell ☐

15   A patient with a hip to waist ratio of 1.1 is obese.

    True ☐   False ☐   Can't tell ☐

16   A patient with a waist measurement over 40 inches is obese.

    True ☐   False ☐   Can't tell ☐

Passage 5. Healthy minds

Mental health problems are the second largest cause of people taking time off work, outnumbered only by muscle-related problems such as back injuries. Depression and anxiety are the most common problems. Less well-known, less common ailments include bi-polar disorder, schizophrenia and paranoia. Stressful life events, suppression of feelings or a difficult family background can lead to neuroses, like depression and anxiety. A family history of mental illness or an imbalance in the body's chemicals may be associated with psychoses such as schizophrenia and bi-polar disorder (formerly manic-depression). The first point of contact with the NHS is usually the doctor's surgery. The patient's GP will try to identify the cause of the problem and treat it. Only 5 per cent of people are referred to a consultant psychiatrist and of these, many are seen at the out-patient clinic. Psychiatric wards are under the control of a consultant psychiatrist who works with a team that includes psychiatric nurses, social workers and occupational therapists.

Psychotic illness can be treated with psychotropic drugs that alter mood, perception and behaviour. With neurosis, psychotherapy sessions encourage a person to talk freely about his or her feelings, and to relate to the experiences that lie behind the distressed state. Most people recover completely from mental distress but some become chronically ill and will always require medication.

Emphasis is placed on care in the community either in people's own homes or in supported housing. Community Psychiatric Nurses (CPNs) visit people at home to provide support through difficult times and to help with medication regimes. Social Workers can assist with housing and financial issues as well as transport, meals and daily chores. Self-help groups and mental health charities like MIND and SANE provide free services for people with mental health problems.

17 Schizophrenia can run in families.

True ☐   False ☐   Can't tell ☐

18 In the NHS, most people with mental health problems attend an out-patient clinic.

True ☐   False ☐   Can't tell ☐

19 A psychiatrist is a qualified medical doctor that works with a team of healthcare professionals.

True ☐   False ☐   Can't tell ☐

20 Psychotherapy could be described as a 'talking treatment'.

True ☐   False ☐   Can't tell ☐

Passage 6. Time and temperature

Food poisoning is still prevalent in the United Kingdom with more than 90,000 reported cases in 2007, though unreported cases could be as much as 10 times higher because most people with mild symptoms fail to report the incident. Millions of bacteria are needed to produce food poisoning. Under favourable conditions, rapid multiplication takes place by binary fission every 10 to 20 minutes. Pathogenic bacteria can grow at temperatures as low as 5°C and as high as 63°C; food kept in this 'danger zone' should never be re-heated. Fridges and cold stores at 1 to 4°C stop the multiplication of pathogenic bacteria but not of food spoilage bacteria. The latter can continue to grow at temperatures as low as minus 18°C below which they remain dormant. Bacteria are not destroyed by freezing and can multiply again after the food thaws out.

Campylobacter is responsible for most of the food poisoning in the United Kingdom with about four times as many cases as occur with salmonella. Campylobacter is also referred to as a 'food-borne' disease because it remains dormant at room temperature but multiplies rapidly at body temperature (37°C); it is destroyed at temperatures above 48°C. Most cases of salmonella food poisoning are caused by storing prepared food at room temperature. Salmonella is quickly destroyed at temperatures above 74°C. Other food-borne pathogens include listeria, E. coli and Clostridium perfringens which is spore forming and can survive cooking.

Both Campylobacter and salmonella are associated with raw meat, poultry, eggs and unpasteurised milk. Examples of cross-contamination include kitchen staff failing to wash their hands when taking eggs out of the fridge, a drop of juice from a fresh chicken at the top of the fridge contaminating cooked foods below, and using the same chopping board to prepare meat and vegetables. Spread is not normally from person to person.

21   Pathogenic and food spoilage bacteria remain dormant below minus 18°C.

    True ☐   False ☐   Can't tell ☐

22   A single cell of Campylobacter can multiply to more than one thousand bacteria in less than two hours on food at room temperature.

    True ☐   False ☐   Can't tell ☐

23   The ingestion of a small number of Campylobacter cells could make you ill.

    True ☐   False ☐   Can't tell ☐

24   Heating food to 75°C will destroy most bacteria responsible for food poisoning in the United Kingdom.

    True ☐   False ☐   Can't tell ☐

Passage 7. Pennies make pounds

In business, it's not just what you spend and earn that counts; it's how you account for it as well. The accounts of a simple business might just keep track of what has been paid out, what has been received and what is due in. Even so, it is easy to get in a mess. A business makes goods or provides a service. It then needs to record the sale invoices sent out in the Sales Day Book and in the customers' Sales Ledger Account (Debtors' account). Upon payment of the invoice the payment is recorded in the Cash Book and in the customers' Sales Ledger Account.

A business will also receive goods or use a service. It then needs to record the invoice received in the Purchase Day Book and in the suppliers' Purchase Ledger Account. On paying the invoice the payment is recorded in the Cash Book and in the suppliers' Purchase Ledger Account. Bank reconciliation checks the accuracy of cash book entries against the bank statements. Differences between the bank columns of the Cash Book and the bank statement may reflect errors made by the business or by the bank; however, they can usually be explained by cheques the business has written out that have yet to be presented to the bank or equally by any uncleared deposits.

A Petty Cash Book is used to maintain an office float, for example £50, to pay for miscellaneous office items like stamps, stationery and travelling expenses. The Petty Cash float cuts down on the need to write out cheques for small items and then have to make numerous book-keeping entries. However, payments received in the form of notes and coins should be paid into the bank in the normal way and not into the petty cash box. Ideally receipts should be provided for Petty Cash claims and a Petty Cash Voucher made out for monies paid out. In this way the sum of the receipts, vouchers and petty cash in the box should always equal the float (£50). When the float runs low the payments recorded in the Petty Cash Book are totalled up and the equivalent sum is withdrawn from the bank to top up the float to its original level.

25   One sale will result in three book-keeping entries in three ledgers.

   True ☐   False ☐   Can't tell ☐

26   The Purchase Ledger Account could be described as a Creditors' Account.

   True ☐   False ☐   Can't tell ☐

27   No notes or coins are paid into the petty cash box.

   True ☐   False ☐   Can't tell ☐

28   There will be no discrepancy between the bank statement and the Cash Book.

   True ☐   False ☐   Can't tell ☐

Passage 8. Bee's knees

Honey is making a comeback as a wound care product. The use of honey for medicinal purposes dates back to Egyptian times when it was used both topically and internally to treat a wide range of health problems ranging from skin infection to gaping wounds and stomach ulcers. However, modern civilizations have regarded honey more as foodstuff than as medicine. Today, medical grade Manuka honey from New Zealand is healing wounds where more conventional treatments have failed. It can be used on partial or full thickness wounds including pressure sores, leg ulcers, surgical wounds, burns and graft sites. The honey is applied directly to the wound bed followed by an occlusive dressing, or as top-up to a honey-impregnated wound dressing.

Honey is able to clean wounds because the high sugar content provides an osmotic potential that draws moisture into the skin. Moisture management is a key feature of wound healing; the benefits of maintaining a warm, moist environment are widely accepted. Infection control is fundamental to wound care and the high acidity or low pH of honey makes it bactericidal. Consequently, honey may be able to control wound infection where antibiotics have failed. Honey has anti-inflammatory properties and it reduces wound exudates, which if not contained can macerate the surrounding skin to increase the risk of infection.

Honey treatments are generally well received by patients, who view them as a natural cure, although body temperature makes honey very runny, creating a sticky mess that may require more frequent dressing changes. The only contra-indication to using honey is a known allergy to bee venom. Some patients may experience an increase in pain due to its osmotic action. Whilst eating honey is not an option for patients with diabetes there are no reports of topical honey increasing blood glucose levels, though the manufacturers advise that these levels are closely monitored.

29   In ancient times honey was used more as a medicine than a foodstuff.

  True ☐   False ☐   Can't tell ☐

30   The application of medical grade Manuka honey to a wound could render it sterile.

  True ☐   False ☐   Can't tell ☐

31   Controlling moisture is the main aim of wound care.

  True ☐   False ☐   Can't tell ☐

32   The possibility of a topical honey dressing increasing the blood sugar level in a patient with diabetes cannot be ruled out.

  True ☐   False ☐   Can't tell ☐

Passage 9. Votes count

The United Kingdom has had a full parliamentary democracy since 1928 when women were allowed to vote in general elections at age 21, the same as men. Women were first given the right to vote in 1918 after the First World War, but only if they were over the age of 30. In 1969 the voting age for men and women was reduced to 18. No person can vote unless their name appears on the electoral register and the earliest you can register is age 16.

Citizens of the Commonwealth and those of the Irish Republic are eligible to vote in all public elections (general and local) as long as they are resident in the United Kingdom. British nationals who move abroad retain the right to vote in British and EU elections for a further 15 years. Some people are disenfranchised, including convicted prisoners (but not those on remand), non-UK EU citizens, Church of England archbishops and bishops, members of the House of Lords and people lacking the mental capacity to vote on polling day. However, all of the above people (convicted prisoners and those lacking mental capacity excepted) can vote in local elections and all EU citizens can also vote in European elections though only in one country and not two.

33 A woman born in 1889 would not have been allowed to vote in the 1918 UK general election.

   True ☐   False ☐   Can't tell ☐

34 A 55-year-old male born in Northern Ireland and domiciled in Spain five years ago is entitled to vote in a UK general election.

   True ☐   False ☐   Can't tell ☐

35 Non-UK EU citizens over age 18 with mental capacity who are not prisoners are entitled to vote in a UK general election.

   True ☐   False ☐   Can't tell ☐

36 A 19-year-old female born in the Irish Republic is entitled to vote in a UK general election.

   True ☐   False ☐   Can't tell ☐

Passage 10. Park and fly

For most people, parking the car is a mundane activity devoid of planning. However, Heathrow Airport has so many car parks and parking options that if you park in the wrong place the charges could exceed the cost of the flight. Terminal 5's car park can hold 2,200 cars and the long-stay car park can hold 3,800 cars and 150 motorcycles so finding a space should never be a problem but the turn-up prices can be much higher than those offered for pre-booking. The multi-storey car parks at Heathrow airport are mainly for short-stay parking where there is a general vehicle height restriction of 2 metres. Charges are designed to discourage a stay of more than six hours and the daily rate is punitive. Vehicles up to 2.4 metres in height can park on the ground floor of car park 3 (serving Terminals 1, 2 and 3).

Customers using Terminal 4 can park vehicles up to 2.6 metres in height on the roof of the car park 4 or alternatively they can use Business Parking where they will be charged the short-stay tariff for stays of up to six hours, after which time long-stay tariffs apply. Terminal 5 customers can also use Business Parking combined with a short courtesy coach transfer. Vehicles up to 2.6 metres in height can use the Terminal 4 forecourt for the purposes of dropping off and picking up only. Vehicles taller than 2.6 metres need to park in the long-stay car parks (one-day minimum stay) or at Business Parking. The former charges a variable daily rate depending on the number of days stayed whilst the latter charges a fixed amount per day for stays between 1 and 13 days and a fixed sum for stays between 14 and 28 days. Stays longer than 28 days incur the fixed sum plus the fixed amount per day charge for the additional days.

37 A vehicle that is 1.9 metres in height can be parked for two days in a multi-story car park.

True ☐   False ☐   Can't tell ☐

38 Vehicles taller than 2.6 metres can park at Business Parking for the purposes of short or long-term parking.

True ☐   False ☐   Can't tell ☐

39 Parking a vehicle at Business Parking costs twice as much for 26 days as it does for 13 days.

True ☐   False ☐   Can't tell ☐

40 A vehicle that is 2.3 metres in height can be parked on the roof of car park 3.

True ☐   False ☐   Can't tell ☐

Passage 11. Minted

Coins have been struck in Britain for over 2,000 years but it was not until the 13th century that a properly instituted mint was formed. Sited in the Tower of London between the inner and outer walls it employed primitive methods of coining money with hand-held tools. In the 17th century, man-powered screw presses were intro-duced that could strike up to 30 coins per minute.

With the advent of the Industrial Revolution, steam-powered machinery was available and a private mint was opened in Birmingham by the entrepreneur Mathew Boulton. He secured contracts for pennies and twopences, producing much higher quality coins than the Tower, which lacked the space for steam-powered presses. A decision was taken to transfer facilities from the Tower to Tower Hill where the Royal Mint began production in 1810. The new presses were capable of striking up to 100 coins per minute. UK coins were circulated in various part of the British Empire, and after the First World War the Royal Mint sought orders from countries all over the world.

In 1964 the government decided to adopt a decimal system of currency and a new Royal Mint was constructed in readiness for decimalization on 15th February 1971. The new Mint was constructed at Llantrisant in South Wales in 1967 and the first phase was opened by the Queen on 17 December 1968. Later, an up-to-date foundry was installed followed by engraving, tool-making and assay departments along with a special section for striking proof coins for the collectors' market. The original site on Tower Hill was run down once the Llantrisant facility had the full range of minting facilities. The last coin was struck at Tower Hill in November 1975.

41   The Royal Mint was not the first to utilize steam power.

   True ☐   False ☐   Can't tell ☐

42   All of the minting facilities had been transferred from Tower Hill to Llantrisant by 1968.

   True ☐   False ☐   Can't tell ☐

43   Only Llantrisant could strike special proof coins.

   True ☐   False ☐   Can't tell ☐

44   The mint at Tower Hill continued to operate after decimalization.

   True ☐   False ☐   Can't tell ☐

Passage 12. Talking rot

Despite its name, dry rot is anything but dry; it needs water to grow. It is caused by the fungus *serpula lacrymans*, which colonizes damp wood in the form of red-brown fruit bodies. Wood consists of cellulose and lignin and the fungus metabolizes the cellulose to its sugar components and eventually to carbon-dioxide and water which the fungus soaks up. The affected timber takes on a dull brown appearance, dries up and rapidly loses mechanical strength. Dry rot can threaten the structure of a building because it can spread beyond its source to penetrate the walls and brickwork.

In the short term, timber affected with dry rot can be removed and the adjacent wood treated with a chemical fungicide. However, prevention is better than cure and dry rot will not grow in an environment with less than 10 per cent moisture. Wet rot is more common in buildings than dry rot but is a far less serious problem because it cannot spread into the brickwork. Like dry rot, wet rot cannot grow in dry wood. Both dry and wet rot can usually be traced to a distinct source of rainwater ingress into a building, for example, broken tiles, guttering or brickwork. Painting timbers with primer and top coat can stop water from penetrating wood, thereby preventing the germination of wood rot spores. However, an intact paint surface can mask fungal penetration that may have entered the wood at an exposed surface, for example, where the timber is embedded in wet brickwork. The presence of dry rot can be confirmed by probing with a screwdriver when the timber will easily give way and also by tapping with a hammer, when it will sound hollow.

45   Both dry and wet rot are caused by the fungus *serpula lacrymans*.

   True ☐   False ☐   Can't tell ☐

46   Dry rot requires an environment with at least 90 per cent moisture.

   True ☐   False ☐   Can't tell ☐

47   Wet rot is not a threat to brickwork.

   True ☐   False ☐   Can't tell ☐

48   Wood with an intact paint surface is free of wood rot.

   True ☐   False ☐   Can't tell ☐

CHAPTER 2

Decision analysis

These tests are about making good judgements in less than ideal circumstances – as is often the case in real life. You have 33 minutes to answer 28 questions, or a little over one minute per question. The goal is to identify which of the sentences is the correct match for the code. There is no need to decipher or break the code. You translate it literally and then compare your translation with the answer choices to find the best fit.

There are two key steps as follows:

Step 1: translate the code words without interpretation.

Step 2: find the best fit, eliminating wrong answers.

One answer will include all the concepts described by the code without leaving any out or introducing new ideas. The answer you choose must translate all the code words. If it fails to do so or includes additional concepts or incorrect concepts you can eliminate it from the answer options.

Example 1: what is the best interpretation of the following coded message:

E1, 5, 7(106), E9.

A I see a large number of problems.

B The group see many new difficulties.

C The players have numerous obstacles.

D We see several stumbling blocks.

E The team envisage numerous difficulties.

Table of codes

Operating	Basic	Specialist
A = Increase	1 = Person	101 = Money
B = Opposite	2 = Eat	102 = Rules
C = Similar	3 = Think	103 = Day
D = Positive	4 = Vehicle	104 = Danger
E = Plural	5 = Vision	105 = Health
F = Always	6 = Time	106 = Number
G = Male	7 = Large	107 = Air
H = Together	8 = Personal	108 = Meal
I = Specific	9 = Problem	109 = Costly

Step 1: write down the code without interpretation.

Step 2: find the best fit, eliminating wrong answers

Step 1: plural person, vision, large number, plural problem.

The following translations are wrong for the reasons given in brackets and would be eliminated from the answer choices:

A 'I see a large number of problems' (no concept of plural person).

B 'The group see many new difficulties' ('new' not coded in the table).

C 'The players have numerous obstacles' (no concept of vision).

D 'We see several stumbling blocks' (poor concept of large number).

The last statement codes for all the concepts correctly:

E 'The team envisage numerous difficulties'.

In addition to translating codes, you can expect a few questions that ask you to identify which code, from the choices given, best translates the message. There is neither time nor need to translate every code; look for the common elements between the answer choices because these are the most likely choices and anticipate what code you would expect to see.

Some answers will be close matches for the code whilst others will be contradictory. Note that the number of concepts to code in the sentence should be reflected in your chosen code.

Example 2: which of the following codes best translates the message:

Your car insurance is expensive.

A   B8, I4, 109

B   B1, C101, 109

C   B8, I4, C101, 109

D   C1, I4, 7(101), 109

E   B8, C102, 109

There are four concepts to code, namely 'Your', 'car', 'insurance' and 'expensive', so answers C and D appear to be the strongest candidates because they have four codes.

C reads: opposite personal, specific vehicle, similar money, expensive.

This code works if 'opposite personal' is taken to be 'Your' (as opposed to 'My'). The code reads opposite personal (*Your*), specific vehicle (*car*), similar money (*insurance*), costly (*expensive*), ie answer C.

A fails to code for insurance (similar money).

B fails to code for car (specific vehicle).

D fails to code the concept of Your (opposite personal).

E fails to code for car (specific vehicle).

In a third type of question, you may be asked to identify which TWO out of five words when added to the table of code words would be the most helpful in coding the sentence. To answer these questions you have to identify which two words in the sentence cannot be coded from any existing code in the table, or failing this, any word that cannot be coded accurately or without difficulty.

Example 3: which TWO codes when added to the previous table of codes would help to translate the message:

Older people are at more risk of food poisoning.

A   Bad

B   Food

C   Older

D   Similar

E   Greater

There is no concept of 'age' in the table so C is one answer.

'Increase danger' (A104) codes well for 'more risk'. 'Meal danger' (104(108)) codes loosely for 'food poisoning'. However, we need to find a second code so add 'bad' to meal (108) to express 'food poisoning'.

Twenty-eight warm-up questions

Test 1 code 1

Use your judgement to identify which of the suggested answers best explains the meaning of the coded messages.

Operating	Basic	Specialist
A = Lessen	1 = Service	101 = Inflation
B = Similar	2 = Commodity	102 = Deflation
C = Reverse	3 = Wide-screen TV	103 = Specific
D = Append	4 = Milk	104 = Situation
E = Parallel	5 = Cigarettes	105 = Unfashionable
F = Add	6 = Banking	106 = Elevated
G = Delete	7 = Landscape gardening	107 = Temperate
H = Future	8 = Pasta	108 = Tiny
	9 = Mobile phone contract	109 = Popular
	10 = Refrigerator	
	11 = Wooden flooring	
	12 = Gasoline	
	13 = Soft furnishings	
	14 = Basket of goods and services	

Q1 CG, 11

A. Delete wooden flooring.
B. Add wooden flooring.
C. Should we add or delete wooden flooring?
D. Reverse the decision to delete wooden flooring.

Answer [   ]

Q2 F8, 5(EG)

A. Delete cigarettes and add pasta.
B. Add cigarettes and delete pasta.
C. Add pasta and delete cigarettes.
D. Remove cigarettes and add pasta.

Answer [   ]

Q3   12, BF, E14

A. Gasoline is on the list.
B. Add gasoline to the inventory.
C. Gasoline is one of the commodities.
D. Put gasoline in the basket of goods and services.

Answer [   ]

Q4   D109, E106, 8

A. Fashionable pasta is all the rage.
B. Promote pasta; it has become all the rage.
C. Pasta has become very popular.
D. Popular, eminent, pasta.

Answer [   ]

Q5   C2, 9, 7

A. Landscape gardening and mobile phone contracts are services.
B. Remove from the basket of goods and services landscape gardening
     and mobile phone contracts.
C. Mobile phone contracts and landscape gardening are not commodities.
D. Mobile phone contracts and landscape gardening are not goods.

Answer [   ]

Q6   6, D(1), B107, 101

A. Banking facilities are experiencing soaring inflation.
B. Pleasant inflation is occurring in banking provision.
C. Inflation is rising in the banking sector.
D. Banking services are experiencing moderate inflation.

Answer [   ]

Q7   4, B105, 101, E(A)

A. Make milk obsolete to cut inflation.
B. Remove milk and you will add to inflation.
C. Decrease inflation by cutting out milk.
D. Increase inflation by promoting milk.

Answer [   ]

Q8   105, 9, 8, C

   A.   Reverse the decision not to include mobile phone contracts and pasta.
   B.   Pasta and mobile phone contracts are popular.
   C.   Mobile phone contracts and pasta are out of favour.
   D.   Pasta and mobile phone contracts are out of date.

                                                                Answer

Q9   13, A(G), 109, E(106), 101

   A.   Soft furnishings are popular but they experience high inflation.
   B.   Soft furnishings are very popular but consider deleting them as they suffer very high inflation.
   C.   Think about deleting soft furnishings; while popular, they have high inflation.
   D.   Don't delete soft furnishings; though they experience inflation they remain very popular.

                                                                Answer

The next question has TWO correct answers.

Q10   E, F, 12

   A.   Include gasoline.
   B.   Put petrol on the list.
   C.   Put gasoline on the list.
   D.   Add petrol.
   E.   Add gasoline.

                                                                Answer

The next question has THREE correct answers.

Q11   13, G, 10

   A.   Delete soft furnishings and refrigerator.
   B.   Delete both soft furnishings and refrigerator.
   C.   Delete refrigerator or soft furnishings.
   D.   Delete soft furnishings not refrigerator.
   E.   Delete refrigerator not soft furnishings.

                                                                Answer

Test 1 code 2

Gasoline and diesel generate large amounts of pollutants and the race is on to find bio-fuel alternatives. Some mathematicians have proposed the following matrix – use it to identify the best interpretation of the messages.

Operating	Basic	Specialist
A = New	1 = Vegetable	101 = Green
B = Gain	2 = Oil	102 = Can
C = More	3 = Octane	103 = May
D = High	4 = Alcohol	104 = Could
E = Equivalent	5 = Ethanol	105 = Contradiction
F = Decrease	6 = Gasoline	106 = Alternative
G = Similar	7 = Diesel	107 = Investment
H = Enlarge	8 = Bio	108 = Tell
I = Turn around	9 = Fuel	109 = Know
J = Join		110 = Few

Q12 3, 4, 6, A, D

   A. The new green fuel is high-octane alcohol.
   B. Interest in high-octane alcohol has long surpassed gasoline and reached a new high.
   C. High-octane alcohol is the new gasoline.
   D. It's high time industry switched from gasoline to high-octane alcohol.

   Answer ☐

Q13 B, I(105), 103

   A. They may deny it but try to gain permission.
   B. You may gain agreement.
   C. This may mean we gain some opposition.
   D. Gain their trust and you may just beat the challenge.

   Answer ☐

Q14 7, C(101), H(106), G(A)

    A. Today we have greener choices than just diesel.
    B. This innovative alternative to diesel is more green.
    C. There are innovative green alternatives to diesel.
    D. Recent alternatives to diesel are greener.

Answer

Q15 107, A, 8, G(109), 9, I(B)

    A. No new investment in bio-fuel is needed.
    B. We know that new investment in bio-fuel is risky.
    C. I know someone who might invest in a new bio-fuel.
    D. Remember investment in bio-fuel is risky.

Answer

Q16 108, I(104)

    A. We couldn't tell the difference from the results.
    B. This might possibly tell between the options.
    C. The test ought to tell them apart.
    D. Tell the project manager that we can do it.

Answer

Q17 101, I(103), 5

    A. Maybe ethanol is not all that green.
    B. Might it be the case that ethanol is not all that green?
    C. Ethanol may not be all that green.
    D. Ethanol may well be the greenest of them all.

Answer

Q18 H(106), H(C), 107, C

    A. Alternatives require more investment.
    B. Most alternatives need more investment.
    C. More investment is required if alternatives are to be found.
    D. Extra investment in alternatives is needed most.

Answer

Q19   B, G(D), I(102), 108, A, 2

A.   The price will soar so gain as much new oil as you can.
B.   Gain as high a price as possible for the new oil product.
C.   You could sell the new oil product but better to wait for the forecast price gains.
D.   We can't tell if oil will gain new highs.

Answer [   ]

The following question has TWO correct answers. Enter the corresponding letter of each correct answer in the answer box.

Q20   G105, G107, 8, 9

A.   The take-up of bio-fuel has been inconsistent.
B.   Disagreement exists over bio-fuel ventures.
C.   There is conflicting evidence about bio-fuel speculation.
D.   The production of bio-fuel is less capital intensive.

Answer [   ]

The following question has THREE correct answers. Enter the corresponding letter of each correct answer in the answer box.

Q21   G110, 5, 107, 106

A.   The minority think ethanol a good alternative investment.
B.   As an alternative investment hardly any think ethanol a good choice.
C.   Only a small amount of investment is required in the alternative ethanol.
D.   As the best investment in the alternative market ethanol is backed by many.

Answer [   ]

Q22   I(B), 7, 9, 6, I(A)

A.   Supplies of gasoline and diesel will dwindle as deliveries of substitute fuel increase.
B.   Production of bio-fuel will increase as production of gasoline and diesel falls.
C.   The decline in traditional gasoline and diesel markets will be sudden and novel.
D.   Sales of all conventional fuel like diesel and gasoline will decrease.

Answer [   ]

The following question has TWO correct answers. Enter the corresponding letter of each correct answer in the answer box.

Q23   5(6), 9, 3D

    A.   Ordinary fuels when blended with ethanol become high-octane.
    B.   An ethanol and gasoline mixture is a high-octane fuel.
    C.   Cars can run on a high-octane ethanol gasoline mix.
    D.   Gasoline and ethanol are both high-octane fuel.

Answer [   ]

Test 1 code 3

You work in the security department of a large corporation and must decode the following messages, which all refer to an employee stealing the personal details of a large number of his colleagues. The letter S is used to signify the thief.

Operating	Basic	Specialist
A = Past	1 = He or S	101 = Online
B = Similar	2 = We	102 = Information
C = Same as	3 = If	103 = Staff
D = Reverse	4 = Know	104 = Week
E = Contract	5 = Try	105 = Ready
F = Expand	6 = Believe	106 = High
G = All	7 = Looks	107 = No
H = Only	8 = Proves	108 = Steal
I = Prefers	9 = Seems	109 = Works

Select *one* of the following answers as in your judgement the best interpretation of the sequence of code.

Q24   102, F5, 1, 101

    A.   S tries to take information from the computer.
    B.   The information he takes is always decrypted.
    C.   He steals the information and e-mails it.
    D.   He is online trying to access information.

Answer [   ]

Q25   109, 1, 9, D104

    A.   It seems S works at the weekend.
    B.   Some days he works later than others.
    C.   Weekly he seems to work from one particular terminal.
    D.   He works as a casual on an hourly contract.

Answer [ ]

Q26   2, C105, 101, 1

    A.   If news goes online that all this personal detail has been stolen we can expect a lot of negative publicity.
    B.   We are online and standing by.
    C.   We are all set for when he next goes online.
    D.   Until S is caught nothing online is safe and we have one major security headache.

Answer [ ]

The following questions have TWO correct answers.

Q27   1, 8, 109

    A.   We proved he operates.
    B.   It proves S works.
    C.   That proves he works.
    D.   It worked as he proved.

Answer [ ]

Q28   2, 4, F107, B1, B108

    A.   We do not know she stole it.
    B.   She thinks he stole it.
    C.   He's not to know we stole it.
    D.   We are nowhere near catching him.

Answer [ ]

28 questions in 33 minutes

Test 2 code 1

Operating	Basic	Specialist
A = Increase	1 = Person	101 = Money
B = Opposite	2 = Eat	102 = Rules
C = Similar	3 = Think	103 = Day
D = Positive	4 = Vehicle	104 = Danger
E = Plural	5 = Wrong	105 = Health
F = Always	6 = Time	106 = Number
G = Male	7 = Large	107 = Air
H = Personal	8 = Water	108 = Meal
J = Together	9 = Speak	109 = Heard
K = Specific	10 = Work	110 = Pain
L = Situation	11 = Fire	201 = Fix
M = Future	12 = House	202 = Light
	13 = Fall	203 = Expensive
	14 = Problem	204 = Old
	15 = Short	205 = Seek
	16 = Few	206 = Notes
	17 = Space	207 = Object
	18 = Travel	

Q1   HE, B7(108), 15(6)

    A.   I eat lunch quickly.
    B.   We have finished our meal.
    C.   We eat breakfast quickly.
    D.   I eat breakfast in the morning.
    E.   We eat small meals in the morning.

Answer [   ]

Q2   (106, 10) 14, B16(E1)

    A.   Some people find numbers hard work.
    B.   Calculations are difficult for people.
    C.   Number work is complicated.
    D.   Equations are hard for many people.
    E.   I find equations hard to solve.

Answer [   ]

Q3   HE, 10(BA), B10(A)

    A.   I should spend less time working.
    B.   People should work less not more.
    C.   People need to work and play.
    D.   We should work less and play more.
    E.   We need less work to do.

Answer [   ]

Q4   14(10), BF, A110, 1

    A.   Nobody likes hard work.
    B.   Hard work never hurt anyone.
    C.   Working hard makes money.
    D.   A little work is pain free.
    E.   There is no gain without pain.

Answer [   ]

Q5   B(HE), B(C105)H

    A.   Others are not as fit as me.
    B.   Most people are healthier than me.
    C.   No people are less healthy than me.
    D.   Many people do not keep fit.
    E.   Few people keep fit and healthy.

Answer [   ]

Q6   BD(7 17), H(7G), 12

    A.   My boyfriend is not coming to stay.
    B.   My husband has left home.
    C.   There is no room in my father's house.
    D.   A small man takes up less space.
    E.   My father's home has plenty of space.

Answer [   ]

Q7 H(BF), B201, C102

    A. Sometimes I break the rules.
    B. I never break the law.
    C. I cannot change the rules.
    D. We should never break the law.
    E. It is not always unlawful.

Answer [　　　　]

Q8 105, 2(B7), 14, A6

    A. It takes time to diet.
    B. I eat a small amount of healthy food.
    C. It is hard to stay on a healthy diet.
    D. I find it hard to eat small, healthy meals.
    E. Healthy people eat small meals.

Answer [　　　　]

Q9 H, B10, B105

    A. I don't like working when I'm ill.
    B. I seldom take sickness absence.
    C. I can play unless I am unwell.
    D. I was off work due to illness.
    E. I hate working when I'm ill.

Answer [　　　　]

Q10 B16, C(E12), 16(7E17)

    A. There are a few buildings and not many open spaces.
    B. There are a few buildings and a few open spaces.
    C. There are many buildings and a few open spaces.
    D. There are many houses in open spaces.
    E. There are few houses in several open spaces.

Answer [　　　　]

Q11 H(10J), A(3C)

    A. My friends and I are in agreement.
    B. My colleagues and I hold the same view.
    C. My work mates and I have similar thoughts.
    D. We work together in the same place.
    E. Working together increases my knowledge.

Answer [　　　　]

Q12 EH, BF, 2, B(105), C2

    A. We never eat healthy food.
    B. We don't eat healthily.
    C. We rarely eat unhealthy food.
    D. We seldom eat fast food.
    E. We never consume unhealthy food.

Answer

Q13 EH, BA(BF), C(11 8)

    A. We seldom drink hot tea.
    B. I rarely drink hot drinks.
    C. We never drink alcohol.
    D. I don't like alcoholic drinks.
    E. We seldom drink juice.

Answer

Q14 B10, A(B13M)

    A. Jobs are hard to find.
    B. The jobless total is rising.
    C. Unemployment is increasing.
    D. Jobs are hard to find quickly.
    E. Unemployment will rise.

Answer

Q15 E1, 4K, 18(7 8)

    A. Boats sail on water.
    B. People sail across oceans.
    C. People take a ferry across the sea.
    D. I went boating on the river.
    E. Most people cross the Channel by ferry.

Answer

Q16 EH, 10(101), C(7 12)

    A. We work for the same company.
    B. We are employed at a hotel.
    C. We work from home.
    D. They work on the shop floor.
    E. We work on a voluntary basis.

Answer

Q17   Which ONE of the following words when added to the table of code words would be the most helpful in coding the sentence?

We sold our home in Scotland and moved away.

A. sell
B. Scotland
C. We
D. home
E. moved

Answer [   ]

Q18   Which ONE of the following words when added to the table of code words would be the most helpful in coding the sentence?

Most people can lose weight with diet and exercise.

A. exercise
B. most
C. diet
D. lose
E. people

Answer [   ]

Q19   (107,14), BD(H107)

A. Car exhaust fumes make breathing difficult.
B. I find it hard to breathe.
C. Exhaust fumes create pollution.
D. Pollution makes breathing difficult for many people.
E. Pollution is bad for my breathing.

Answer [   ]

Q20   E1, B10, B15(4), 18

A. People rest on coaches.
B. People sleep on train journeys.
C. Many people use public transport.
D. Trains stop for short periods.
E. We travel long distance.

Answer [   ]

Q21   2, 15(6), B204(108)

A. Food should not be eaten beyond its use by date.
B. Old food is bad to eat.
C. Expiry dates are always shown on food.
D. Fresh food should be eaten soon.
E. Food should be eaten fresh.

Answer

Q22   B16, B7(E1), 10(BD 101)

A. Many young people do voluntary work.
B. Many young people are out of work.
C. Some children work for free.
D. Many young people receive little wages.
E. Most young people are paid less.

Answer

Q23   BD(105,A), E1(2,11,108)

A. It is unhealthy for me to eat hot dinners.
B. Eating undercooked food is a health hazard.
C. Food poisoning is dangerous for old people.
D. Eating barbecued food made them ill.
E. Food poisoning bacteria can kill.

Answer

Q24   (108, K, 105,14), B(202), E1, C(104)

A. Large people eat too much.
B. People with diabetes should watch their diet.
C. Eating too much makes people look overweight.
D. Obese people risk diabetes.
E. Diabetes is linked with obesity.

Answer

Q25   C(BK), B105, M, H, B103, 17

A. After a night out I felt generally unwell.
B. Generally there was lack of space at night.
C. My diabetes required overnight treatment.
D. I stayed in hospital last night to recover.
E. I was admitted to the General Hospital.

Answer

Q26   BD(105), C(BD,14), E1

    A.   The solution was obvious to everyone.
    B.   The team diagnosed the problem.
    C.   We all understood the difficulty.
    D.   The health problem was obvious.
    E.   Doctors diagnose illness.

Answer

Q27   E108, 202, BD(14), E(1,2)BA

    A.   Breakfast is the smallest meal of the day.
    B.   Diets are easy for poor eaters.
    C.   Light meals leave you feeling empty.
    D.   Small snacks are eaten between meals.
    E.   Lunch was an easy meal to prepare.

Answer

Q28   3, 14, 10, 106, 205, E1

    A.   Large numbers are difficult to manipulate.
    B.   Mental arithmetic is hard for some people.
    C.   Maths questions are the most problematic.
    D.   Numerical solutions are hard to find.
    E.   People find maths confusing.

Answer

28 questions in 33 minutes

Test 3 code 1

Operating	Basic	Specialist
A = Increase	1 = Person	101 = Money
B = Opposite	2 = Eat	102 = Rules
C = Similar	3 = Think	103 = Day
D = Positive	4 = Vehicle	104 = Danger
E = Plural	5 = Wrong	105 = Health
F = Always	6 = Time	106 = Number
G = Male	7 = Large	107 = Air
H = Personal	8 = Water	108 = Meal
J = Together	9 = Speak	109 = Heard
K = Specific	10 = Work	110 = Pain
L = Situation	11 = Fire	201 = Fix
M = Future	12 = House	202 = Light
	13 = Fall	203 = Expensive
	14 = Problem	204 = Old
	15 = Short	205 = Seek
	16 = Few	206 = Notes
	17 = Space	207 = Object
	18 = Travel	● = Happy
	19 = Take	■ = Lonely
	20 = Vision	◆ = Friendly
	21 = Vessel	♥ = Anxious

Q1   Which of the following codes best translates the message:

Happy people are not depressed.

A. ●E1, BD(B●)
B. ●E1, B(B●)
C. ●1, BD(B●)
D. ●E1, BD(●)
E. ●E1, B(BD●)

Answer ⬚

Q2   Which TWO of the following words when added to the table of code words would be the most helpful in coding the sentence?

My old car passed its test.

A.   My
B.   old
C.   car
D.   failed
E.   test

Answer [   ]

Q3   Which TWO of the following words when added to the table of code words would be the most helpful in coding the sentence?

We sold our home in the city and moved to the countryside to live.

A.   sell
B.   city
C.   moved
D.   countryside
E.   live

Answer [   ]

Q4   Which TWO of the following words when added to the table of code words would be the most helpful in coding the sentence?

Neither of us found the restaurant meals appetising.

A.   food
B.   appetising
C.   neither
D.   both
E.   restaurant

Answer [   ]

Q5   Which of the following codes best translates the message:

A thoughtful person avoids a dangerous situation.

A.   3E1, BD(205), 104L
B.   3(1), BD(205), 104L
C.   1(BM3) BD(205), 104L
D.   1(BM3), L(205), 104L
E.   1(BM3), 14(205), 104L

Answer [   ]

Q6   Which of the following codes best translates the message:

Women earn less money than men.

A.   BG, BA(101), G
B.   B(G E1), BA(101), G E1
C.   BG, 14(101), G
D.   BG, 10, BA(101), G
E.   B(G E1), 10, BA(101), G E1

Answer

Q7   Which of the following codes best translates the message:

Children should be seen and not heard.

A.   B7(E1), C20, B109
B.   B204(E1), D(C20), BD109
C.   B204(E1), BD109, C20
D.   B7(E1), C20, BD109
E.   15(E1), BD109, D(C20)

Answer

Q8   Which of the following codes best translates the message:

New light bulbs use less energy.

A.   CM, 202(K4), BA(20)
B.   B204, 202(207), DA(K106)
C.   KM, 202(K4), K10, 14
D.   KM, 202(C4), K10, 205
E.   B204, 202(207), BA(K10)

Answer

Q9   BD(10)E1, BD(203), 105 206

A.   Health advice is available for free.
B.   A sick note is required if you take time off work.
C.   Health records are freely available.
D.   Illness causes unemployment and lack of money.
E.   Prescriptions are free for unemployed people.

Answer

Q10 (18,6) (207,110) C(B102)

A. Carrying a weapon is a crime.
B. Time travellers feel no pain.
C. An assault is a criminal offence.
D. Heavy cargo should not be transported.
E. Criminals carry weapons that inflict injuries.

Answer

Q11 M, B7(8), 7(106), M(103)

A. Most of the country will be short of water.
B. There will be very little water for us.
C. Showers are forecast for tomorrow.
D. Tomorrow we will have plenty to drink.
E. It was raining earlier in the day.

Answer

Q12 ♦ E1, ♦ BA, 12J

A. Friendly people make excellent housemates.
B. Our neighbours are unfriendly people.
C. Friendly people make satisfactory neighbours.
D. I am a good friend to my neighbour.
E. My friends live in the same house.

Answer

Q13 BD(107A), H, BD(H107)

A. Air pressure decreases at high altitude.
B. Exercise increases my breathing rate.
C. Expiration follows inspiration.
D. I suffer from shortness of breath.
E. I can't breathe without oxygen.

Answer

Q14 17(18), 18E1, H18, BM(103)

A. Space travel will be available to everyone.
B. Long distances take several days on foot.
C. We travelled by train yesterday.
D. We walked across the bridge yesterday.
E. There is no future in space travel.

Answer

Q15   H(E14), 20M, 7, 106

    A.   I envisaged numerous problems.
    B.   We will experience many more problems.
    C.   I found the high number of questions problematic.
    D.   We anticipated more difficulties in the future.
    E.   There are many more problems to come.

Answer

Q16   104, BM(3), BD1

    A.   A negative person thinks about risk.
    B.   I find the hazards depressing.
    C.   Nobody had considered it risky.
    D.   We heard that it was dangerous.
    E.   It pays not to think about it.

Answer

Q17   Which TWO of the following words when added to the table of code words would be the most helpful in coding the sentence?

A reservoir provided the town with a source of fresh water.

    A.   source
    B.   reservoir
    C.   water
    D.   town
    E.   fresh

Answer

Q18   Which TWO of the following words when added to the table of code words would be the most helpful in coding the sentence?

We were unconcerned with the possibility of deterioration and complications.

    A.   possibility
    B.   complications
    C.   deterioration
    D.   concerned
    E.   we

Answer

Q19   Which TWO of the following words when added to the table of code words would be the most helpful in coding the sentence?

Clients' health records are filed away separately.

A.   separate
B.   client
C.   health
D.   store
E.   records

Answer [   ]

Q20   Which TWO of the following words when added to the table of code words would be the most helpful in coding the sentence?

Nobody protested as the better player won.

A.   player
B.   protest
C.   good
D.   nobody
E.   won

Answer [   ]

Q21   Which of the following codes best translates the message:

The women could see more with the light on.

A.   BD(G1), 20D, 202A
B.   B(G E1), 20A, 202D
C.   B(G E1), 20A, 7(202)
D.   B(G E1), 20A, 202L
E.   BD(G1), 20A, 202A

Answer [   ]

Q22   Which of the following codes best translates the message:

A burn takes a long time to heal.

A.   11(110), 19, B15, 6, 201
B.   11(110), 19, B16(6), 105(201)
C.   11(110), 19, B(15,6), 201(105)
D.   11(110), 19, B15, 6, 105
E.   11(110,7), 19, B15, 6, 105

Answer [   ]

Q23   Which of the following codes best translates the message:

The young woman solicited our help for her sick mother.

A.   B204(B G1), 205(BM), L♦, B105, H(7,BG).
B.   B204(B G1), 205, L♦, B105, H(7,BG).
C.   B204(B GE1), 205(BM), L♦, B105, H(7,BG).
D.   B204(B G1), 205(BM), L♦, B105, H(7,G).
E.   B204(B G1), 205(BM), C♦, B105, B(7,G).

Answer

Q24   Which of the following codes best translates the message:

We ate by candlelight.

A.   E1, 19(108), L(C11)
B.   BM(2), L(C11, 202)
C.   E1, 19(108), L(C11, 202)
D.   E1, BM(2), L(C11, 202)
E.   E1, BM(2), K(C202)

Answer

Q25   H■, BJ, B103 6

A.   I felt lonely after becoming separated.
B.   I feel lonely on my own in the evening.
C.   Night-time is a lonely time of day.
D.   I feel all alone when we part.
E.   People feel lonely at night-time.

Answer

Q26   B(16), E1, BD(105), 14(B●)

A.   Many ill people are depressed.
B.   Many sad people are ill.
C.   Depression is an illness that makes many people sad.
D.   Some people are unhappy with their health.
E.   Depression makes all people feel sad.

Answer

Q27   E1, J, A(A●)

    A.   Couples like to be together.
    B.   Married people are happier.
    C.   People are happiest when together.
    D.   Married people are happy people.
    E.   Married people are the happiest.

Answer

Q28   H, J(E1), B♦(E1)

    A.   My neighbours are unfriendly towards me.
    B.   I am not friends with my neighbours.
    C.   I find neighbours unfriendly.
    D.   My neighbours are unfriendly people.
    E.   My neighbours are not my friends.

Answer

CHAPTER 3

Quantitative reasoning

Objectives

At the end of this chapter you will be able to answer questions that use the GCSE maths skills required for the UKCAT quantitative reasoning section, principally on the following subjects:

A Addition, subtraction, multiplication and division

B Fractions, decimals and percentages

C Proportion and ratios

D Graphs, charts and tables

The intention of this chapter is to give you skills necessary to maximize your score by practising the type of mathematical operations you will meet in the quantitative reasoning test.

The test

The test consists of 36 multiple-choice questions divided up into nine blocks of four questions for which you will have 23 minutes, ie 2½ minutes per block, or just under 40 seconds per question.

As there are no penalties for incorrect answers, you have nothing to lose by guessing answers if you are short of time towards the end.

Format

Each block of questions starts with a brief description of the scenario and then some information, often in the form of a table. There are then four multiple-choice questions with five possible answers, A, B, C, D, E, of which only one is correct. This is the format used here for the examples.

The test is described by the UKCAT consortium as being more about testing your problem-solving ability than your numerical faculty. It is the intention of this chapter to develop not only your problem-solving ability, but also your numerical ability. Time is of the essence! The more familiar you are with number and mathematical concepts the quicker you will be in all numerical questions.

The questions in this chapter start easily and rapidly become more difficult at a level equivalent to at least a 'good GCSE' as described by UKCAT consortium. You are aiming to get into a competitive field in a numerical subject; you need this ability with numbers.

There are a total of 100 questions, including some which are in the form of timed mini sub-tests. Good luck.

Questions 1 to 4 concern the population of a certain town which can be divided into the age groups shown in the table:

Age group	Population	Age group	Population
0–4	6,450	50–54	10,150
5–9	7,600	55–59	9,600
10–14	8,450	60–64	7,950
15–19	7,400	65–69	7,450
20–24	5,550	70–74	7,100
25–29	6,150	75–79	6,450
30–34	8,100	80–84	4,500
35–39	8,750	85 and over	2,750
45–49	8,400		

Q1   How many people are younger than 20?

    A. 5,550
    B. 7,400
    C. 29,000
    D. 29,900
    E. 30,000

                                              Answer [   ]

Q2   If the total population is 131,250, approximately what percentage are under 25?

    A. 10%
    B. 15%
    C. 20%
    D. 25%
    E. 30%

                                              Answer [   ]

Q3   If everyone retires at 65, approximately what fraction of the population is within 10 years of retiring?

    A. 1/4
    B. 1/5
    C. 1/7
    D. 1/10
    E. 1/20

                                              Answer [   ]

Q4   What is the ratio of schoolchildren (5–19) to retired people (65+)?

    A. 4 : 5
    B. 4 : 3
    C. 1 : 1
    D. 2 : 1
    E. 1 : 2

                                              Answer [   ]

Questions 5 to 8 concern the cost of calling abroad. A student has two possible phone companies' cards she can use to call her home country:

	Green		Black	
	£10 card	£20 card	£10 card	£20 card
Connection cost (p)	10	10	8	6
Cost per minute (p)	0.4	0.35	0.5	0.4

Q5   If she intends to call home 10 minutes every day, which card offers the cheapest calls?

A.   Green £10
B.   Green £20
C.   Black £10
D.   Black £20
E.   Black £20 or Green £20, the same price

Answer

Q6   Again assume that she calls home for 10 minutes a day. If she chooses the Black £10 card, but it is only valid for a month, what percentage of the cost will she have wasted, to the nearest 5%?

A.   40%
B.   60%
C.   45%
D.   55%
E.   50%

Answer

Q7   She records her phone calls for a year in the following table. What is the average length of call in minutes?

A.   270.1
B.   10.0
C.   27.0
D.   10.1
E.   9.9

Answer

Month	No. of calls	Total duration (mins)
January	20	226
February	25	320
March	40	330
April	32	450
May	33	290
June	29	237
July	23	211
August	5	37
September	26	233
October	26	256
November	30	338
December	36	315

Q8   If the Black company increases its prices per minute by 70%, which card would now be the cheapest for the calls described in question 5?

A.   Green £10

B.   Green £20

C.   Black £10

D.   Black £20

E.   Black £20 or Green £20, the same price

Answer [   ]

Questions 9 to 12 concern the type of employment in a particular region. The breakdown by industry is in thousands of people:

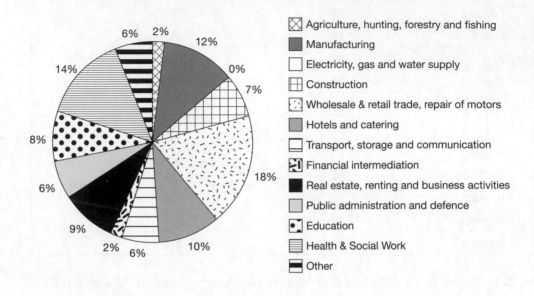

Q9 If the total population is 200,000, how many sectors employ more than 19,000 people?

A. 3
B. 4
C. 5
D. 6
E. 7

Answer [   ]

Q10 If those working in manufacturing generate a third more revenue per person than those in agriculture, fishing, etc, how much more total revenue do they generate?

A. 8 times
B. 7 times
C. 6 times
D. 7.2 times
E. 6.75 times

Answer [   ]

Q11 Half of the agricultural produce is sold to continental Europe. If the total revenue for the sector is £100m, calculate the revenue generated from these European sales in euros (1 pound = 1.25 euros).

A. 12.5m
B. 75m
C. 125m
D. 60m
E. 62.5m

Answer

Q12 The average number of people employed per employer in hotels and catering is 20. How many employers are there (assume the total population is 200,000)?

A. 1,000
B. 4,000
C. 10,000
D. 400
E. 2,000

Answer

Questions 13 to 16 concern the salt content in grams of some supermarket pre-prepared foods per 100g:

Budget's Best Chicken Tikka with Pilau Rice	2.0
Charlie's Champion Chilli	1.2
Red Dragon Lo-salt Vegetable Chow Mein	0.3
Luigi Lambretta's Pasta Carbonara	1.8
Thai Me Up Prawn Curry	1.1
Barry's Bargain Range Paella	1.9
Cheap As Chips Shepherd's Pie	1.6
Luigi Lambretta's Spaghetti Bolognese	1.5
Sadek's Fish Curry	1.2
Mo's Cushy Couscous	1.7
John Bull's British Classics Toad In The Hole	1.8

Q13 Expressed as a decimal, what fraction of the above products are high in salt, ie greater than or equal to 1.5%?

A. 0.4
B. 0.55
C. 0.54
D. 0.64
E. 0.63

Answer [   ]

Q14 If the maximum recommended daily intake of salt is 6g, what percentage does a 350g portion of Chicken Tikka with Pilau Rice represent?

A. 35%
B. 117%
C. 86%
D. 111%
E. 33%

Answer [   ]

Q15 The Fish Curry is twice as expensive as the Paella, which itself is 10% more expensive than the Shepherd's Pie. If the pie costs £1.50, how much does the curry cost?

A. £3.00
B. £1.65
C. £3.60
D. £3.30
E. Can't tell

Answer [   ]

Q16 The Toad in the Hole is also sold in continental Europe. The price in Britain is £2.65 and the exchange rate used to print the prices is £1 = 115.0 cents. If the actual exchange rate is £1 = 112.5 cents, how much more is the rest of Europe paying for Toad in the Hole than it should be if the actual exchange rate is used?

A. 2.5 cents
B. 4.5 cents
C. 6.6 cents
D. 5.9 cents
E. 3.1 cents

Answer [   ]

Questions 17 to 20 concern the number of people in different groups. 106 people were stopped in the street and the following information obtained: 62 were born in this country, 50 were taller than 1.6m and 14 were left-handed.

Q17 What percentage were 1.6m or under?

A. 36%
B. 64%
C. 60%
D. 53%
E. 34%

Answer [   ]

Q18   If three people were taller than 1.6m, born in this country and left-handed, how many people were only one of these things?

    A.   62
    B.   76
    C.   103
    D.   89
    E.   Can't tell

Answer [   ]

Q19   What percentage of those born in this country were left-handed?

    A.   13%
    B.   60%
    C.   20%
    D.   25%
    E.   Can't tell

Answer [   ]

Q20   There are three people who are left-handed, born in this country and taller than 1.6m, and two people who are left-handed and taller than 1.6m. There are twice as many people who are just left-handed as are left-handed and born in this country. How many are just left-handed?

    A.   6
    B.   14
    C.   9
    D.   5
    E.   Can't tell

Answer [   ]

Questions 21 to 24 concern the prices of different foods:

Q21 If an order of three cod and two portions of chips costs a total of £12.85 and two cod with three chips costs £10.40, what would be the formulae for determining the different prices?

    A. 2C + 3F = 12.85, 3C + 2Y = 10.40
    B. C + F = 7.85, F = 1.3
    C. X + Y = £5.00, 2X + 2Y = £10
    D. F = £3.50, C = £1.05
    E. 3X + 2Y = 1285, 2X + 3Y = 1040

Answer [   ]

Q22 If the price of cod increases to £4.26, what is the percentage increase in the price of cod?

    A. 10%
    B. 20%
    C. 15%
    D. 25%
    E. 5%

Answer [   ]

Q23 What is the ratio of the old price to the new price for a portion of cod and chips?

    A. 1 : 1.15
    B. 1.55 : 1
    C. 1.15 : 1
    D. 1 : 1.17
    E. 1.2 : 1

Answer [   ]

Q24 If a shop accepts euros at an exchange rate of 1.20 euros = 1 pound, how much would a tourist pay at the original prices for three cod and two chips?

    A. 13.95
    B. 16.74
    C. 15.42
    D. 16.08
    E. 19.20

Answer [   ]

Questions 25 to 28 concern fuel prices in Europe:

Country	Fuel price (p/l)	Country	Fuel price (p/l)
Austria	75	Hungary	83.5
Belgium	95	Italy	87.5
Czech Rep	71.5	Luxembourg	76.5
Denmark	92.2	Norway	94.8
Eire	74.5	Poland	79.5
Finland	89.4	Portugal	85.8
France	85.2	Spain	66.4
Germany	90	Sweden	82.1
Greece	65.7	Switzerland	72.1
Netherlands	100.3	United Kingdom (Av)	96.5

Q25 Which formula correctly identifies what would be the cost of driving a car that does 30 miles per gallon a distance of 95 miles in Italy if one gallon is 4.55 litres?

A. $(95 / 30) \times (87.5 / 4.55)$
B. $(95 \times 30) / (87.5 \times 4.55)$
C. $(95 \times 30 \times 4.55) / 87.5$
D. $(87.5 \times 4.55) / (95 / 30)$
E. $(95 \times 87.5 \times 4.55) / 30$

Answer ⬚

Q26 If the table concerning fuel prices in Europe was taken to show the increase in price in one month, which group of countries (A–E) has seen the greatest increases?

A. Hungary, Luxembourg, Germany
B. Sweden, Spain
C. Belgium, Finland, United Kingdom, Italy
D. Luxembourg, Germany, United Kingdom, Italy
E. Belgium, Finland, Germany

Answer ⬚

Q27 If the price of fuel were continue to rise at 7% per month in the UK, what would be the percentage increase to drive 100 miles with the car in question 25 after three months?

    A. 14.0%
    B. 21.0%
    C. 21.7%
    D. 22.5%
    E. 28.0%

Answer

Q28 If the driver is planning to drive 210 miles in the Netherlands starting at the German border, how much cheaper would it be to buy the fuel in Germany using the car and prices in question 25?

    A. 297p
    B. 328.1p
    C. 333.275p
    D. 10.3p
    E. Can't tell

Answer

Questions 29 to 32 concern two tests to detect the presence of a certain substance:

SUBSTANCE PRESENT	Yes	Allcheck = 95% Truespot = 92%	Allcheck = 10% Truespot = 2%
	No	Allcheck = 5% Truespot = 8%	Allcheck = 90% Truespot = 98%
TRIAL RESULTS		Positive result	Negative result
		RESULTS OF TRIAL	

Q29 A trial was carried out on 780 samples using Allcheck. How many would be identified as having the substance present?

    A. 702
    B. 741
    C. 78
    D. 62
    E. Can't tell

Answer

Q30 If 500 of the 780 have the substance present, how many results samples would be expected to be incorrect using Truespot?

A. About 43
B. 40
C. About 46
D. 10
E. Can't tell

Answer [　　　　　]

Q31 If half the 780 samples had the substance present, what would be the difference in the number of wrong results for Allcheck compared to Truespot?

A. About 10 more
B. About 5 less
C. About 8 less
D. About 20 more
E. Can't tell

Answer [　　　　　]

Q32 In another trial of 800 samples, Allcheck identifies 475 with the substance. How many are likely to have the substance present?

A. About 488
B. About 465
C. About 475
D. About 325
E. Can't tell

Answer [　　　　　]

Questions 33 to 36 concern the video game-playing habits of students:

Time playing video games per week	
Hours	Number of students
10–14	2
15–19	12
20–24	23
25–29	60
30–34	77
35–39	38
40–44	8

Q33 What is the approximate average time spent playing games per week?

   A. 30
   B. 27
   C. 26
   D. 25
   E. 24

Answer

Q34 How many play less than 20 hours a week?

   A. 35
   B. 37
   C. 14
   D. 206
   E. 24

Answer

Q35 What fraction plays more than the average?

   A. 3/7
   B. 5/7
   C. 3/4
   D. 1/2
   E. 5/9

Answer

Q36   If, during exam term, the three heaviest user groups reduce their playing by 10%, the three least-heavy user groups by 20% and the middle group remains unchanged, what would be the approximate average number of hours spent playing?

    A.   24
    B.   25
    C.   26
    D.   27
    E.   28

Answer [   ]

Questions 37 to 40 concern the measure of Body Mass Index (BMI) – the mass of a person (kg) divided by the square of the height (m^2). Normal range is 18.5–24.9, overweight is 25–29.9, obese is 30.0 or more:

Person	Height (m)	Weight (kg)
A	1.45	45
B	1.50	50
C	1.55	55
D	1.70	60
E	1.80	70

Q37   Which person has the greatest BMI?

    A.   A
    B.   B
    C.   C
    D.   D
    E.   E

Answer [   ]

Q38   If an adolescent's height increases by 10% and their mass by 10%, by how much will their BMI change?

    A.   Plus 11%
    B.   Plus 10%
    C.   Minus 10%
    D.   Minus 9%
    E.   Unchanged

Answer [   ]

Q39 Person A has a BMI index of 28, but would like to be in the 'normal' range, 18.5–24.9. If person A weighs 80 kg, how much do they need to lose?

A. 9 kg
B. 8 kg
C. 7 kg
D. 6 kg
E. 5 kg

Answer _____

Q40 A 1.8 m person has a BMI of 24.9, at the top end of the 'normal' range. By what fraction will their weight have to increase to be in the 'obese' range?

A. 1/3
B. 1/4
C. 1/5
D. 1/6
E. 1/7

Answer _____

Questions 41 to 44 concern house prices in two different regions:

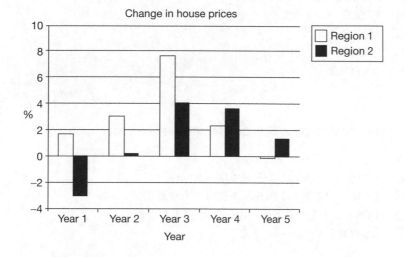

Q41 Where and when did prices fall most?

A. Region 1, year 3
B. Region 2, year 3
C. Region 2, year 2
D. Region 1, year 5
E. Region 2, year 1

Answer

Q42 Which year had the greatest difference in price changes between the two regions?

A. Year 1
B. Year 2
C. Year 3
D. Year 4
E. Year 5

Answer

Q43 If a region 1 house and a region 2 house are both worth £200,000 at the start of year 3, what will be the difference in value at the end?

A. £15,000
B. £7,000
C. £8,000
D. £7,500
E. Can't tell

Answer

Q44 What is the total price change over the five years for region 1?

A. $1.5 + 3 + 7.5 + 2.3 - 0.1$
B. $1.015 \times 1.03 \times 1.075 \times 1.023 \times -1.01$
C. $1.015 \times 1.03 \times 1.075 \times 1.023 \times 0.99$
D. $1.05 + 1.03 + 1.075 + 1.023 + -1.01$
E. Can't tell

Answer

Questions 45 to 48 concern the exchange rates at different bureaux de change:

Financial institution	Exchange rate: £1 = 1.18€ to 1.22€
Happy Holidays	×1.20€ 3% commission and £1.20 fee
Better Bank	×1.18€ no commission and no fee
X-Change	×1.22€ 2% commission and £2.50 fee
Four Eyes Currency	×1.22€ 3% commission and no fee
Concurrency	×1.20€ no commission and £2.00 fee

Q45   Which of the following equations gives the number of euros (€) for £200 with Happy Holidays?

A. $(200 \times 1.20) - (0.03 \times 200)$
B. $0.03 \times 200 \times 1.20 - 1.20$
C. $0.97 \times 200 \times 1.20 + 1.20$
D. $200 \times 1.2 \times 0.97 - 1.20 \,(1.2)$
E. $200 \times 1.20 - 1.20 \,(1.2)$

Answer ☐

Q46   Which would be the most worthwhile for converting a large sum?

A.   Happy Holidays
B.   Better Bank
C.   X-change
D.   Four Eyes Currency
E.   Concurrency

Answer ☐

The table below shows the number of euros for different sterling transactions:

£	Bureau de change €				
	HH	BB	XC	FEC	CON
10	10.24	11.80	8.97	11.64	10.00
20	21.88	23.60	20.92	23.28	22.00
30	33.52	35.40	32.88	34.92	34.00
40	45.16	47.20	44.84	46.56	46.00
50	56.80	59.00	56.79	58.20	58.00
60	68.44	70.80	68.75	69.84	70.00
70	80.08	82.60	80.70	81.48	82.00
80	91.72	94.40	92.66	93.12	94.00
90	103.36	106.20	104.62	104.76	106.00
100	115.00	118.00	116.57	116.40	118.00
110	126.64	129.80	128.53	128.04	130.00
120	138.28	141.60	140.48	139.68	142.00
130	149.92	153.40	152.44	151.32	154.00
140	161.56	165.20	164.40	162.96	166.00
150	173.20	177.00	175.70	177.50	177.60
160	184.84	188.80	188.31	186.24	190.00
170	196.48	200.60	200.26	197.88	202.00
180	208.12	212.40	212.22	209.52	214.00
190	219.76	224.20	224.18	221.16	226.00
200	231.40	236.00	236.13	232.80	238.00
210	243.04	247.80	248.09	244.44	250.00
220	254.68	259.60	260.04	256.08	262.00
230	266.32	271.40	272.00	267.72	274.00
240	277.96	283.20	283.96	279.36	286.00
250	289.60	295.00	295.91	291.00	298.00

Q47 What is the biggest difference between the different bureaux for changing £150?

A. 2.5%
B. 4.4%
C. 3%
D. 3.5%
E. 2%

Answer [   ]

Q48 If the exchange rate is €1.22 to the pound, approximately what fraction is lost when changing £20 with Concurrency, reading directly from the table?

A. 1/5
B. 1/10
C. 1/4
D. 1/7
E. 1/3

Answer [   ]

Questions 49 to 52 concern the market share of different soft drinks:

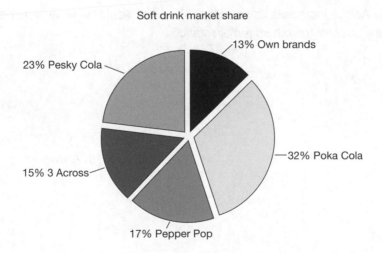

Soft drink market share

13% Own brands
23% Pesky Cola
32% Poka Cola
15% 3 Across
17% Pepper Pop

Q49 Approximately what fraction of the market do the colas represent?

A. 1/3
B. 1/2
C. 3/4
D. 1/5
E. 5/9

Answer [   ]

Q50 If Pepper Pop increases its market share by 3% at the expense of 3 Across, what would be the new ratio of Pepper Pop to 3 Across?

A. 4 : 3
B. 1.67 : 1
C. 3 : 5
D. 20 : 15
E. 17 : 15

Answer

Q51 A new brand is launched which succeeds in capturing 5% of the market within a year. If the ratio of Pesky Cola to Pepper Pop to 3 Across to Poker Cola remains the same, what is the maximum market share of the own brands?

A. 8%
B. 15%
C. 20%
D. 25%
E. 95%

Answer

Q52 If 3 Across increases its sales by 15%, what would be its new market share, if the sales of the others remain static?

A. 15%
B. 16%
C. 17%
D. 20%
E. 30%

Answer

Questions 53 to 56 concern the reliability of various brands based on the number of warranty claims of various brands of car:

Brand	Claims per 100	Average claim cost (£)
Bonza	9.9	325
Havanaisday	16.2	135
Frort	36.4	223
Perja	30.8	228
MT	37.7	433

Q53 Which brand has the lowest cost per 100?

A. Bonza
B. Havanaisday
C. Frort
D. Perja
E. MT

Answer [   ]

Q54 If the cost of the claims has not been factored in to the original price of the car, how much will MT have to add to the price of a car to take this into account?

A. £143
B. £149
C. £155
D. £160
E. £163

Answer [   ]

Q55 Through improved quality and better working practices, Frort is able to reduce the number of claims per hundred to 25 and the cost per claim to £200. What is the fractional saving?

A. 2/5
B. 1/4
C. 3/10
D. 1/3
E. 4/9

Answer [   ]

Q56 Perja decides to offer an additional insurance policy beyond the warranty period. If the probability of a breakdown with an average repair cost of £250 is 1 in 12 per year, what price should the premium be to make a 20% return?

    A. £25
    B. £20.74
    C. £30.92
    D. £20.10
    E. £27

Answer

Questions 57 to 60 concern exchange rates:

Dollally	Kroni	Pounze	Robbers	Yangs	Barts
1	5.91	1.97	23.69	104.93	33.15

Q57 What is the exchange rate from Robbers to Yangs?

    A. 0.226
    B. 4.429
    C. 0.262
    D. 23.69
    E. 4.492

Answer

Q58 If the exchange rate from Dollally to Pounze drops by 20% and the rate from Dollally to Yangs increases by 25%, by how much will the Pounze–Yangs rate change?

    A. 56%
    B. 45%
    C. 5%
    D. 20%
    E. 25%

Answer

Q59 A virtual currency is defined as the value of Dollally times Robbers divided by Pounze times Kroni. If the value of the Pounze drops 20% against the Dollally, by how much will this virtual currency change?

A. Up 1/4
B. Up 1/5
C. Down 1/5
D. Down 1/4
E. Down 1/3

Answer [   ]

Q60 A tourist changes 100 Dollally to Barts. If the tourist then returns home and changes the remaining 100 Barts back to Dollally, how much would they have lost in total if the commission is 3% in both directions?

A. 6.00 Dollally
B. 3.00 Dollally
C. 3.09 Dollally
D. 6.33 Dollally
E. 4.27 Dollally

Answer [   ]

Mini-tests

Mini-test 1

You have four minutes to answer eight questions in the two sections below.

Questions 61 to 64 concern the sale of ice cream:

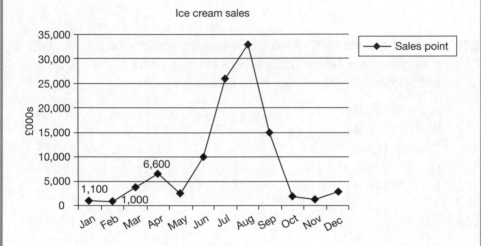

Ice cream sales

Q61 What fraction were the minimum sales of the maximum?

A. 1/10
B. 1/20
C. 1/30
D. 1/40
E. 1/25

Answer [   ]

Q62 By how much do sales increase from January to April?

A. 500%
B. 600%
C. 60%
D. 450%
E. 550%

Answer [   ]

Q63 If the company needs £5m sales per month to break even, how much profit does it make in the year?

A. £0.5m
B. £400m
C. £500,000
D. £5m
E. £45m

Answer [   ]

Q64 If inflation rises at 0.1% per month, which formula correctly calculates the increase in cost at the end of the year?

A. 1.001^{12}
B. 12×0.1
C. 1.1^{12}
D. 0.1^{12}
E. $1 + (12 \times 0.001)$

Answer [   ]

Questions 65 to 68 compare the time taken for various journeys:

Journey	Distance (miles)	Time (hours and mins)
A	115	1h 55m
B	97	2h 6m
C	65	1h 11m
D	88	1h 45m
E	95	1h 35m

Q65 Which journey has the highest average speed?

A. A
B. A and E
C. E and C
D. C
E. E

Answer [   ]

Q66   Which formula gives the average speed for journey C in miles per hour?

    A. s = 65 / 1.11
    B. s = 65 / 1 + (11/60)
    C. s = 65 / (1 + (11/60))
    D. s = 65 × 1.11
    E. s = 65 / (1 × (11/60))

Answer [   ]

Q67   The time taken for journey C can vary by as much as plus or minus 20%. By how much will the corresponding average speed change?

    A. +20%, −20%
    B. +25%, −25%
    C. +25%, −17%
    D. +17%, −20%
    E. Can't tell

Answer [   ]

Q68   If there are 1.609 km to a mile, what is the average speed for journey E in metres per second?

    A. 26.82 m/s
    B. 1609 m/s
    C. 96552 m/s
    D. 25.66 m/s
    E. 95562 m/s

Answer [   ]

End of test

Mini-test 2

You have five minutes to answer eight questions.

Questions 69 to 72 concern traffic on the internet through a particular server during the day (1 TeraByte = 1,000 GigaBytes):

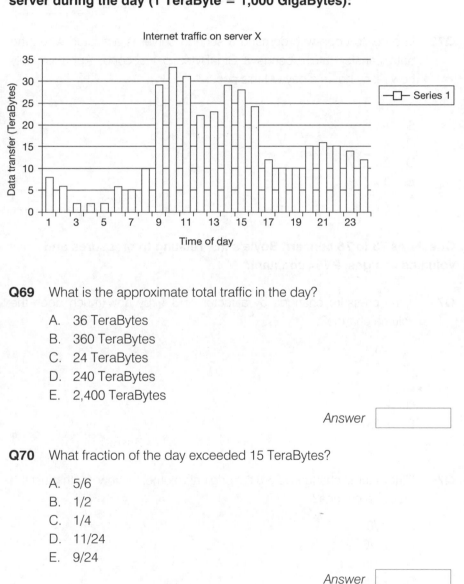

Internet traffic on server X

Q69   What is the approximate total traffic in the day?

A.   36 TeraBytes
B.   360 TeraBytes
C.   24 TeraBytes
D.   240 TeraBytes
E.   2,400 TeraBytes

Answer

Q70   What fraction of the day exceeded 15 TeraBytes?

A.   5/6
B.   1/2
C.   1/4
D.   11/24
E.   9/24

Answer

Q71 Between which times did the traffic increase the most?

A. 8 and 9
B. 5 and 6 or 8 and 9
C. 5 and 6
D. 16 and 17
E. 30%

Answer [   ]

Q72 In order to cope with demand a second server is activated when the data transfer rate exceeds 3 GigaBytes per second. Approximately how many hours a day will this occur?

A. 14
B. 10
C. 3
D. 2
E. 0

Answer [   ]

Questions 73 to 76 concern Boyle's law relating to pressures and volumes of a gas, PV = constant:

Q73 If the pressure changes by a factor of 3/4, by how much does the volume change?

A. 3/4
B. 4/3
C. 1.5
D. 2
E. 1.25

Answer [   ]

Q74 If the volume changes to 5/6 the original volume, by how much must the pressure change?

A. −1/6
B. +1/6
C. +1/5
D. +5/6
E. −5/6

Answer [   ]

Q75 The following results were taken during an experiment. It appears that the experimenter has made a mistake. Where?

A. The volume 0.020 should read 0.200.
B. The pressure 100 should read 10.
C. The volume 0.022 should read 0.220.
D. The volume 0.133 should read 0.013.
E. Can't tell.

Answer ⬚

Pressure (kPa)	Volume (m³)
100	0.020
95	0.021
90	0.022
65	0.031
150	0.133

Q76 The pressure in the above experiment is increased to 900 kPa. If the experimenter only reads to three decimal places, what percentage error will this introduce?

A. 10%
B. 15%
C. 5%
D. 2%
E. 3%

Answer ⬚

End of test

Mini-test 3

Questions 77 to 80 concern the results of a comparison test between two populations and two types of orange juice. The percentages give the number who preferred the particular juice:

	Population X	Population Y
Juice A	85%	55%
Juice B	10%	30%

Q77   What fraction of population Y was undecided?

   A.   85/100
   B.   25/100
   C.   1/5
   D.   3/20
   E.   15/50

   Answer [   ]

Q78   If the population Y were twice as big as population X, what would be the average preference percentage for Juice A for the entire population of X and Y together?

   A.   83%
   B.   79%
   C.   65%
   D.   70%
   E.   67%

   Answer [   ]

Q79 The polling company then carried out a later test where juice A was identified as being 10% more expensive than juice B and the question asked as to which juice people would buy. Which population has shown the greatest points percentage change?

	Population X	Population Y
Juice A	65%	62%
Juice B	29%	32%

A. Population X for juice A
B. Population X for juice B
C. Population Y for juice B
D. Population Y for juice A
E. Can't tell

Answer [   ]

Q80 What percentage change in revenue would be achieved by making Juice A 10% more expensive for populations X and Y combined?

A. Around 10% more
B. Around 10% less
C. Around 7% more
D. Around no change
E. Can't tell

Answer [   ]

Questions 81 to 84 concern the results of a particular competition:

Team	Won	Drawn	Lost	Points
A	2	2	0	26
B	0	4	1	21
C	0	3	3	18
D	1	2	1	19
E	2	1	0	21

Q81 How many points are there for a draw?

A. 1   B. 2   C. 3   D. 4   E. 5

Answer

Q82 How many matches are left to play if each team plays the others twice?

A. 9   B. 8   C. 7   D. 6   E. 5

Answer

Q83 What is the maximum total number of points obtainable by any team in this season?

A. 64   B. 61   C. 62   D. 58   E. 60

Answer

Q84 If all the remaining matches are drawn, what fraction of the teams will have less than 30 points?

A.   1/5
B.   2/5
C.   3/5
D.   4/5
E.   Can't tell

Answer

End of test

Mini-test 4

Questions 85 to 88 concern a set of exam results:

Student	Result (%)	Student	Result (%)
A	44	K	36
B	46	L	38
C	55	M	48
D	91	N	57
E	88	O	87
F	66	P	83
G	57	Q	55
H	80	R	61
I	72	S	59
J	55	T	54

Q85 If the exam board intends that only 10% of students should receive the maximum grade, what mark should be the minimum to achieve this grade?

A. 80
B. 87.5
C. 88
D. 87
E. 85.5

Answer [   ]

Q86 If 10% also fail, what is the range between the mark separating the top group and the mark separating the bottom group?

A. 49
B. 48
C. 47.5
D. 48.5
E. 50

Answer [   ]

Q87   A second set of results was obtained as follows. What percentage has achieved more than half marks?

Result (%)	Result (%)
37	58
39	60
45	62
49	67
50	73
55	82
56	85
56	89
56	90
58	93

A.   60%
B.   70%
C.   75%
D.   80%
E.   90%

Answer

Q88   If all the scores in the first set improved by 3%, how many would now achieve the top grade if the dividing mark/original grade boundary remained unchanged?

A.   2
B.   3
C.   4
D.   5
E.   Can't tell

Answer

Questions 89 to 92 concern rates of interest:

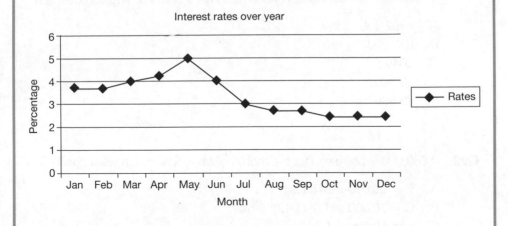

Interest rates over year

Q89 Which four months had the highest rates of interest?

A. January, February, March, April
B. February, March, April, May
C. March, April, May, June
D. April, May, June, July
E. September, October, November, December

Answer

Q90 What fraction of the May interest rate is the September rate?

A. 11/20
B. 1/2
C. 3/5
D. 2.5/5
E. 6/10

Answer

Q91   If the average interest rate over the year can be used to determine the interest paid on borrowings, how much will be paid on a £250,000 loan?

A.   £102,000
B.   £10,200
C.   £840
D.   £8,500
E.   £9,600

Answer [   ]

Q92   If £50,000 is borrowed for the month of May, how much will it cost?

A.   C = 50,000 × 5(1/12)
B.   C = 50,000 × 1.05(1/12)
C.   C = 50,000 × 5 / 12
D.   C = 50,000 × 1.05 / 12
E.   Can't tell

Answer [   ]

End of test

Mini-test 5

You have four minutes to answer eight questions in the two sections below.

Questions 93 to 96 concern the activity of a typical student during a college day:

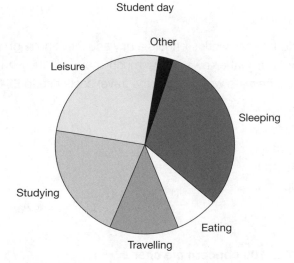

Student day

Q93   How much more time is spent on leisure than on travelling?

    A. 100%
    B. 400%
    C. 40%
    D. 200%
    E. 25%

                                                    Answer   [   ]

Q94   If the travelling time is doubled at the expense of leisure time, what is now the ratio of leisure to travel?

    A. 4 : 1
    B. 3 : 2
    C. 2 : 1
    D. 2 : 3
    E. 1 : 2

                                                    Answer   [   ]

Q95   During the holidays the study time is replaced by working at £6.50 per hour. If the travel costs are £1.20 to get to work, how long does the student have to work to pay the travel costs?

A.   10.5 minutes
B.   20 minutes
C.   18.5 minutes
D.   11 minutes
E.   15.5 minutes

Answer [   ]

Q96   If the student can work six hours a day and they find a job which is more lucrative but further away, how much more will they have to earn to make the new job worthwhile if the travel costs rise to £3.00?

A.   10p/hour
B.   15p/hour
C.   20p/hour
D.   25p/hour
E.   30p/hour

Answer [   ]

Questions 97 to 100 concern pie charts

Carbon-dioxide, nitrous oxide, methane and fluorocarbons are the main gases that contribute to global warming. The combined emission of these gases constitutes the household carbon-dioxide emission. Each of these four gases has a different impact on global warming depending upon how much heat they trap. Fluorocarbon emissions are particularly damaging to the environment because they trap 1,000 times as much heat as carbon-dioxide. The ability to trap heat relative to carbon-dioxide is as follows:

carbon-dioxide × 1

methane × 22

nitrous oxide × 300

fluorocarbons × 1,000

The carbon footprint is found by multiplying the household carbon-dioxide emissions by 12/44 or 0.273 (the ratio of the atomic weights of carbon and carbon dioxide). Household X generated 5,241 kg of carbon-dioxide from room heating during the year.

Pie chart showing household Y's emissions of greenhouse gases during the year

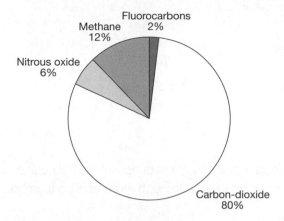

Pie chart showing carbon footprint activities of household X

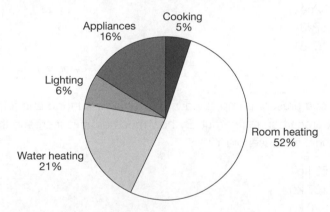

Pie chart showing carbon footprint activities of household Y

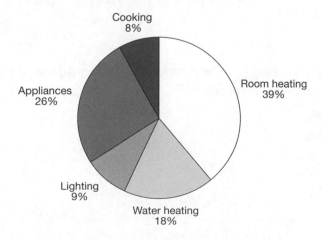

Q97 What was the carbon footprint of household X in kilograms of carbon during the year?

A. 2751
B. 3160
C. 5241
D. 8793
E. 10079

Answer

Q98 What was the carbon footprint of household Y if household Y generated 20% less carbon-dioxide through room heating than household X?

A. 2747
B. 2935
C. 3264
D. 5793
E. 10751

Answer

Q99 The compressor pump failed in household Y's fridge and it lost 0.5 kg of fluorocarbon refrigerant. By how much did this increase the carbon footprint of household Y?

A. 65 kg
B. 137 kg
C. 326 kg
D. 500 kg
E. 1000 kg

Answer

Q100 What percentage of household Y's carbon-dioxide emissions are attributable to fluorocarbons?

A. 2%
B. 6%
C. 12%
D. 36%
E. 48%

Answer

CHAPTER 4

Abstract Reasoning

The abstract reasoning sub-test is described as being intended to assess an ability to identify patterns amongst abstract shapes. The way the UKCAT sub-test does this is by asking the candidate to identify to which group a particular shape, or set of shapes, belongs.

For each set, A and B, there will be five test shapes and you will have to click on one of three buttons, A, B or C, to indicate whether you think the test shape belongs to set A, set B or neither (C).

What you have to do, therefore, is to try to identify a particular rule, or set of rules, that govern the contents of the cells in each set. For example Set A may contain an even number of shapes and set B an odd number of shapes, or set A may contain shapes containing a right angle and set B shapes without a right angle.

The questions are easy to answer if you have identified the distinguishing features of each set correctly. If you have problems choosing an answer then look at the set again to see if you need to change the rationale. Avoid the temptation to study the test shape in an attempt to characterise the sets because it is unlikely to provide further insights. Instead concentrate on each set in turn, starting with either A or B. If you start with set A but are unable to characterise it, then switch to set B. When you have characterised one set it will be easier to characterise the other.

Some rules will be readily apparent, but others, equally crucial for determining whether or not a particular test shape belongs, will be more obscure and will require careful scrutiny of *all* the cells in the set.

The kinds of things you should be looking for include:

number of shapes;

size of shapes;

shape of shapes;

shaded or not;

number of sides;

rotation symmetry;

reflection symmetry;

number of intersections or overlapping regions;

number of shaded regions;

relationships between shapes (eg shapes in pairs);

direction (pointing up or down, left or right, etc.)

position in the cell.

You have 55 questions to answer in 13 minutes. Simply dividing the time available by the number of test shapes to consider would give about 14 seconds for each shape. What you should do, however, is to spend about half the time trying to establish the rules for each set and then more quickly determine the appropriate responses (Set A, Set B or Neither) for each of the five test shapes. Aim to spend anything up to three-quarters of a minute on characterising the two sets. Once this has been done, it only takes a few seconds to identify to which set each test shape belongs. In some instances all five test shapes can be characterised in half a minute.

The following warm-up exercise starts with a few easy questions where the rules are fairly obvious, followed by more difficult questions where the rules become increasingly obscure. You should attempt to complete all 55 questions in no more than 13 minutes. If you cannot find the rule in under one-minute then move on to the next question. On test day, do not leave any questions unanswered as you have a one in three chance of choosing the correct answer and there is no penalty for wrong answers.

Warm-up questions

Exercise 1 (easy) – 55 questions in 13 minutes

Q1

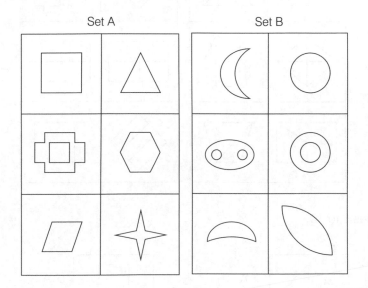

Test shapes 1 to 5

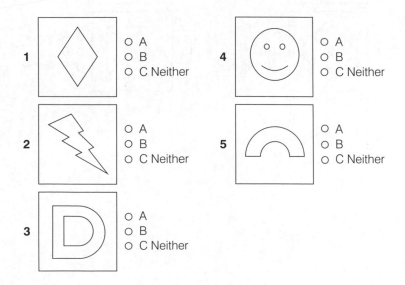

1
  ○ A
  ○ B
  ○ C Neither

2
  ○ A
  ○ B
  ○ C Neither

3
  ○ A
  ○ B
  ○ C Neither

4
  ○ A
  ○ B
  ○ C Neither

5
  ○ A
  ○ B
  ○ C Neither

Q2

Set A   Set B

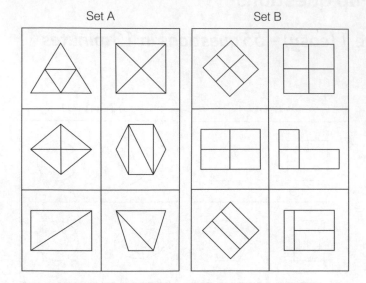

Test shapes 6 to 10

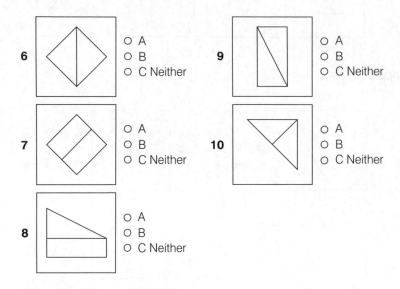

6   ○ A
     ○ B
     ○ C Neither

9   ○ A
     ○ B
     ○ C Neither

7   ○ A
     ○ B
     ○ C Neither

10   ○ A
     ○ B
     ○ C Neither

8   ○ A
     ○ B
     ○ C Neither

Q3

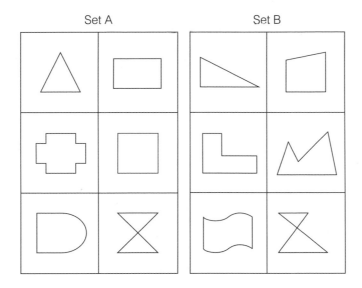

Set A   Set B

Test shapes 11 to 15

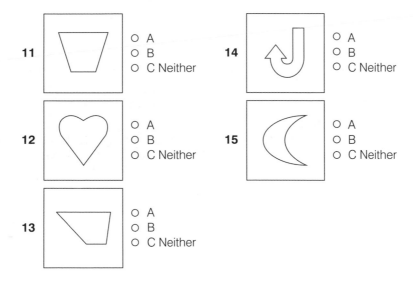

11
○ A
○ B
○ C Neither

14
○ A
○ B
○ C Neither

12
○ A
○ B
○ C Neither

15
○ A
○ B
○ C Neither

13
○ A
○ B
○ C Neither

Q4

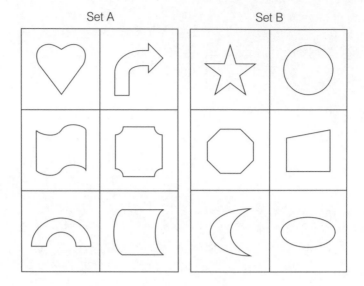

Set A   Set B

Test shapes 16 to 20

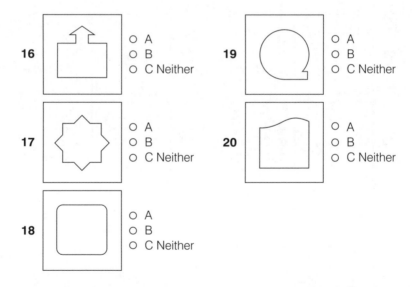

16   ○ A
     ○ B
     ○ C Neither

17   ○ A
     ○ B
     ○ C Neither

18   ○ A
     ○ B
     ○ C Neither

19   ○ A
     ○ B
     ○ C Neither

20   ○ A
     ○ B
     ○ C Neither

Q5

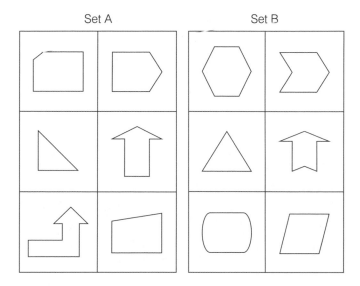

Set A   Set B

Test shapes 21 to 25

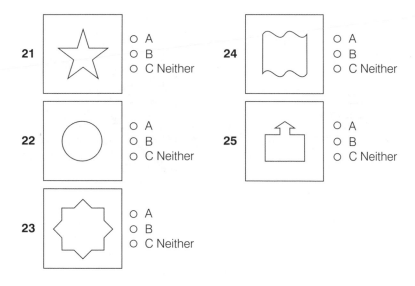

21 ○ A
        ○ B
        ○ C Neither

22 ○ A
        ○ B
        ○ C Neither

23 ○ A
        ○ B
        ○ C Neither

24 ○ A
        ○ B
        ○ C Neither

25 ○ A
        ○ B
        ○ C Neither

Q6

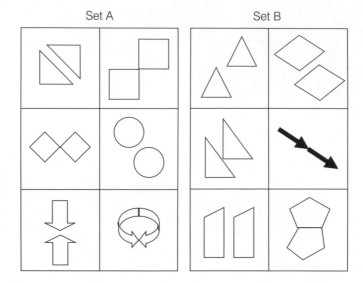

Test shapes 26 to 30

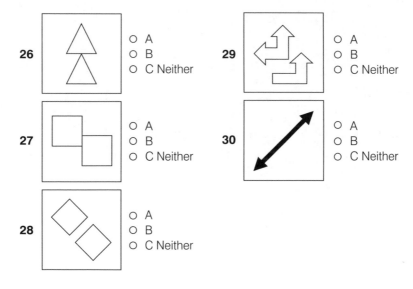

Q7

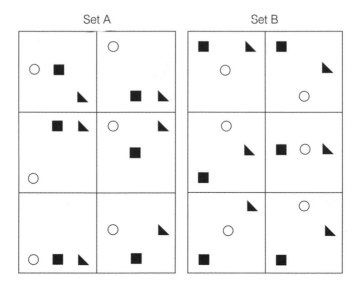

Test shapes 31 to 35

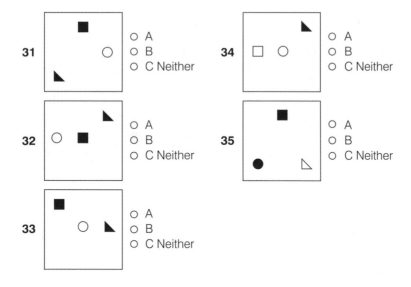

Q8

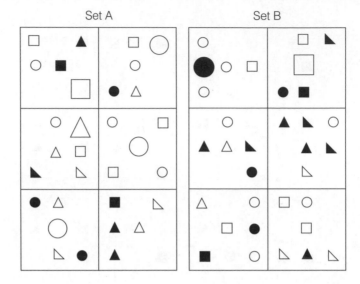

Test shapes 36 to 40

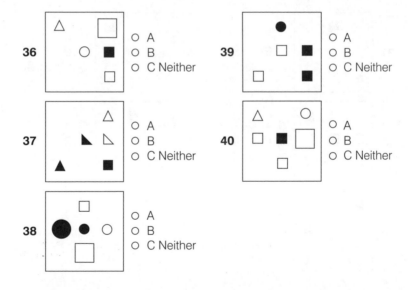

Q9

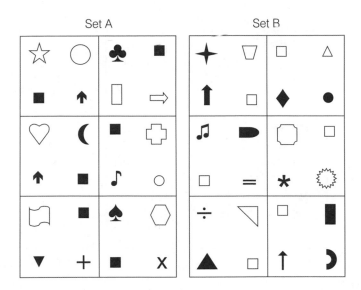

Test shapes 41 to 45

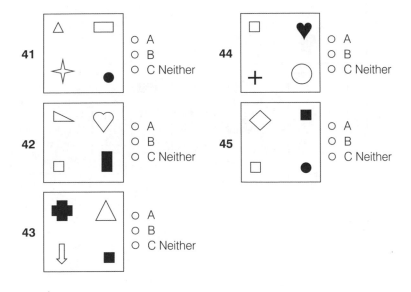

Q10

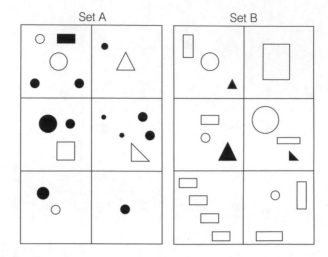

Test shapes 46 to 50

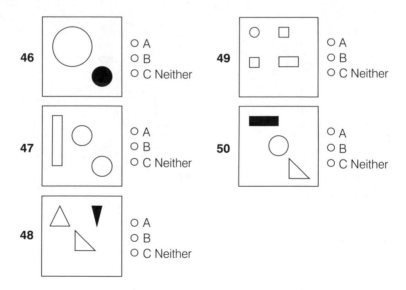

Q11

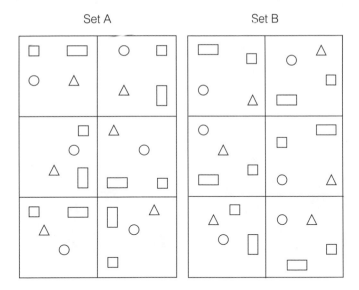

Set A   Set B

Test shapes 51 to 55

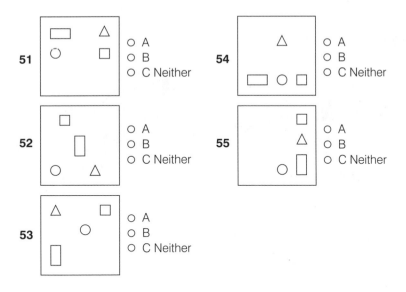

51   ○ A
     ○ B
     ○ C Neither

52   ○ A
     ○ B
     ○ C Neither

53   ○ A
     ○ B
     ○ C Neither

54   ○ A
     ○ B
     ○ C Neither

55   ○ A
     ○ B
     ○ C Neither

Exercise 2 (more difficult) – 55 questions in 13 minutes

Q1

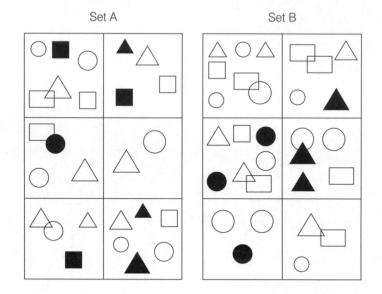

Test shapes 1 to 5

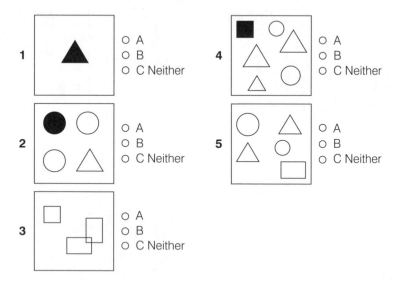

Q2

Set A   Set B

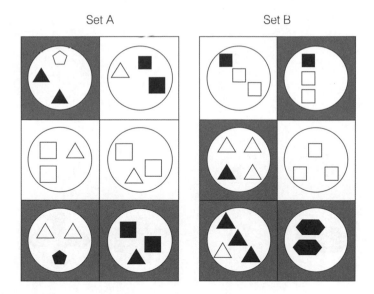

Test shapes 6 to 10

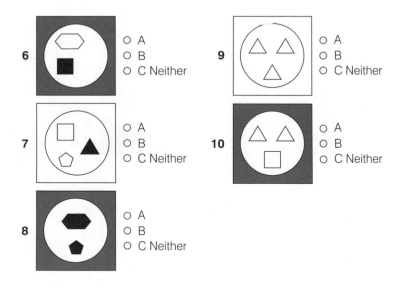

6
○ A
○ B
○ C Neither

9
○ A
○ B
○ C Neither

7
○ A
○ B
○ C Neither

10
○ A
○ B
○ C Neither

8
○ A
○ B
○ C Neither

Q3

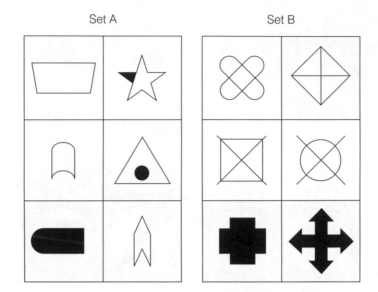

Test shapes 11 to 15

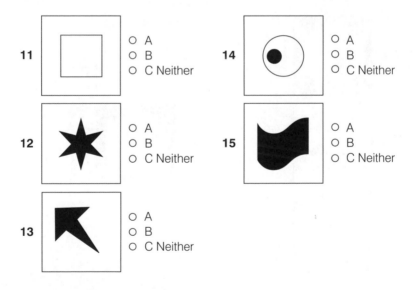

Q4

Set A   Set B

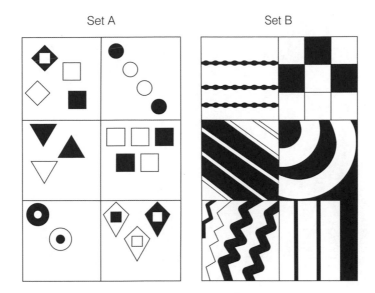

Test shapes 16 to 20

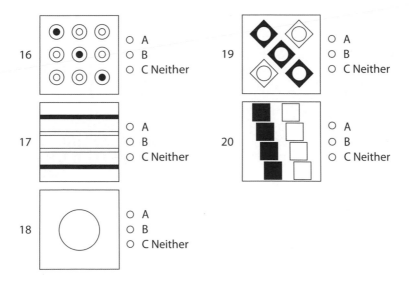

16   ○ A
     ○ B
     ○ C Neither

17   ○ A
     ○ B
     ○ C Neither

18   ○ A
     ○ B
     ○ C Neither

19   ○ A
     ○ B
     ○ C Neither

20   ○ A
     ○ B
     ○ C Neither

Q5

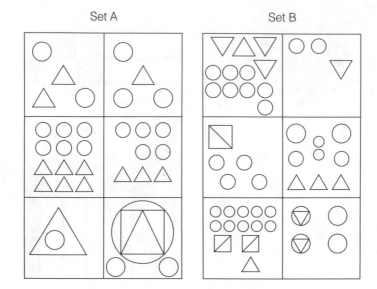

Set A   Set B

Test shapes 21 to 25

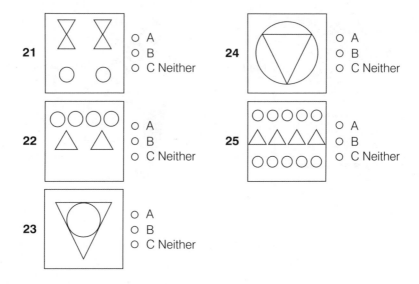

21
○ A
○ B
○ C Neither

22
○ A
○ B
○ C Neither

23
○ A
○ B
○ C Neither

24
○ A
○ B
○ C Neither

25
○ A
○ B
○ C Neither

Q6

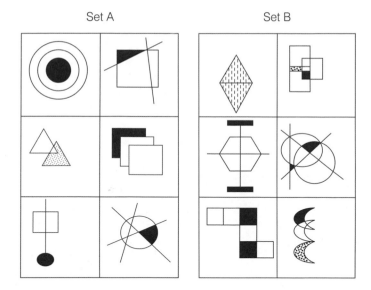

Set A   Set B

Test shapes 26 to 30

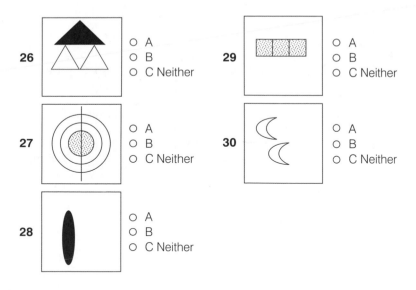

26   ○ A
          ○ B
          ○ C Neither

27   ○ A
          ○ B
          ○ C Neither

28   ○ A
          ○ B
          ○ C Neither

29   ○ A
          ○ B
          ○ C Neither

30   ○ A
          ○ B
          ○ C Neither

Q7

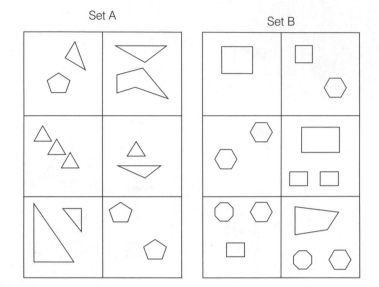

Set A   Set B

Test shapes 31 to 35

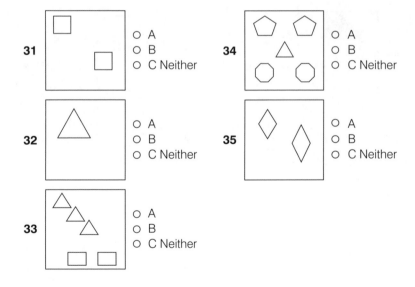

31   ○ A
         ○ B
         ○ C Neither

32   ○ A
         ○ B
         ○ C Neither

33   ○ A
         ○ B
         ○ C Neither

34   ○ A
         ○ B
         ○ C Neither

35   ○ A
         ○ B
         ○ C Neither

Q8

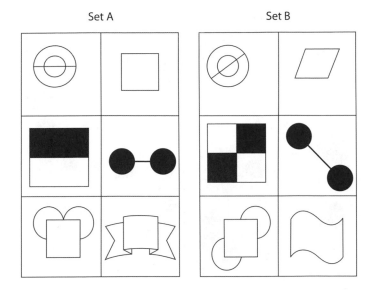

Set A   Set B

Test shapes 36 to 40

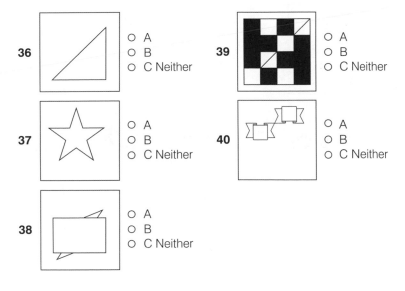

36   ○ A
          ○ B
          ○ C Neither

37   ○ A
          ○ B
          ○ C Neither

38   ○ A
          ○ B
          ○ C Neither

39   ○ A
          ○ B
          ○ C Neither

40   ○ A
          ○ B
          ○ C Neither

Q9

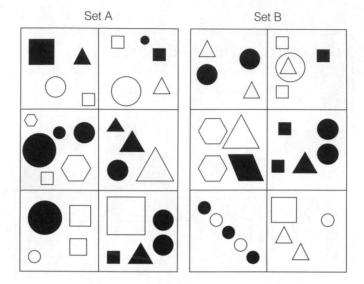

Test shapes 41 to 45

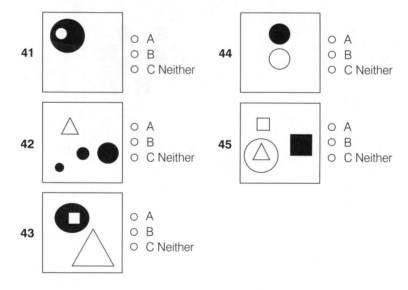

Q10

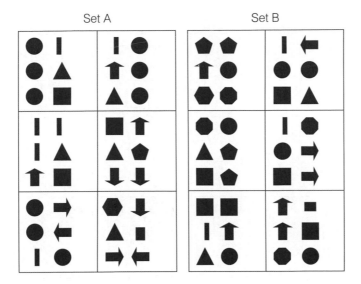

Set A   Set B

Test shapes 46 to 50

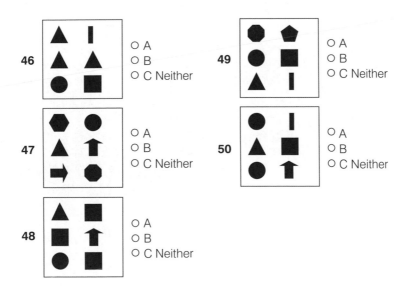

46
○ A
○ B
○ C Neither

47
○ A
○ B
○ C Neither

48
○ A
○ B
○ C Neither

49
○ A
○ B
○ C Neither

50
○ A
○ B
○ C Neither

Q11

Set A Set B

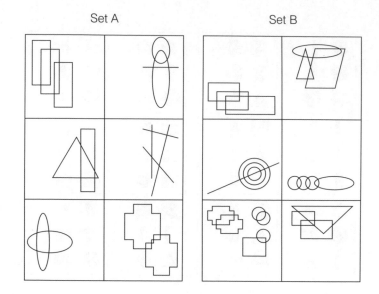

Test shapes 51 to 55

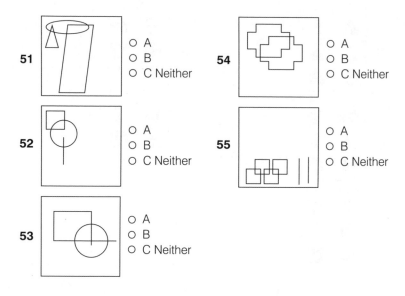

51 ○ A
○ B
○ C Neither

54 ○ A
○ B
○ C Neither

52 ○ A
○ B
○ C Neither

55 ○ A
○ B
○ C Neither

53 ○ A
○ B
○ C Neither

CHAPTER 5

Situational judgement analysis

The situational judgement test is the newest and perhaps the most daunting of all the sections as it introduces the highest levels of ambiguity you will have to face on a regular basis. The format is already familiar to medical students and doctors, and is involved as part of the professional assessment for selecting Foundation trainees to the deanery areas of their choice, and indeed later in selecting trainees to specialties.

Essentially, you are given a scenario and forced to make a life-like decision with regards to two elements: appropriateness or importance.

In appropriateness type items, you will be given a choice of the following four responses to the passage you are faced with:

● ***A very appropriate thing to do.*** A very appropriate answer means that this will definitely be helpful in the situation, and should be done. (Importantly, it does not mean it will be the only thing to do, and there may be multiple actions of various levels of appropriateness.)

    For example, if you are given a scenario about breaking bad news to a patient, listening and giving time for the patient to talk is a very appropriate thing to do.

● ***Appropriate, but not ideal.*** An appropriate, but not ideal answer means that it is fine to do this, but it's not the optimal solution for the problem. For example, when breaking bad news to a patient, you could be reading the facts out from the medical notes rather than looking at the patient. Appropriate as you are ensuring the facts are correct, but not ideal as eye contact for empathy and reading the situation would be better.

- **_Inappropriate, but not awful._** An inappropriate, but not awful answer means that you should not do this, but in the event that it did happen, it would not be awful. For this type of answer, keep in mind things which would annoy or upset patients or colleagues, but would not harm them.

  For example, when breaking bad news to a patient, you could be constantly checking your beeper or smartphone. This is not a very nice thing to do, but probably not life (or licence) threatening.

- **_A very inappropriate thing to do._** A very inappropriate thing to do answer means you should really not do what it says, and the result of which can be detrimental, unprofessional or harmful to the people in the situation. For example, when breaking bad news to a patient, you could ask a medical student who has not seen the patient to read up the notes and go and break the news, rather than do it yourself. This potentially harms both the patient and the student, and could cause serious mis-information and distress. Very inappropriate indeed, and an order of magnitude more than the above.

As you can imagine, the highest level of ambiguity will be between responses 2 and 3, and indeed it is often very tricky to isolate the desired response from the examiners. A general rule is to use the mindset of 'non-optimal but still does the trick' for _appropriate and not ideal_, and 'doesn't help, even though no-one suffers too badly' for _inappropriate but not awful_. The usefulness of what you are doing determines if it is appropriate or not.

Importance is the second type of response you will be asked to give, and much like the appropriateness test above, it is of critical relevance to your day-to-day life as a clinician. Similarly, there are four levels of response:

- Very important. _A very important_ answer means that you cannot miss this out, and that missing it may lead to highly negative effects.

  For example, in a scenario where you are managing multiple patients on a ward at once, prioritizing life-threatening, limb-threatening, sight-threatening and other permanent problems over temporary ones should always be the case. This is one way to filter 'very important' from important: life-threatening is more important than limb-threatening, which is more important than temporary illness.

- Important. An _important_ answer means that you can miss it out without terrible consequences, but it would be helpful to do or know.

  For example, when taking a history from a cancer patient, knowing their family history and if anyone has died of cancer in the family is important as many cancers have significant genetic components. You will find out other information and symptoms, and investigate the patient further: however, it is still important.

- Of minor importance. An *of minor importance* answer means that whilst having the information could be used in some way, it is not of particular consequence either way. For example, in the same cancer patient, you could ask about their travel in the past 10 years, as certain viruses which are prevalent in other countries can give you a higher chance of getting certain cancers such as Hepatitis B or C and liver cancer. If someone comes to you with cancer-like symptoms or you are suspicious, this will not tip the balance, and you will still investigate them fully. However, it is a minor piece to the puzzle, which makes it different from the answer below.

- Not important at all. A *not important at all* answer means exactly what it says, even if you know or do this, it will not have the slightest impact on the outcome. In a cancer patient, this could be non-sensical questions such as 'do you like classical music', or even pseudo-medical questions with no bearing such as 'frequency of exercise'.

As with all sections of this book, and the UKCAT, practice makes perfect. Knowing the general principles is one thing, but a careful calibration of your senses to what the examiners want can only be achieved through going through questions and adapting to the feedback, especially when you find yourself wrong. Resist the urge to 'argue' with the answer and impose your sense of appropriateness or importance on it: rather, try to do as many questions as available, and adapt yourself to the global picture of what is important or appropriate. (This is a UKCAT only technique; in life you should of course do what you think is appropriate and important!)

You will spend 26 minutes (plus one for instruction reading) to undertake 67 items from 20 scenarios, which is quite a high pace. This further emphasizes the need for practice and development of 'reading' situations. This chapter contains seven practice scenarios, each of which has between four and six related questions. For further, relevant reading on similar situational judgement tests, you can consider *Ultimate Psychometric Tests*, also published by Kogan Page.

Fifteen warm-up questions

Scenario 1

Phillip is a first-year medical student on a ward round. Another student, Aisha, has not rolled up her shirt-sleeves in accordance with the hospital's 'bare below the sleeves' infection control guidelines. When questioned by Phillip, Aisha says that it is allowed because she's Muslim.

How appropriate are each of the following responses by Phillip to the situation?

Q1   Bleep infection control to let them know that your colleague is non-compliant with infection control guidelines.

    A.   A very appropriate thing to do

    B.   Appropriate but not ideal

    C.   Inappropriate, but not awful

    D.   A very inappropriate thing to do

Q2   Do nothing because there is a lack of scientific evidence to indicate that staff clothes are a serious source of cross-infection.

    A.   A very appropriate thing to do

    B.   Appropriate but not ideal

    C.   Inappropriate, but not awful

    D.   A very inappropriate thing to do

Q3   Inform Aisha that disposable over-sleeves are available for patient contact.

    A.   A very appropriate thing to do

    B.   Appropriate but not ideal

    C.   Inappropriate, but not awful

    D.   A very inappropriate thing to do

Q4   Ask the Ward Manager if the infection control policy is any different for Muslim doctors.

    A.   A very appropriate thing to do

    B.   Appropriate but not ideal

    C.   Inappropriate, but not awful

    D.   A very inappropriate thing to do

Q5   Review the hospital's infection control policy in the Ward Manager's office.

    A.   A very appropriate thing to do

    B.   Appropriate but not ideal

    C.   Inappropriate, but not awful

    D.   A very inappropriate thing to do

Scenario 2

Lucy is the on call doctor when Mrs Jones phones to request an update on her husband's condition. Lucy has never met Mrs Jones and does not recognize her voice. The hospital's policy is not to give out confidential patient information to a third party without confirming the identity of the caller.

How appropriate are each of the following responses by Lucy to the situation?

Q6   Ask the nurse in charge to see if she can confirm the identity of the caller.

A.   A very appropriate thing to do

B.   Appropriate but not ideal

C.   Inappropriate, but not awful

D.   A very inappropriate thing to do

Q7   Ask Mr Jones if he can come to the phone to speak to his wife or call her back later.

A.   A very appropriate thing to do

B.   Appropriate but not ideal

C.   Inappropriate, but not awful

D.   A very inappropriate thing to do

Q8   Give out the minimum amount of information to the caller.

A.   A very appropriate thing to do

B.   Appropriate but not ideal

C.   Inappropriate, but not awful

D.   A very inappropriate thing to do

Q9   Politely inform the caller that no patient information can be given out over the phone.

A.   A very appropriate thing to do

B.   Appropriate but not ideal

C.   Inappropriate, but not awful

D.   A very inappropriate thing to do

Scenario 3

Carl is a medical student on clinical placement. He confides in his friend Damien that he does not get on with his mentor. He says he that he feels unsupported and that his work is suffering.

How appropriate are each of the following responses by Damien to the situation?

Q10 Ask Carl exactly what the problem is and why.

    A. A very appropriate thing to do

    B. Appropriate but not ideal

    C. Inappropriate, but not awful

    D. A very inappropriate thing to do

Q11 Advise Carl to look towards other members of the team for additional help and support.

    A. A very appropriate thing to do

    B. Appropriate but not ideal

    C. Inappropriate, but not awful

    D. A very inappropriate thing to do

Q12 Advise Carl to explain to his mentor that he needs more support and that he is concerned about his lack of progress.

    A. A very appropriate thing to do

    B. Appropriate but not ideal

    C. Inappropriate, but not awful

    D. A very inappropriate thing to do

Q13 Advise Carl to inform the mentor in writing that he needs better mentorship.

    A. A very appropriate thing to do

    B. Appropriate but not ideal

    C. Inappropriate, but not awful

    D. A very inappropriate thing to do

Q14 Suggest Carl speaks to his academic supervisor about the difficulties he is experiencing on placement.

    A. A very appropriate thing to do

    B. Appropriate but not ideal

    C. Inappropriate, but not awful

    D. A very inappropriate thing to do

Q15 Advise Carl to do nothing as it is only a communication problem and should sort itself out given time.

A. A very appropriate thing to do

B. Appropriate but not ideal

C. Inappropriate, but not awful

D. A very inappropriate thing to do

20 practice questions in 8 minutes

Scenario 4

Zak is junior doctor on a urology ward. His patient's catheter is not draining and it needs to be removed urgently and replaced. He asks a student nurse to perform the procedure but she declines to do it stating that she is not competent with catheters.
How appropriate are each of the following responses by Zak to the situation?

Q16 Replace the catheter himself even though he has never done it before.

A. A very appropriate thing to do

B. Appropriate but not ideal

C. Inappropriate, but not awful

D. A very inappropriate thing to do

Q17 Tell the student nurse it is a simple procedure and she must do it.

A. A very appropriate thing to do

B. Appropriate but not ideal

C. Inappropriate, but not awful

D. A very inappropriate thing to do

Q18 Wait until a suitably trained member of staff returns from lunch break.

A. A very appropriate thing to do

B. Appropriate but not ideal

C. Inappropriate, but not awful

D. A very inappropriate thing to do

Q19 Ask the student nurse to find a competent colleague on the ward.

A. A very appropriate thing to do

B. Appropriate but not ideal

C. Inappropriate, but not awful

D. A very inappropriate thing to do

Scenario 5

Emma is a student doctor working a night-shift in the Emergency Department. Mike, a staff nurse, has fallen asleep at the nurses' station. Emma manages to rouse Mike but he remains a little drowsy. He has a bottle of tablets in his hand.

How important to take into account are the following considerations for Emma when deciding how to respond to the situation?

Q20   A patient's bed-light is on and Mike needs to attend.

A.   Very important

B.   Important

C.   Of minor importance

D.   Not important at all

Q21   It has been an exceptionally busy night and Mike has been working very hard.

A.   Very important

B.   Important

C.   Of minor importance

D.   Not important at all

Q22   Mike has never fallen asleep on duty before.

A.   Very important

B.   Important

C.   Of minor importance

D.   Not important at all

Q23   Mike is on his break but sleeping is not permitted in the Emergency Department and Mike knows this.

A.   Very important

B.   Important

C.   Of minor importance

D.   Not important at all

Q24   Mike has a bad back and takes strong pain killers regularly.

A.   Very important

B.   Important

C.   Of minor importance

D.   Not important at all

Scenario 6

Jasmine, a third-year medical student, is clinically obese and smokes. She works on a vascular ward where patients need to watch their weight and stop smoking. Melanie, Jasmine's colleague is unhappy that Jasmine avoids discussing health promotion issues with the patients and always leaves it to her.

How important to take into account are the following considerations for Melanie when deciding how to respond to the situation?

Q25 Jasmine is a competent practitioner in every respect other than health promotion.

A. Very important
B. Important
C. Of minor importance
D. Not important at all

Q26 It is part of a doctor's role to promote the health of patients and the public.

A. Very important
B. Important
C. Of minor importance
D. Not important at all

Q27 Jasmine has never made any attempt to watch her weight or quit smoking.

A. Very important
B. Important
C. Of minor importance
D. Not important at all

Q28 Obesity runs in Jasmine's family.

A. Very important
B. Important
C. Of minor importance
D. Not important at all

Q29 Jasmine's weight increased dramatically when she split up with her boyfriend three years ago.

A. Very important
B. Important
C. Of minor importance
D. Not important at all

Scenario 7

A Senior Nurse overhears a consultant speaking disrespectfully to a patient. Rate the importance of the following considerations in dealing with the situation:

Q30 He is particularly busy that day and obviously feeling stressed.

A. Very important

B. Important

C. Of minor importance

D. Not important at all

Q31 He is usually considerate towards staff and patients.

A. Very important

B. Important

C. Of minor importance

D. Not important at all

Q32 The patient is known to suffer from a mental illness and to be challenging

A. Very important

B. Important

C. Of minor importance

D. Not important at all

Q33 He is a senior consultant and highly respected for his expertise.

A. Very important

B. Important

C. Of minor importance

D. Not important at all

Q34 Immediately after this he returned to the patient and apologised.

A. Very important

B. Important

C. Of minor importance

D. Not important at all

Q35 The consultant was of Indian heritage, and the patient had demanded to 'be seen by someone English'.

A. Very important

B. Important

C. Of minor importance

D. Not important at all

CHAPTER 6

Mock exam

Verbal reasoning

(11 sets of four questions in 21 minutes.)

1. ET

From a space exploration point of view, a satellite is a man-made object placed into orbit around a planet, for example the Earth, Saturn or Jupiter. In astronomy, a satellite is any celestial body orbiting around a planet or star, so the moon is a natural or non-artificial satellite of the Earth; the other planets encircling the sun are natural satellites of the sun. Mercury and Venus are the only planets to have no moons. Mars has two small asteroid-like moons called Phobos and Deimos. Saturn has at least 30 orbiting moons. The largest of Saturn's moons, Titan, is 1.5 times larger than the Earth's moon, making it the second largest moon in the solar system. Titan is larger than the planets Mercury and Pluto. The four largest of Jupiter's 60 moons are Ganymede, Io, Callisto and Europa. These four Galilean satellites were discovered in 1610 and are all planet-sized. Europa has an icy surface at minus 170°C. However, heat linked to volcanic activity on Europa may be sufficient to maintain a layer of liquid water below the ice sheet, making it one of the few places in the solar system capable of sustaining life. This possibility featured in the 1984 science fiction film *2010*, based on an Arthur C Clarke novel. NASA now plans to send a probe to Europa to see if it harbours life.

Q1   The Earth's moon is the third largest moon in the solar system.

True ☐   False ☐   Can't tell ☐

Q2   Jupiter has more moons than any other planet.

True ☐   False ☐   Can't tell ☐

Q3   The low number of craters on the surface of Europa results from volcanic activity and larvae flows.

True ☐   False ☐   Can't tell ☐

Q4   The atmosphere on Europa is capable of sustaining life.

True ☐   False ☐   Can't tell ☐

2. Burning issues

Fire extinguishers come in several different types depending on the nature of the material that can combust. There are six classifications of combustible material as described below:

Class A: flammable organic solids (eg wood, paper, coal, plastics, textiles).

Class B: flammable liquids (eg petrol, spirits) but not cooking oil.

Class C: flammable gas (eg LPG, butane).

Class D: combustible metals (eg magnesium, titanium).

Class E: electrical equipment (eg computers, photocopiers).

Class F: cooking oil and fat.

Pressurized water fire extinguishers can only be used to tackle Class A fires; carbon-dioxide extinguishers are especially suitable for Class E fires as they do not damage electrical equipment such as computers; they can find limited use with type B fires though there is a risk of re-ignition due to a lack of cooling; foam-filled fire extinguishers are suitable for Class B fires and can be used on Class A fires though not in confined spaces; they are not for electrical equipment fires or cooking oil; dry powder fire extinguishers can be used for Class A, B, C and E fires, with specialist powders for Class D fires; dry powder fire extinguishers smother the fire but do not cool it or penetrate very well so there is a risk of re-ignition; wet chemical fire extinguishers are designed specifically to tackle cooking oil fires, especially high temperature with deep fat fryers.

Q5   Class F fires can be extinguished with wet chemical fire extinguishers.

   True ☐   False ☐   Can't tell ☐

Q6   Class A fires can be tackled with three types of fire extinguisher.

   True ☐   False ☐   Can't tell ☐

Q7   Foam-filled fire extinguishers should not be used on Class D fires.

   True ☐   False ☐   Can't tell ☐

Q8   Flammable liquids are more likely to re-ignite than flammable solids.

   True ☐   False ☐   Can't tell ☐

3. World's language

The pre-eminence of the English language globally may be under threat. Mandarin is the dominant language of China and there are 1 billion speakers of Mandarin in the world compared with 330 million English speakers. If economic trends continue then China is set to dominate world trade and quite possibly global communication with it. It is perhaps a surprising fact that learning English is growing fast in China where there are more English Language teaching jobs than in any other country. The International English Language Testing System or IELTS is taken by more than 1 million people worldwide and last year 270,000 tests were taken in China. This fact belies the notion that the number of speakers of a language determines its status. English is set to remain influential because it is seen as the language of academia, diplomacy and especially science, where 95 per cent of scientific publications worldwide are written in English.

The language of English is robust because it has great literary heritage and prestige (though notably so did Latin, which subsequently declined), and it is the main language of the prosperous and stable nations of the West. The use of English became widespread following the expanse of the British Empire and it remains the primary language of at least 45 countries and the official language of many international organizations. Above all else, it is the popularity of English as a second and third language that confirms its status as the world's language. Globally there are almost three times as many non-native speakers of English as native speakers. The number of people who can speak English in India now exceeds the number in the United States. In Nigeria, more people can speak English (Pidgin) than in the United Kingdom.

Q9   There are fewer English Language teaching jobs in the UK than in China.

True ☐   False ☐   Can't tell ☐

Q10   The language of Latin was gradually displaced by English.

True ☐   False ☐   Can't tell ☐

Q11   More people speak English outside of the UK than in the UK.

True ☐   False ☐   Can't tell ☐

Q12   In terms of English speakers, four countries are ranked as follows: India, US, Nigeria, UK (highest number first).

True ☐   False ☐   Can't tell ☐

4. Waterways

At the height of the Industrial Revolution in the mid-19th century, huge quantities of coal had to be transported from the pithead for iron smelting, manufacturing and domestic use. Coastal shipping, navigable rivers and horse-drawn carts were either slow or restrictive in comparison to the new purpose-built canals. A horse could pull a narrowboat weighing 50 times as much as a cart. The UK soon developed a national network of canals and by the middle of the 19th century almost all major towns and cities had a canal. At the same time, there was controversy as to the rival merits of transporting coal by canal or by railway. Stephenson's 'locomotive' could transport vast quantities of coal and other goods quicker than by canal and also offered a new means of passenger transport. The canal network was doomed and investment was redirected into railways with local lines laid down in the coal districts developed into a national system for the whole of the country.

Road haulage in the 20th century brought more competition for canals and only a few remained open until the Second World War. Further declines were inevitable and the use of canals for industrial purposes was minimal in the 1960s. However, interest in canals for leisure purposes had begun to grow and some were restored and reopened by volunteers in the 1970s. This trend has continued with canals attracting government funding for restoration projects. Canals are now a major tourist industry with more than 10 million visitors per year and 30,000 craft. Today there are more boats on the canals than at the height of the Industrial Revolution.

Q13   A network of canals was in place before a national system of railways.

True ☐   False ☐   Can't tell ☐

Q14 The 1960s saw more interest in canals for leisure than for industry.

True ☐   False ☐   Can't tell ☐

Q15 Stephenson's locomotive succeeded because it could transport vast quantities of coal.

True ☐   False ☐   Can't tell ☐

Q16 There are more narrowboats on the canals today than at the height of the Industrial Revolution.

True ☐   False ☐   Can't tell ☐

5. Internet chat

The transmission control protocol/internet protocol (TCP/IP) is a spin-off from military communications. TCP/IP is an electronic handshake that connects networks using routers. It defines what happens when data packets are transmitted and received and includes data formatting, timing, and error checking. An in-house TCP/IP network is called an intranet and it allows members of an organization to access a private website. An internet service provider (ISP) is required to share public web pages on the internet. In a Local Area Network or LAN, several computers or workstations, and their associated peripherals (eg printers) are connected together in the same building. In a Wide Area Network or WAN, multiple LANs are connected over a large area of several kilometres.

Topology is a term that refers to the physical layout of the network or the architecture of its cabling system. Problems with the cabling can lead to a network 'going down'. There are three basic types of LAN topology, which are the star, ring and bus and each have their own advantages and disadvantages. With a star topology each workstation has its own cable connected to a central hub. Signals pass into the hub and then out to each of the workstations. Failure of a single system will not affect any of the other workstations but the failure of the hub will disconnect every computer. A star topology makes adding more workstations easy, though only one computer can send and receive data from the hub at any one time. In a ring topology, or closed loop network each workstation is joined to a common ring at a node. If one computer fails, it can bring the entire network down. In a bus topology the workstations are 'daisy chained' together with all the computers connected to a backbone or bus cable; if two computers try to send a signal along the cable at the same time a collision occurs; every collision slows the network down. Network faults are difficult to troubleshoot with a bus topology because the workstations share a cable, unlike the star and ring topologies.

Q17   In a star topology, a computer can be disconnected from the network without causing the system to go down.

True ☐   False ☐   Can't tell ☐

Q18   In a star topology, several computers can send and receive data from the hub at any one time.

True ☐   False ☐   Can't tell ☐

Q19   If too many computers are 'daisy chained' together on a bus cable then the network system might grind to a halt.

True ☐   False ☐   Can't tell ☐

Q20   In a ring topology with six workstations, every node in the network is connected to two other nodes.

True ☐   False ☐   Can't tell ☐

6. Beneficence

In the 18th century, there were great improvements in surgery, midwifery and hygiene. In London between 1720 and 1745, Guy's, Westminster, St George's, The London and Middlesex general hospitals were all founded. Other hospitals were established in Exeter (1741), Bristol (1733), Liverpool (1745) and York (1740). In the course of 125 years after 1700, at least 154 new hospitals and dispensaries were founded in towns across Britain. These were not municipal undertakings; they were benevolent efforts that relied on voluntary contributions and bequests. It worked well for 250 years prior to the creation of the NHS in 1948.

The first medical school in England was the London Hospital Medical college founded in 1785. The teaching and practice of medicine and surgery were improving but treatments remained limited encouraging medical fakers with homemade remedies. There was minimal knowledge of the disease process and diagnosis remained poor so the same medication was given regardless of the ailment. The most popular treatment was laudanum, a mixture of an opiate-based drug and alcohol, prescribed for pain relief and common ailments such as headaches and diarrhoea. Unfortunately some people became dependent on it and died from overdoses.

Anaesthetics (chloroform and ether) were not used to relieve pain in surgery until 1847. Suturing of wounds was common practice though needles and thread were not sterile so infection was rife. Hygiene and infection control remained non-existent until the 1870s when Louis Pasteur's germ theory of disease had become widely accepted. A Scottish surgeon named Joseph Lister atomized carbolic acid (phenol) for use as an antiseptic, leading to a major decline in blood poisoning following surgery that had normally proved fatal. The hygiene and nursing practices of Florence

Nightingale were adopted by hospitals and led to a reduction in cross-infection and an improvement in recovery rates.

Q21   On average at least one new hospital per year was founded in Britain between 1700 and 1825.

True ☐   False ☐   Can't tell ☐

Q22   A hospital in Exeter was established before a hospital in Liverpool but after hospitals in Bristol and York.

True ☐   False ☐   Can't tell ☐

Q23   In the 1870s the germs responsible for a disease could be identified.

True ☐   False ☐   Can't tell ☐

Q24   Operations prior to 1847 were carried out without any pain relief.

True ☐   False ☐   Can't tell ☐

7. Drive alive

The monotony of driving along straight roads and motorways, especially with driver aids like cruise control, increases the chances of falling asleep at the wheel. Working night shifts and driving home afterwards can be particularly risky. Younger drivers are more likely to feel tired in the morning and older drivers can doze off in the afternoon. A period of increased drowsiness and fighting sleep pre-empts falling asleep. It is important to recognize these warning signs and to stop driving. Winding the window down for cold air and turning the radio up provide only temporary relief from drowsiness. Drivers should act responsibly and stop driving to prevent an accident. One solution is to take a short break (15 minutes) with a cup of coffee (caffeine stimulant). The same counter measures can be employed every two hours during daytime driving.

   Long journeys should be planned in advance to avoid hold-ups, which increase the time spent behind the wheel. Other preventative measures include sharing the driving with others, turning the heat down or the air conditioning on, not driving after a large meal or heavy exercise, and avoiding even the smallest amount of alcohol. Some medications, such as cold and flu remedies, antihistamines and motion sickness tablets, can cause drowsiness as a side-effect. Ideally, it is better not to upset the body's natural circadian rhythm by driving at a time normally spent sleeping, for example, in the early hours of the morning, and to limit the total number of hours spent behind the wheel to a maximum of eight per day. Self-awareness of one's vulnerability to falling asleep and of fighting sleep is also important. Feeling sleepy is perfectly natural but, narcolepsy accepted, nobody falls asleep without prior warning.

Q25   Ideally, a driver spending a maximum of eight hours per day behind the wheel should take three 15-minute coffee breaks at regular intervals.

True ☐   False ☐   Can't tell ☐

Q26   Driving home after a night shift with the window of the car open and the radio turned up will prevent you from falling asleep.

True ☐   False ☐   Can't tell ☐

Q27   Driving in the early hours of the morning upsets the circadian rhythm.

True ☐   False ☐   Can't tell ☐

Q28   Reaction times are slower in the early hours of the morning.

True ☐   False ☐   Can't tell ☐

8. Non-PC

Political correctness has eroded our freedom of speech. In the UK, political correctness came to the fore in the 1980s when it sought to protect minority groups from offensive language, attitudes and discrimination as well as banish stereotypes. In recent times it has influenced language, ideas and behaviour to the extent that only one viewpoint can be tolerated, ie that of the politically correct majority, and as such has seriously undermined our freedom of expression. The government has pandered to the 'PC brigade' who, more often than not, fail to consult the minority groups they claim to support.

The NHS has not escaped the culture of political correctness. Equality and diversity are the latest NHS buzzwords. Anti-discrimination laws have been in place since the 1970s and they were updated in 2003, so much of the new material covers old ground. Furthermore, the PC brigade has failed to understand that the best way to prevent discrimination is to stop looking for it at every turn. For example, why should NHS employees and patients be asked to tick boxes that request information about sexuality or ethnic origin? Highlighting differences is a form of discrimination in itself.

The pervasiveness and absurdity of political correctness was highlighted recently when the NHS suspended a nurse for offering to pray for an elderly patient. In this case, the NHS discriminated against the nurse on the basis of her religious beliefs whilst at the same time claiming to respect equality and diversity. Clearly the PC brigade within the NHS believes that spiritual needs are at odds with their equality and diversity policy; hospital chaplains beware. The only PC the NHS should concern itself with is Patient Care. The NHS should not waste resources pandering to political correctness when all that is required is a little more common sense.

Q29   The author believes that equality and diversity within the NHS are largely within the scope of anti-discrimination laws.

True ☐   False ☐   Can't tell ☐

Q30   NHS patients must declare their sexuality by ticking a box.

True ☐   False ☐   Can't tell ☐

Q31   The nurse was suspended for breaching the NHS equality and diversity policy.

True ☐   False ☐   Can't tell ☐

Q32   The author believes that political correctness is contrary to freedom of thought.

True ☐   False ☐   Can't tell ☐

9. Pink ladies

In 1973, the antipodean John Cripps crossbred the Australian Lady Williams apple with the American Golden Delicious to combine the best features of both apples in the Cripps Pink. Today it is one of the best-known varieties of apples and is grown extensively in Australia, New Zealand, and in California and Washington in the United States. By switching from northern hemisphere fruit to southern hemisphere fruit the apple is available at its seasonal best all year round. The highest-quality apples are marketed worldwide under the trademark Pink Lady™ and in order to preserve its premium appeal and price, about 65 per cent of the apples that do not meet the highest standard are sold under the name Cripps Pink™. These standards are based on colour intensity and flavour. Both the Pink Lady™ and the Cripps Pink™ have become increasing popular with UK consumers. The Pink Lady™ held approximately 10 per cent of the UK apple market in 2005.

The Cripps Red variety also known as Cripps II sells equally as well as the Pink Lady™, with which it shares the same parentage. The premium grade is marketed as the Sundowner™. This apple is harvested in late May to early June, three weeks after Cripps Pink and a few weeks before Lady Williams™. It can be cold-stored for longer than Cripps Pink and has an excellent shelf life. Cripps Red is sweeter than Lady Williams™ but not as sweet as Golden Delicious. Unlike the genuinely pink Pink Lady™, the Sundowner™ is a classic bi-coloured apple, about 45 per cent red from Lady Williams™ and 55 per cent green from Golden Delicious™. Apples that fall outside of this colour ratio are rejected at the packing station and used for juice whilst the smaller apples are retained for the home market.

Q33   Approximately two-thirds of the Cripps Pink variety fail to meet the highest standards required of the Pink Lady™ trademark.

True ☐   False ☐   Can't tell ☐

Q34   Pink Lady™ is more expensive than Sundowner™.

True ☐   False ☐   Can't tell ☐

Q35   The Pink Lady™ is equally as popular as the Sundowner™.

True ☐   False ☐   Can't tell ☐

Q36   Colour is an important factor in determining whether an apple can be sold as a Pink Lady™ or as a Sundowner™.

True ☐   False ☐   Can't tell ☐

10. Blighty

Are the British Isles, the UK, Great Britain and Britain one and the same thing? Well, no, actually. The British Isles is a non-political, geographical term that refers to an archipelago, or cluster of islands, that include the two main islands that encompass England, Wales and Scotland and the whole of the island of Ireland, as well as all of the many, small surrounding islands.

The UK is an abbreviated form of the United Kingdom of Great Britain and Northern Ireland, whereas Great Britain is England, Wales and Scotland (and their adjacent islands) but not Northern Ireland, making Great Britain a geographical term but not a political entity. The adjacent islands referred to include the Isle of Wight, the Isles of Scilly, the Isle of Anglesey (Ynys Mon in Welsh) and the Isles of Scotland (Orkney and Shetland Islands and the Inner and Outer Hebrides). The term Britain is often used to mean Great Britain, though strictly speaking Britain covers England and Wales but not Scotland because Britain stems from the Roman word Britannia that did not include the area now called Scotland, which was never conquered. To add to the confusion, the term British Islands encompasses the United Kingdom, the Channel Islands (Jersey and Guernsey) and the Isle of Man; these islands are not part of Great Britain, the UK or Europe but are self-governing British Crown Dependencies. Finally, the term Ireland defines both a political entity, ie the Republic of Ireland (or Eire) that is Southern Ireland and the geographical entity that is both Northern and Southern Ireland, the single land mass.

Q37   The British Islands include Northern Ireland while the British Isles include all of Ireland.

True ☐   False ☐   Can't tell ☐

Q38   The Isle of Anglesey is not part of Great Britain.

True ☐   False ☐   Can't tell ☐

Q39   Northern Ireland is not part of Great Britain but it is part of the UK.

True ☐   False ☐   Can't tell ☐

Q40   Jersey is not part of Great Britain but it is part of the British Isles.

True ☐   False ☐   Can't tell ☐

11. Fumes

The word smog was first used to describe the 'smoke fog' that arose from the burning of coal during the early 19th century. Today's smog is associated more with vehicle exhaust emissions and industrial pollutants that combine in the presence of sunlight to produce a 'photochemical smog'. This modern smog has implications for human health and global warming.

Car exhausts emit unburned hydrocarbons, carbon-monoxide, carbon-dioxide and oxides of nitrogen (NOx). Hydrocarbons can cause liver damage and carbon-monoxide is harmful to people with ischaemic heart disease (IHD). Carbon-dioxide is a major greenhouse gas and nitrogen oxides contribute to acid rain. Power stations release sulphur dioxide, which is an irritant when inhaled and can cause breathing difficulties. Sulphur dioxide is oxidized to sulphur trioxide which combines with water vapour in the atmosphere to form sulphuric acid, giving rise to acid rain. The acid is environmentally damaging and can become a risk to human health if it leaches carcinogenic metals into the food chain.

Volatile organic compounds (VOCs) constitute the volatile components in paints, aerosol sprays and solvents and they are released when fuel is not completely burnt. VOCs can be split into two groups – methane-containing and non-methane-containing. Methane is a significant greenhouse gas and contributes to global warming. Some non-methane VOCs react with nitrogen oxides in the presence of sunlight to form ozone, which can exacerbate chronic obstructive pulmonary disease (COPD) and asthma.

The formation of ozone and acid rain is not instantaneous so concentrations of secondary pollutants are highest downwind of the precursor chemicals. Consequently, choosing to live in the countryside where there are fewer sources of pollutants no longer guarantees good air quality.

Q41   The passage states that carbon-monoxide is a major greenhouse gas.

True ☐   False ☐   Can't tell ☐

Q42   Non-methane-containing VOCs do not contribute to global warming.

True ☐   False ☐   Can't tell ☐

Q43   Sulphur dioxide is the only pollutant that forms acid rain.

True ☐   False ☐   Can't tell ☐

Q44   The precursor chemicals referred to in the final paragraph include nitrogen oxides, sulphur dioxide and methane.

True ☐   False ☐   Can't tell ☐

Decision analysis

Operating	Basic	Specialist
A = Increase	1 = Person	101 = Money
B = Opposite	2 = Eat	102 = Rules
C = Similar	3 = Think	103 = Day
D = Positive	4 = Vehicle	104 = Danger
E = Plural	5 = Wrong	105 = Health
F = Always	6 = Time	106 = Number
G = Male	7 = Large	107 = Air
H = Personal	8 = Water	108 = Meal
J = Together	9 = Speak	109 = Heard
K = Specific	10 = Work	110 = Pain
L = Situation	11 = Fire	201 = Fix
M = Future	12 = House	202 = Light
	13 = Fall	203 = Expensive
	14 = Problem	204 = Old
	15 = Short	205 = Seek
	16 = Few	206 = Notes
	17 = Space	207 = Object
	18 = Travel	■ = Happy
	19 = Take	● = Lonely
	20 = Vision	♦ = Friendly
	21 = Vessel	♥ = Anxious

What is the best interpretation of the following coded messages?

Q1   HG, A(C18), 12

   A.   He was evicted from the house.
   B.   They were asked to leave their home.
   C.   The man quickly left his house.
   D.   He was ordered to leave the home.
   E.   They were forced out of the premises.

   Answer ▢

Q2   101(BA), 102(BD), 18B, K4

   A.   You must pay for parking your car.
   B.   There are fines for illegally parking your car.
   C.   You can be fined for parking your car.
   D.   There are fines for illegally parking a vehicle.
   E.   You can receive a ticket for illegal parking.

   Answer ▢

Q3   8(B13), 8(14A)

   A.   The rising water caused great damage.
   B.   More floods caused water damage.
   C.   Flooding by water increased the damage.
   D.   The rising tide caused water damage.
   E.   Rising tides caused flooding.

   Answer ▢

Q4   EH17(11 107), 104 105

   A.   Smoke inhalation is dangerous.
   B.   Smoking kills many people.
   C.   We do not smoke as it is unhealthy.
   D.   Smoking cigarettes is hazardous to health.
   E.   Passive smoking is a health risk.

   Answer ▢

Q5   B7(G), 19(5), H(G7), 7(101)

    A.   The small boy stole the large man's money.
    B.   The son inherited his father's money.
    C.   The boy stole his father's money.
    D.   The son inherited his father's estate.
    E.   The son stole his father's fortune.

Answer

Q6   C(9), 18(MB), BA(12 2)

    A.   The letter will be posted shortly.
    B.   The e-mail was sent from an internet café.
    C.   The e-mail was sent from my computer.
    D.   The e-mail was opened at an internet café.
    E.   He sent the e-mail from an internet café.

Answer

Q7   C(102,12), H(BD5), (14,102)

    A.   The court found him not guilty of the crime.
    B.   He said he was not guilty of the crime.
    C.   The judge found him not guilty of the crime.
    D.   The court decided he was not guilty.
    E.   The court found him guilty as charged.

Answer

Q8   G(E1), 19(C12), A(C101), BG(E1)

    A.   Men earn more than women.
    B.   Men buy larger houses than women.
    C.   Men take home more pay than women.
    D.   Males take home similar money to females.
    E.   Males earn the same money as females.

Answer

Q9   7(12 101), (14 101), A16(7 6)

    A.   A mortgage is a loan paid back in instalments.
    B.   A large house takes years to buy.
    C.   An expensive house is hard to pay for.
    D.   A mortgage is a loan paid back over many years.
    E.   A mortgage is taken out to buy a home.

Answer

Q10 1E(B105), C19, C(105 12), BD(B103)

    A. Outpatients receive hospital care during the day.
    B. Patients receive medical care but not at night.
    C. Patients need less hospital care at night.
    D. Outpatients attend hospital during the day.
    E. Outpatients receive hospital care except at night.

Answer

Q11 E1(B7), C19, B(7 101), (15 6)

    A. Pupils receive little money for school meals.
    B. Young people are paid a minimum weekly wage.
    C. Children receive weekly pocket money.
    D. Children have little time to spend their money.
    E. Children receive pocket money from their parents.

Answer

Q12 A16(E1), 18(10), B(E)1, 4

    A. Some people drive to work by car.
    B. A few people catch the bus to work.
    C. Some people ride a motorcycle to work.
    D. Most people drive to work.
    E. Some people walk to work.

Answer

Q13 10J, BD(18), B10

    A. The workforce went on strike.
    B. The team-mates did not travel together.
    C. The workmen turned up late for work.
    D. Team working saves time and effort.
    E. The management stopped the strike.

Answer

Q14 B(7 1), H18, C(MB), 9

    A. Some young people can see into the future.
    B. Most children learn to walk and speak.
    C. A child walks before it talks.
    D. Children soon learn to walk and speak.
    E. A child can walk and talk.

Answer [ ]

Q15 Which TWO of the following words when added to the table of code words would be the most helpful in coding the sentence?

Successful business people are optimistic about the future.

    A. optimistic
    B. business
    C. future
    D. people
    E. successful

Answer [ ]

Q16 Which TWO of the following words when added to the table of code words would be the most helpful in coding the sentence?

Penalty points are on your licence for three years.

    A. penalty
    B. on
    C. three
    D. points
    E. your

Answer [ ]

Q17 Which TWO of the following words when added to the table of code words would be the most helpful in coding the sentence?

Time spent studying for the test is time spent well.

    A. test
    B. time
    C. well
    D. study
    E. spend

Answer [ ]

Q18 Which TWO of the following words when added to the table of code words would be the most helpful in coding the sentence?

Parents can harm their child's development.

A. growth
B. child
C. hinder
D. their
E. parent

Answer

Operating	Basic	Specialist
A = Increase	1 = Person	101 = Money
B = Opposite	2 = Eat	102 = Rules
C = Similar	3 = Think	103 = Day
D = Positive	4 = Vehicle	104 = Danger
E = Plural	5 = Wrong	105 = Health
F = Always	6 = Time	106 = Number
G = Male	7 = Large	107 = Air
H = Personal	8 = Water	108 = Meal
J = Together	9 = Speak	109 = Heard
K = Specific	10 = Work	110 = Pain
L = Situation	11 = Fire	201 = Fix
M = Future	12 = House	202 = Light
	13 = Fall	203 = Expensive
	14 = Problem	204 = Old
	15 = Short	205 = Seek
	16 = Few	206 = Notes
	17 = Space	207 = Object
	18 = Travel	■ = Happy
	19 = Take	● = Lonely
	20 = Vision	♦ = Friendly
	21 = Vessel	♥ = Anxious

Q19 Which of the following codes best translates the message:

We paid a small deposit on the house.

A. E1, 12, B(19,7)101
B. E1, B7, 101, 12
C. E1, B19, 101,12
D. E1, B19, 7(101)
E. E1, B(19)101, B7(101)

Answer [   ]

Q20 Which of the following codes best translates the message:

I eat one hot meal at night.

A. H, 2, 11(108), 103
B. H, 2, 11(108), B(103)
C. H, 2, BE, 11, 108, B(103)
D. E1, 2, 11(108), 103
E. 2, H, B(103)

Answer [   ]

Q21 Which of the following codes best translates the message:

The meeting was held in cramped conditions.

A. E1, C19, B7(17)
B. E1(J), BM19, L(B7,17)
C. E1, 7(106), J, C(B7,17)
D. E1(BJ), 7(17)
E. E1, BM19, BA(17)

Answer [   ]

Operating	Basic	Specialist
A = Increase	1 = Money	Σ = Opposite
B = Reverse	2 = Hobby	π = Better
C = Plural	3 = Drink	θ = Intention
D = Negative	4 = Computer	Ω = Improve
E = Present	5 = Possession	◊ = Communication
F = Decrease	6 = Fluid	∞ = Less
G = Light	7 = Technology	λ = Special
H = Travel	8 = Person	α = Intense
J = Equipment	9 = Gift	¥ = Function
K = Miss	10 = Behaviour	
L = Personal	11 = Issue	
M = Future	12 = Female	
N = Solution	13 = Body	
O = Issue	14 = Jewellery	
P = Hospital	15 = Vehicle	
	16 = Other	
	17 = Future	
	18 = Happy	
	19 = Information	

Q22   ΩK(Σ3),π,C11(16)

    A.   Better to skip some meals in favour of alternatives.

    B.   It is worse not to drink and better to drink more.

    C.   Missing droughts is preferable to other issues.

    D.   Many others increasingly miss eating.

    E.   Fluid requirements are higher for people who do not drink.

Answer ☐

Q23   π17, ◊4, C8

    A.   We use modern computers to communicate with people.

    B.   In the future we will have far better computers.

    C.   It will be easier to e-mail in the future.

    D.   The internet generation have a bright future.

    E.   There will be a new era of electronic messaging.

Answer ☐

Q24 C8, (◊10 A 7), 17(ΣN)

    A.   The internet has become popular for looking up problems.

    B.   In the future, more people will have trouble accessing telecommunications.

    C.   Years from now the problems with communication between people will increase.

    D.   People behave as if the technology for communication will always be available in the future.

    E.   People's increased use of mobile phones will cause problems in the future.

Answer

Q25 λ3(Ω ¥ 8) m Ω 11

    A.   Juice helps me to think about solving problems.

    B.   Coffee aids me with solving problems.

    C.   Water helps a person to improve themselves.

    D.   Coke has improved its problems and works well.

    E.   Tea helps me towards improving certain issues.

Answer

Q26 AH, λ, 15, C8, π1

    A.   Travelling by bus is a good option for some people.

    B.   People should buy four-wheel drive cars for rough terrain.

    C.   I don't like to travel in a fast car bought by rich people.

    D.   For more passengers, a minivan is a better purchase.

    E.   Coaches are good value for people on long journeys.

Answer

Q27 Which TWO codes when added to the table of codes would help to translate the following message?

Men and women can solve problems with counselling and medication.

    A.   Counsellor

    B.   Men

    C.   Fix

    D.   Drug

    E.   Through

Answer

Q28 Which TWO codes when added to the table of codes would help to translate the following message?

Vans are better than cars for travelling in the country.

A. Wilderness
B. People
C. High
D. Best
E. Distance

Answer

Quantitative reasoning

(Nine sets of four questions in 23 minutes.)

1. Three Rs

A school has recorded the performance of its pupils in reading, writing and arithmetic, and presented the information in the table shown below.

TABLE 6.1 Class 4a: Attainment level

Name	Reading	Writing	Arithmetic
Alan	6	5	5
Barry	5	4	5
Charlie	5	6	6
Ethan	4	6	4
Harry	5	5	6
Joshua	5	4	5
Leanne	6	6	6
Nicola	5	6	7
Phoebe	7	7	7
Soraya	5	5	4
Yasmin	4	4	5
Zara	6	6	5
% at level 5 or above		75.0	83.3
% at level 6 or above	25.0	50.0	41.7

Questions

Q1   What proportion of the pupils achieved level 5 or above in reading?

    A. 58.3%
    B. 66.7%
    C. 83.3%
    D. 75.0%
    E. 90.0%

Answer

Q2   What proportion of the pupils who achieved level 5 or above in reading also achieved level 5 or above in arithmetic?

    A. 58.3%
    B. 66.7%
    C. 83.3%
    D. 75.0%
    E. 90.0%

Answer

Q3   What proportion of the pupils achieved level 5 or above in all three subjects?

    A. 58.3%
    B. 66.7%
    C. 83.3%
    D. 75.0%
    E. 90.0%

Answer

Q4   What proportion of the pupils who achieved level 5 or above in all three subjects achieved level 6 or above in arithmetic?

    A. 41.6%
    B. 50.0%
    C. 66.7%
    D. 71.4%
    E. 83.3%

Answer

2. Onwards and upwards

FIGURE 6.1   Pie chart showing destination of year 11 pupils

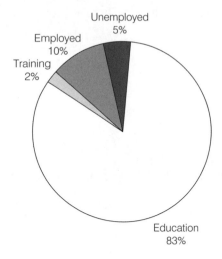

FIGURE 6.2   Pie chart showing destination of year 13 pupils

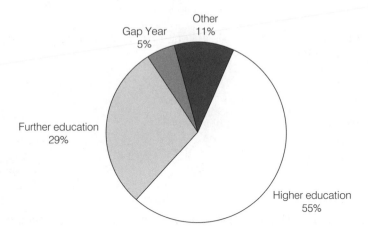

After completing their education at Robert Nubegin School, pupils in year 11 have several options available to them including staying on in full-time education, training for a job or finding employment. Of the pupils who chose to continue their education, three out of seven did so at Robert Nubegin School.

Questions

Q5   In year 11, the number of pupils who did not stay on in full-time education was 1,701. How many pupils were there in year 11?

    A.   7,074
    B.   8,506
    C.   9,748
    D.   10,006
    E.   11,080

Answer [   ]

Q6   How many pupils in year 11 left the school to find employment or training?

    A.   1,101
    B.   1,201
    C.   1,301
    D.   1,401
    E.   1,501

Answer [   ]

Q7   What percentage of the pupils in year 11 at Robert Nubegin School decided to stay on at the school beyond year 11?

    A.   27.7%
    B.   29.4%
    C.   35.6%
    D.   38.8%
    E.   42.9%

Answer [   ]

Q8   Assuming that all the pupils who stay on at Robert Nubegin School after year 11 remain until the end of year 13, how many of these students are likely to end up in higher education, including those who take a gap year?

    A.   2,136
    B.   2,095
    C.   2,042
    D.   2,004
    E.   1,986

Answer [   ]

3. Young Man's Game

Company ABC Ltd has carried out an audit of its sales staff, measuring average weekly sales in relation to sex and age. All the sales people under age 35 are men and all the sales people over 44 are women. Two-thirds of the sales staff aged 35 to 44 are men.

FIGURE 6.3   Age distribution of ABC sales staff versus sales

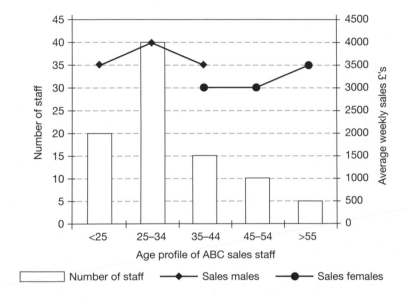

Questions

Q9   What was the total weekly sales revenue of all the sales staff under age 35?

   A. £160,000
   B. £170,000
   C. £200,000
   D. £230,000
   E. £260,500

Answer _____

Q10 What was the total weekly sales revenue of the female staff?

    A. £42,500
    B. £62,500
    C. £92,500
    D. £102,500
    E. £112,500

Answer

Q11 What percentage of the company's weekly sales is generated by the male workforce?

    A. 61%
    B. 71%
    C. 75%
    D. 81%
    E. 86%

Answer

Q12 In the following year, sales by the men remained unchanged while sales by the women rose 10 per cent. What was the annual sales total?

    A. £14.63 million
    B. £15.99 million
    C. £17.36 million
    D. £18.95 million
    E. £20.15 million

Answer

4. Sip it

Ensure Twocal™ and Calogen™ are two high-energy nutritional supplements. Taken together they can provide the recommended daily calorific intake of 1,940 kilocalories (kcal) for women and 2,550 kilocalories (kcal) for men. Ensure Twocal is supplied in 200 ml bottles. The recommended dose of Calogen is 3 × 30 ml per day. Nutritional data is as follows:

Nutrition per 100 ml	Carbs	Protein	Fat
Twocal™	21 g	8.4 g	8.9 g
Calogen™	0 g	0 g	50 g

Fat provides more calories per gram than carbohydrate and protein, as shown below.

Nutrient	Carbs	Protein	Fat
kcal per g	4	4	9

Questions

Q13 How many kcal are provided by the recommended daily dose of Calogen?

A. 400
B. 405
C. 410
D. 425
E. 450

Answer [   ]

Q14 A male patient, who cannot eat solid food, consumes the recommended daily dose of Calogen and six bottles of Twocal. What percentage of the recommended daily calorific intake will he achieve?

A. 69%
B. 79%
C. 89%
D. 99%
E. 109%

Answer [   ]

Q15   What proportion of the calorific content of Twocal is supplied by its fat content?

   A.   41%
   B.   46%
   C.   51%
   D.   56%
   E.   61%

Answer [   ]

Q16   How many ml of Twocal will a female patient need to consume to achieve 100 per cent of her recommended daily calories if she takes 30 ml of Calogen per day?

   A.   684 ml
   B.   779 ml
   C.   824 ml
   D.   913 ml
   E.   980 ml

Answer [   ]

5. Duplicated

The table shows the annual amount of photocopying done by office workers in five different companies. The cost per copy is based on single-sided copies and it is equal to the cost of the photocopying paper at £5 per ream of 500 sheets plus the cost of toner, which varies from company to company.

Company	Cost per copy in pence	Copies per employee	Number of employees
Valu	2 p	8,000	2,000
Wilats	3.5 p	6,000	3,000
Xsels	1.5 p	10,000	1,000
Yamit	2.5 p	4,000	5,000
Zonika	3 p	5,000	6,000

Questions

Q17 Which company spent the most money on photocopying?

A. Valu
B. Wilat
C. Xsels
D. Yamit
E. Zonika

Answer [   ]

Q18 What proportion of Wilats photocopying costs went on toner?

A. 71%
B. 73%
C. 75%
D. 77%
E. 79%

Answer [   ]

Q19 To reduce its copying costs Xsels asks its staff to make duplex copies (double-sided) to cut its paper costs in half. How much money will Xsels save annually?

A. £25,000
B. £50,000
C. £60,000
D. £75,000
E. £90,000

Answer [   ]

Q20 To reduce copying costs, Yamit asks its office staff to reduce all its documents to A5 size to get two copies on to one A4 sheet. This cuts paper costs in half and reduces the consumption of toner by 50 per cent. How much money will Yamit spend on toner annually?

A. £50,000
B. £75,000
C. £100,000
D. £125,000
E. £150,000

Answer [   ]

6. Skin you're in

The Mosteller equation can be used for estimating body surface area (BSA) in metres squared, when the height and weight of a patient are known. It is given by the square root of the height in centimetres (cm) multiplied by the weight in kilograms (kg), divided by 3,600. Alan is 1.8 metres tall and weighs 80 kg.

$$\text{BSA (m}^2) = \sqrt{\frac{cm \times kg}{3600}} \text{ or BSA}^2 \times 3600 = cm \times kg$$

$$= 1/60 \times \sqrt{cm \times kg}$$

Patient	Height in metres	Weight in kg
Alan	1.8	80
Jack	1.7	–
Paula	1.6	60

Questions

Q21   What is Alan's BSA in metres squared?

   A.   1.8
   B.   2.0
   C.   √3
   D.   √8
   E.   2√2

   Answer [   ]

Q22   How heavy is Jack if he has the same body surface area (BSA) as Alan?

   A.   79.5 kg
   B.   80.2 kg
   C.   83.0 kg
   D.   84.7 kg
   E.   85.0 kg

   Answer [   ]

Q23   What is Paula's BSA in metres squared?

  A. 2.25
  B. $2/3\sqrt{3}$
  C. $\sqrt{5}/2$
  D. $\sqrt{7}/2$
  E. $4/\sqrt{6}$

            Answer ☐

Q24   How much weight must Paula put on to reach a BSA of 1.732?

  A. 1.0 kg
  B. 2.5 kg
  C. 5.0 kg
  D. 7.5 kg
  E. 10.0 kg

            Answer ☐

7. Making hay

A straw merchant has to transport hay bales on a trailer 11 metres long and 2.4 metres wide. The bales are stacked one bale high and must not overhang the sides of the trailer. Bales come in five sizes as shown in the table.

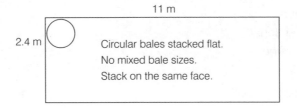

Bale type	Dimensions (cm)	£ per bale
Small	80 × 80 × 80	10
Medium	120 × 80 × 60	12
Conventional	200 × 80 × 60	20
Large cube	100 × 100 × 100	22
Circular	120 diameter	30

Questions

Q25 How many small bales will fit on the trailer?

    A. 39
    B. 42
    C. 45
    D. 47
    E. 50

Answer

Q26 How much will the merchant sell his straw for if he stacks the trailer with circular bales?

    A. £420
    B. £460
    C. £500
    D. £540
    E. £580

Answer

Q27 Which size bale should the merchant transport if he wants to sell hay with the highest value?

    A. small
    B. medium
    C. conventional
    D. large cube
    E. circular

Answer

Q28 The straw merchant can stack the conventional bales in one of three ways. Proportionally how much less money will he receive from the sale of one trailer load if he stacks them in the least inefficient of the three ways?

    A. 32%
    B. 48%
    C. 50%
    D. 63%
    E. 76%

Answer

8. Mine's a double

Daily limits for sensible drinking are 3 to 4 units for men and 2 to 3 units for women. One unit is 10 ml or 8 g of pure alcohol. The table shows the alcohol content by volume (ABV) of selected liquors. A standard single measure is 25 ml, a large single measure is 35 ml and a double measure is 50 ml.

Liquor	Percentage alcohol (ABV)
Bailey's Irish Cream	17%
Cointreau	40%
Malibu	21%
Pimm's No 1	25%
Southern Comfort	37%
Tia Maria	26.5%

Questions

Q29 How many grams of alcohol are there in a large single measure of Cointreau?

    A. 8.0 g
    B. 11.2 g
    C. 14.9 g
    D. 32.0 g
    E. 1.12 g

Answer [   ]

Q30 How many large single measures of Bailey's Irish Cream are equivalent to the maximum sensible drinking limit for women?

    A. 2
    B. 3
    C. 4
    D. 5
    E. 6

Answer [   ]

Q31 The ingredients of a Mudslide cocktail are one-and-a-half measures of Vodka (40% ABV), one-half measure of Tia Maria and one-half measure of Bailey's Irish Cream. What is the alcohol content (ABV) of a Mudslide cocktail?

A. 27.5%

B. 29.6%

C. 32.7%

D. 35.5%

E. 36.7%

Answer

Q32 John completes his meal with a 150 ml cup of Bailey's coffee (one-third Bailey's Irish Cream and two-thirds black coffee) followed by a double measure of Cointreau. What fraction of the maximum sensible drinking limit has he drunk?

A. 71%

B. 73%

C. 75%

D. 77%

E. 79%

Answer

9. Student travel

Five students travel from a hall of residence to the Faculty of Medicine, a distance of two miles, for the 09.15 lecture. Their chosen mode of transport is shown below along with each person's departure time and average speed in miles per hour.

	Mode	Speed (mph)	Departure
Barbara	walks	3	08.15
Phillip	walks	3.25	08.15
Aran	cycles	10	08.40
Luke	bus	20	08.40
Katie	car	30	08.55

Questions

Q33 Who is the last person to arrive at the Faculty of Medicine?

    A. Barbara
    B. Phillip
    C. Aran
    D. Luke
    E. Katie

Answer [   ]

Q34 On Tuesday, Aran leaves five minutes later but cycles 10 per cent faster. What time does Aran arrive?

    A. 08.56
    B. 08.57
    C. 08.58
    D. 08.59
    E. 09.00

Answer [   ]

Q35 On Monday morning it starts to rain so Barbara decides to stop en route and catch the bus. She has walked a distance of one mile before catching the bus. What is her average speed for the two-mile journey?

    A. 5.3 mph
    B. 6.3 mph
    C. 8.6 mph
    D. 9.3 mph
    E. 11.5 mph

Answer [   ]

Q36 On Tuesday morning Katie leaves 10 minutes earlier than usual and stops en route to give Barbara a lift. How far has Barbara walked when she is given a lift?

    A. 1.0 miles
    B. 1.25 miles
    C. 1.33 miles
    D. 1.5 miles
    E. 1.67 miles

Answer [   ]

Abstract reasoning

Mock test

Q1

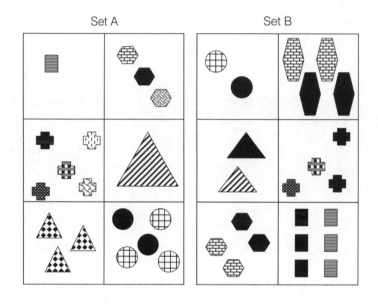

Test shapes 1 to 5

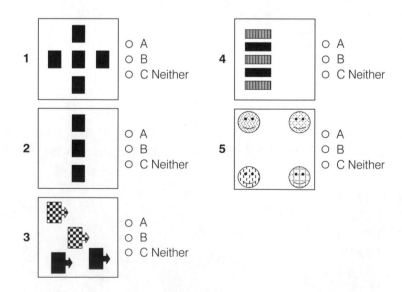

Q2

Set A   Set B

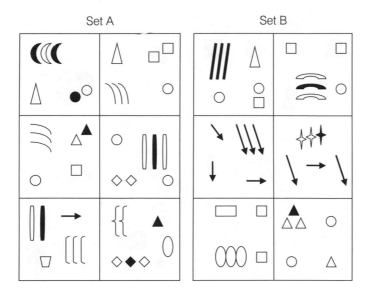

Test shapes 6 to 10

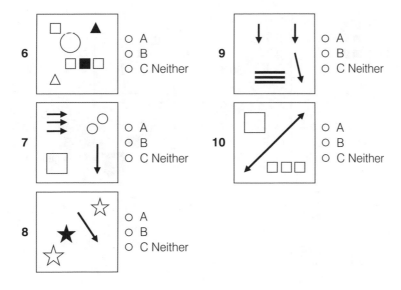

6   ○ A
        ○ B
        ○ C Neither

7   ○ A
        ○ B
        ○ C Neither

8   ○ A
        ○ B
        ○ C Neither

9   ○ A
        ○ B
        ○ C Neither

10 ○ A
        ○ B
        ○ C Neither

Q3

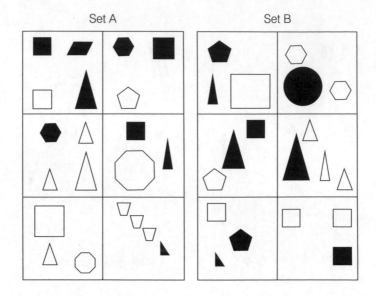

Set A   Set B

Test shapes 11 to 15

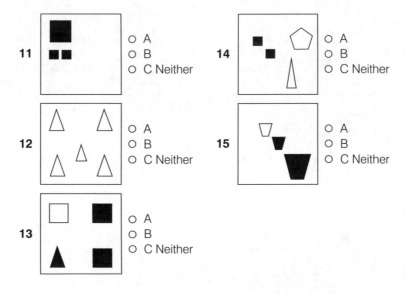

11 ○ A
    ○ B
    ○ C Neither

12 ○ A
    ○ B
    ○ C Neither

13 ○ A
    ○ B
    ○ C Neither

14 ○ A
    ○ B
    ○ C Neither

15 ○ A
    ○ B
    ○ C Neither

Q4

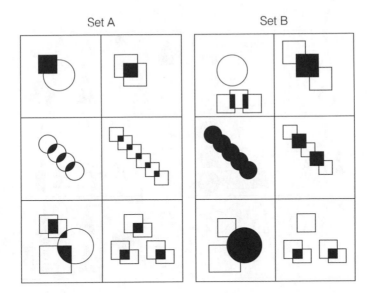

Set A   Set B

Test shapes 16 to 20

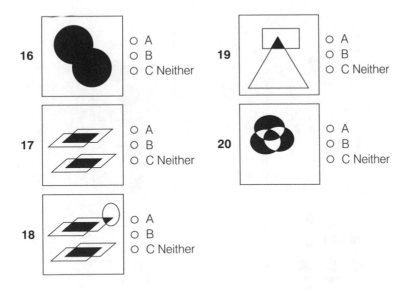

16 ○ A
    ○ B
    ○ C Neither

17 ○ A
    ○ B
    ○ C Neither

18 ○ A
    ○ B
    ○ C Neither

19 ○ A
    ○ B
    ○ C Neither

20 ○ A
    ○ B
    ○ C Neither

Q5

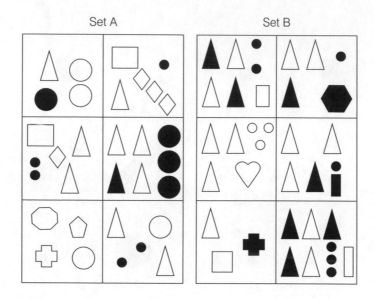

Set A   Set B

Test shapes 21 to 25

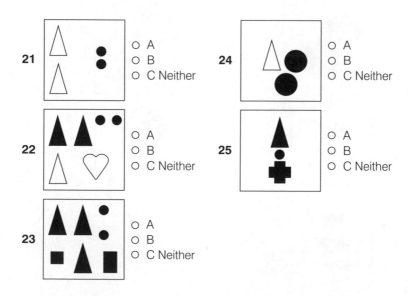

21   ○ A
         ○ B
         ○ C Neither

22   ○ A
         ○ B
         ○ C Neither

23   ○ A
         ○ B
         ○ C Neither

24   ○ A
         ○ B
         ○ C Neither

25   ○ A
         ○ B
         ○ C Neither

Q6

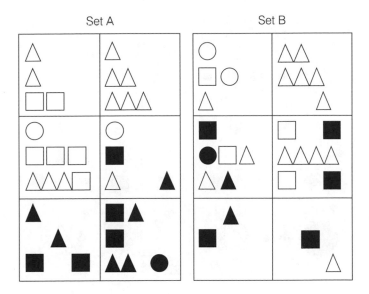

Test shapes 26 to 30

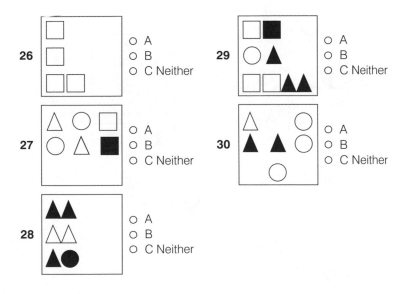

Q7

Set A Set B

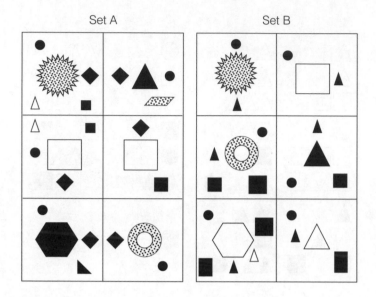

Test shapes 31 to 35

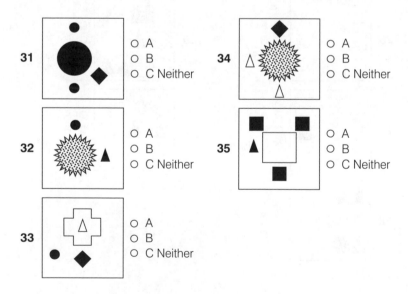

31 ○ A
○ B
○ C Neither

32 ○ A
○ B
○ C Neither

33 ○ A
○ B
○ C Neither

34 ○ A
○ B
○ C Neither

35 ○ A
○ B
○ C Neither

Q8

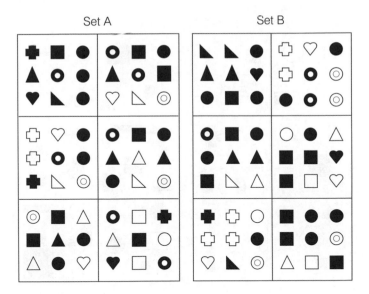

Set A   Set B

Test shapes 36 to 40

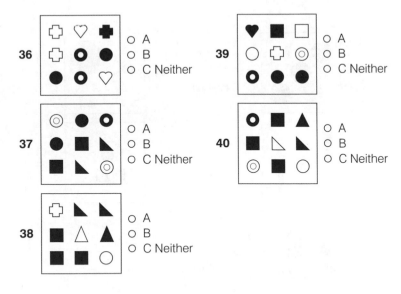

36
○ A
○ B
○ C Neither

37
○ A
○ B
○ C Neither

38
○ A
○ B
○ C Neither

39
○ A
○ B
○ C Neither

40
○ A
○ B
○ C Neither

Q9

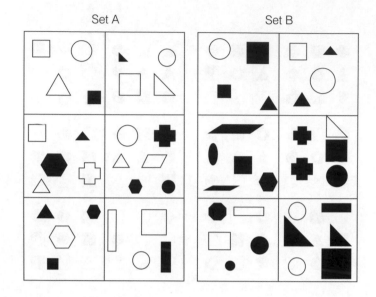

Set A   Set B

Test shapes 41 to 45

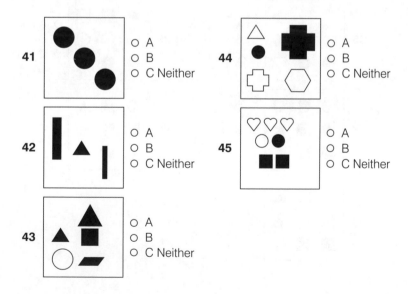

41   ○ A
         ○ B
         ○ C Neither

42   ○ A
         ○ B
         ○ C Neither

43   ○ A
         ○ B
         ○ C Neither

44   ○ A
         ○ B
         ○ C Neither

45   ○ A
         ○ B
         ○ C Neither

Q10 Choose ONE drawing that best completes the statement:

46

47 (△) is to △ as ◇ is to ◇ ◇ ◇ ◇ ◇
                          1   2   3   4   5

48 is to as is to
                          1   2   3   4   5

49 is to as is to
                          1   2   3   4   5

Find the ODD ONE OUT.

50   1   2   3   4   5

51   1   2   3   4   5

52   1   2   3   4   5

Q11   Which of the five numbered drawings comes next in the series?

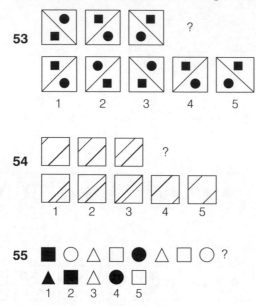

Situational judgement

Scenario 1

A parent makes a doctor's appointment for their adult child who has a long history of mental health problems. After the appointment the parent calls back the surgery receptionist to ask about the outcome of the consultation.

Q1   He would not look on the patient's file but instead tell them something vaguely reassuring.

A.   Very appropriate
B.   Appropriate but not ideal
C.   Inappropriate but not awful
D.   A very inappropriate thing to do

Q2   He would look on the patient's file and if they were doing well tell them there was nothing to worry about.

A.   Very appropriate
B.   Appropriate but not ideal
C.   Inappropriate but not awful
D.   A very inappropriate thing to do

Q3   He would look up the outcome and discuss it with them.

    A. Very appropriate ☐

    B. Appropriate but not ideal ☐

    C. Inappropriate but not awful ☐

    D. A very inappropriate thing to do ☐

Scenario 2

A clinician comes into the waiting area after seeing a patient and comments to the surgery manager 'how very brave the patient is'. Two other patients sitting nearby may well have overheard what the clinician said.

Q4   He would do nothing.

    A. Very appropriate ☐

    B. Appropriate but not ideal ☐

    C. Inappropriate but not awful ☐

    D. A very inappropriate thing to do ☐

Q5   He would interrupt the clinician and immediately point out these other patients may have heard his remark.

    A. Very appropriate ☐

    B. Appropriate but not ideal ☐

    C. Inappropriate but not awful ☐

    D. A very inappropriate thing to do ☐

Q6   He would take the clinician aside and tell them that their remark may have been overheard.

    A. Very appropriate ☐

    B. Appropriate but not ideal ☐

    C. Inappropriate but not awful ☐

    D. A very inappropriate thing to do ☐

Q7   He would ask him why he thought the patient was brave?

    A. Very appropriate ☐

    B. Appropriate but not ideal ☐

    C. Inappropriate but not awful ☐

    D. A very inappropriate thing to do ☐

Scenario 3

A clinic administrator discovers that an important test result is missing from a patient's file.

Q8   He resolves to raise the matter at the next practice meeting.

    A. Very appropriate

    B. Appropriate but not ideal

    C. Inappropriate but not awful

    D. A very inappropriate thing to do

Q9   He initiates an investigation to find out who is responsible for losing this vital data.

    A. Very appropriate

    B. Appropriate but not ideal

    C. Inappropriate but not awful

    D. A very inappropriate thing to do

Scenario 4

A senior nurse in a busy department already finds it hard to complete his work. Management have introduced an additional form that has to be completed when a patient registers and he can't see how he is going to have the time to complete this extra task nor what benefit this form will have.

Q10   He works through his lunch hour and stays late to get the job done.

    A. Very appropriate

    B. Appropriate but not ideal

    C. Inappropriate but not awful

    D. A very inappropriate thing to do

Q11   He asks his team leader to explain the purpose of the new form and to help him manage the additional work.

    A. Very appropriate

    B. Appropriate but not ideal

    C. Inappropriate but not awful

    D. A very inappropriate thing to do

Q12   He raises the difficulties with his team mates and they discuss how to support one another.

   A.   Very appropriate
   B.   Appropriate but not ideal
   C.   Inappropriate but not awful
   D.   A very inappropriate thing to do

Scenario 5

A consultant is not sure the patient has fully understood what was being said at her last consultation. The follow-up meeting is due.

Q13   She arranges for extra time with the patient at the follow-up meeting.

   A.   Very appropriate
   B.   Appropriate but not ideal
   C.   Inappropriate but not awful
   D.   A very inappropriate thing to do

Q14   She calls the patient to check her understanding and discuss her support needs for the next meeting.

   A.   Very appropriate
   B.   Appropriate but not ideal
   C.   Inappropriate but not awful
   D.   A very inappropriate thing to do

Q15   At the next meeting she takes the first few minutes to go over the information again.

   A.   Very appropriate
   B.   Appropriate but not ideal
   C.   Inappropriate but not awful
   D.   A very inappropriate thing to do

Q16   She discusses the situation with colleagues and asks how they have dealt with similar situations in the past so that she can decide on the best strategy.

   A.   Very appropriate
   B.   Appropriate but not ideal
   C.   Inappropriate but not awful
   D.   A very inappropriate thing to do

Scenario 6

A clinician notices that a patient attending next week's clinic with a standard condition has some complications, however he will be on holiday that day. This means another clinician will have to see the patient.

Q17   He changes the appointment to a date when he is on duty.

A. Very appropriate

B. Appropriate but not ideal

C. Inappropriate but not awful

D. A very inappropriate thing to do

Q18   He writes a note to his colleague bringing the complications to his attention

A. Very appropriate

B. Appropriate but not ideal

C. Inappropriate but not awful

D. A very inappropriate thing to do

Q19   He prepares detailed notes on how the consultation should proceed and the preferred treatment.

A. Very appropriate

B. Appropriate but not ideal

C. Inappropriate but not awful

D. A very inappropriate thing to do

Q20   He leaves the matter to his colleagues and enjoys his holiday.

A. Very appropriate

B. Appropriate but not ideal

C. Inappropriate but not awful

D. A very inappropriate thing to do

Scenario 7

Medical student Stefan confides in a colleague Tomos that he takes the 'smart drug' Modafinil to keep himself alert when working a 12-hour shift. He purchases Modafinil online because it is a prescription-only drug and is not available over the counter (OTC).

How important to take into account are the following considerations for Tomos when deciding how to respond to the situation?

Q21 Prescription-only drugs should only be taken with the advice of a doctor who knows your medical history.

A. Very important

B. Important

C. Of minor importance

D. Not important at all

Q22 There are ethical issues surrounding performance enhancing drugs.

A. Very important

B. Important

C. Of minor importance

D. Not important at all

Q23 The long-term side effect of taking the drug are unknown and it could become addictive.

A. Very important

B. Important

C. Of minor importance

D. Not important at all

Scenario 8

A purse containing money was found by a receptionist, who bought the whole department a box of chocolates with it.

Q24 There was no identification in the purse so the owner could not be traced.

A. Very important

B. Important

C. Of minor importance

D. Not important at all

Q25 After a month, nobody had returned to claim it

A. Very important

B. Important

C. Of minor importance

D. Not important at all

Q26   The total sum in the purse was less than £10

A. Very important ☐

B. Important ☐

C. Of minor importance ☐

D. Not important at all ☐

Scenario 9

A terminally ill patient insistently asks a member of staff if she is dying. In deciding whether to tell her he takes into consideration:

Q27   How anxious and prone to becoming upset the patient is.

A. Very important ☐

B. Important ☐

C. Of minor importance ☐

D. Not important at all ☐

Q28   The next of kin has stated that they wish to be present when the patient is informed.

A. Very important ☐

B. Important ☐

C. Of minor importance ☐

D. Not important at all ☐

Q29   That the patient has previously indicated that they do want full disclosure about their disease.

A. Very important ☐

B. Important ☐

C. Of minor importance ☐

D. Not important at all ☐

Scenario 10

A patient discloses that their father is violent towards their mother. Decide the importance of the following items in informing the clinician's response.

Q30   The patient is 14 years of age.

A.   Very important

B.   Important

C.   Of minor importance

D.   Not important at all

Q31   The patient asks the clinician to promise not to tell anyone.

A.   Very important

B.   Important

C.   Of minor importance

D.   Not important at all

Q32   The patient's mother always denies that violence occurs.

A.   Very important

B.   Important

C.   Of minor importance

D.   Not important at all

Scenario 11

A four-month pregnant junior doctor is attempting to take a blood sample from a patient in accident and emergency. The patient is needlephobic, extremely nervous and shaky, and as a result the doctor pricks herself with the needle which has also been in contact with the patient's blood. A fellow doctor comes to assist her as she is visibly upset.

How appropriate are each of the following responses by the doctor's colleague in this situation.

Q33   Insisting on locating and safely disposing of the needle before comforting the doctor involved.

A.   Very appropriate

B.   Appropriate but not ideal

C.   Inappropriate but not awful

D.   A very inappropriate thing to do

Q34   Taking blood samples from both the patient and the doctor as soon as possible to be tested for a variety of infectious diseases.

   A. Very appropriate
   B. Appropriate but not ideal
   C. Inappropriate but not awful
   D. A very inappropriate thing to do

Q35   Accepting the request of the doctor to not report the incident to the head of department, on the grounds that it would reflect negatively on the skill of the doctor, whereas in reality it was the fault of the needle-phobic patient.

   A. Very appropriate
   B. Appropriate but not ideal
   C. Inappropriate but not awful
   D. A very inappropriate thing to do

Q36   Remind the patient that thousands of patients in the hospital, including children, have needles put in them every day and that he should try to manage his fear for his own safety as well as those of the people caring for him.

   A. Very appropriate
   B. Appropriate but not ideal
   C. Inappropriate but not awful
   D. A very inappropriate thing to do

Scenario 12

A university student is applying for a prestigious financial scholarship and sends in a cover letter and CV. The rules of the award state that there is no interview process, but each candidate will be judged on four major areas of achievement as demonstrated by their application: leadership, research skills, academic publications and teamwork.

   How appropriate are each of the following actions by the student in this situation.

Q37   Comparing his application to those successful seniors and very closely adopting the style, tone and structure of the best application letter.

   A. Very appropriate
   B. Appropriate but not ideal
   C. Inappropriate but not awful
   D. A very inappropriate thing to do

Q38 Overstating his role in a previous project by claiming he was the originator of the idea, rather than one of the three co-founders.

- A. Very appropriate ☐
- B. Appropriate but not ideal ☐
- C. Inappropriate but not awful ☐
- D. A very inappropriate thing to do ☐

Q39 Making up a learning-point from an activity which they actually participated in, by stating they learned about the role of teamwork in a laboratory placement when they were in fact attached to a single research scientist working alone.

- A. Very appropriate ☐
- B. Appropriate but not ideal ☐
- C. Inappropriate but not awful ☐
- D. A very inappropriate thing to do ☐

Scenario 13

A second year student in medical school is part of a problem-based learning group. She had been assigned to undertake a group presentation, and attended all the meetings, contributed fully with several important ideas and is progressing well with the presentation slides. One of her colleagues then e-mails the group to say that she is being lazy and making others carry her share of the work.

How appropriate are each of the following responses by the medical student to this situation.

Q40 E-mailing the group back and requesting other members to share their opinion of her work.

- A. Very appropriate ☐
- B. Appropriate but not ideal ☐
- C. Inappropriate but not awful ☐
- D. A very inappropriate thing to do ☐

Q41 Emailing the group back to arrange an in-person discussion at the next PBL meeting

- A. Very appropriate ☐
- B. Appropriate but not ideal ☐
- C. Inappropriate but not awful ☐
- D. A very inappropriate thing to do ☐

Q42   Immediately reporting the incident to her PBL tutor

    A. Very appropriate

    B. Appropriate but not ideal

    C. Inappropriate but not awful

    D. A very inappropriate thing to do

Scenario 14

A patient is awaiting an MRI scan, but left the ward to buy some snacks from the hospital shop, therefore missing her slot. The radiology department puts her on standby for the next available space, and asks the junior doctor to request that she stays on the ward whilst waiting for this appointment. After several hours of waiting, she tries to leave the ward. When requested by the junior doctor to remain on the ward, she threatens him with a formal complaint.

   How appropriate are each of the following responses by the junior doctor to this situation.

Q43   Physically restraining the patient from leaving the ward if she continues to insist.

    A. Very appropriate

    B. Appropriate but not ideal

    C. Inappropriate but not awful

    D. A very inappropriate thing to do

Q44   Threatening the patient that if she goes off and misses her MRI once again, she is at risk of not being treated for a serious injury.

    A. Very appropriate

    B. Appropriate but not ideal

    C. Inappropriate but not awful

    D. A very inappropriate thing to do

Q45   Attempting to reason with the patient, and offering to check with the radiology department for updates.

    A. Very appropriate

    B. Appropriate but not ideal

    C. Inappropriate but not awful

    D. A very inappropriate thing to do

Scenario 15

A patient who is suffering from chronic leg pain for six months goes to see a GP, and explains that his pain medication is not relieving his symptoms. He states that his friend was relieved by taking herbal medicines and acupuncture, and would like to try these therapies.

How important are each of the following actions by the GP in this situation.

Q46 Explaining to the patient that herbal medicines are unlicensed in the UK and can carry serious adverse health risks including liver failure.

A. Very important
B. Important
C. Of minor importance
D. Not important at all

Q47 Offering a trial of changing his current pain medication

A. Very important
B. Important
C. Of minor importance
D. Not important at all

Q48 Checking the latest clinical trial evidence on acupuncture and herbal medicine in the management of chronic pain before discussing this issue.

A. Very important
B. Important
C. Of minor importance
D. Not important at all

Scenario 16

A patient comes into an accident an emergency unit, suffering from a high fever, sweating, cough, vomiting and diarrhoea. He looks severely unwell and dehydrated and a junior doctor attends him.

How important are each of the following actions by the junior doctor in this situation.

Q49   Giving the patient several oral medications designed to relieve his symptoms.

    A. Very important

    B. Important

    C. Of minor importance

    D. Not important at all

Q50   Asking if he has been abroad in the last six months.

    A. Very important

    B. Important

    C. Of minor importance

    D. Not important at all

Q51   Asking if he has eaten any unusual foods in the last few days

    A. Very important

    B. Important

    C. Of minor importance

    D. Not important at all

Q52   Informing senior doctors to review the patient.

    A. Very important

    B. Important

    C. Of minor importance

    D. Not important at all

Scenario 17

An 8-year-old girl is being treated in the Emergency Medicine department for a fracture of her left tibia and fibula, which occurred as she tripped and fell down the stairs according to her parents. The doctor notes that this is her third admission to hospital in six months and is concerned that this could be a case of child abuse.

    Rate the importance of the following actions by the treating doctor.

Q53   Examining the notes of the previous admissions.

    A. Very important

    B. Important

    C. Of minor importance

    D. Not important at all

Q54   Asking the parents questions regarding their occupation and educational background.

    A.   Very important

    B.   Important

    C.   Of minor importance

    D.   Not important at all

Q55   He examines the girl for signs of other injuries.

    A.   Very important

    B.   Important

    C.   Of minor importance

    D.   Not important at all

Scenario 18

A medical student tells his roommate that he was sent a copy of this year's examination by a lecturer who he is close to. He offers to share the test with his roommate.

    How appropriate are each of the following responses by the medical student to this situation.

Q56   Refusing to take the test, but not revealing the information to anyone else.

    A.   Very appropriate

    B.   Appropriate but not ideal

    C.   Inappropriate but not awful

    D.   A very inappropriate thing to do

Q57   Accepting the test and sharing it within his close circle of friends.

    A.   Very appropriate

    B.   Appropriate but not ideal

    C.   Inappropriate but not awful

    D.   A very inappropriate thing to do

Q58   Reporting the student to the Dean of the medical school.

    A.   Very appropriate

    B.   Appropriate but not ideal

    C.   Inappropriate but not awful

    D.   A very inappropriate thing to do

Q59   Discussing the ethics of the situation with his roommate, and trying to convince him to report the situation.

A. Very appropriate
B. Appropriate but not ideal
C. Inappropriate but not awful
D. A very inappropriate thing to do

Scenario 19

A young GP is treating a patient who flirts with her throughout the consultation period. At the end of the consultation, the patient politely asks for her telephone number and if she would be interested in meeting for a coffee at some point.

How appropriate are each of the following responses by the GP to this situation.

Q60   Telling the patient that doctor–patient relationships are not appropriate and therefore she would not be allowed to meet him in this manner.

A. Very appropriate
B. Appropriate but not ideal
C. Inappropriate but not awful
D. A very inappropriate thing to do

Q61   Lying to the patient by saying that she is married and is therefore not interested in such meetings.

A. Very appropriate
B. Appropriate but not ideal
C. Inappropriate but not awful
D. A very inappropriate thing to do

Q62   Bluntly refusing the patient by saying that she is not interested in him.

A. Very appropriate
B. Appropriate but not ideal
C. Inappropriate but not awful
D. A very inappropriate thing to do

Q63 Ignoring the statement altogether, stating that she will see him next time and hopes he recovers soon.

A. Very appropriate ☐
B. Appropriate but not ideal ☐
C. Inappropriate but not awful ☐
D. A very inappropriate thing to do ☐

Scenario 20

A medical student is on a trans-atlantic flight when a passenger collapses, and a call is put out for a 'doctor on board'. He is the only person with medical experience, and comes to the aid of the passenger.

Rate the importance of the following actions by the medical student.

Q64 Identifying himself as a student doctor and explaining the limits of his knowledge.

A. Very important ☐
B. Important ☐
C. Of minor importance ☐
D. Not important at all ☐

Q65 Identifying other members of the public with first-aid training, such as the cabin crew, to assist him.

A. Very important ☐
B. Important ☐
C. Of minor importance ☐
D. Not important at all ☐

Q66 Locating any friends or relatives of the passenger.

A. Very important ☐
B. Important ☐
C. Of minor importance ☐
D. Not important at all ☐

Q67 Considering the amount of inconvenience caused if he recommends the pilot descend for the emergency treatment of the passenger.

A. Very important ☐
B. Important ☐
C. Of minor importance ☐
D. Not important at all ☐

CHAPTER 7

Answers and explanations

Chapter 1: Verbal reasoning warm-up questions

Passage 1

Q1 *Answer*: Can't tell

Explanation: The passage states that it is now possible to relocate without affecting earning power but the reason for this new development is not given in the passage. It might be because of new technology but we cannot rule out the possibility that there are other causes; for example, the reason might be that it is the introduction of new legislation that allows workers a better work–life balance. Because we cannot establish new technology as the reason we must conclude that we cannot tell if the statement is true or false.

Q2 *Answer*: False

Explanation: Two reasons for these locations' popularity are mentioned in the passage, although the passage dwells mainly on one of them, commuters; the other is second-home owners.

Q3 *Answer*: True

Explanation: This is a tough question, so don't be too hard on yourself if you got it wrong. Although the passage does not mention a traditional high street with local shops, it is reasonable to conclude that this concept might form part of 'an idea of an unspoilt civic centre'. The statement starts with 'an idea' not 'the idea' and states it 'could include' not 'does or should include'. These are weak assertions and allow for many possibilities and for this reason the correct answer is true.

Q4   *Answer*: Can't tell

Explanation: the passage states commuters continue to commute despite the disadvantages but that does not mean that the benefits outweigh the disadvantages.

Passage 2

Q5   *Answer*: True

Explanation: The passage states three kinds of pests that affect asparagus.

Q6   *Answer*: Can't tell

Explanation: The passage states that the most sought-after domesticated varieties prefer a ph of 6.5, but we cannot tell or infer from the information given if other varieties of wild asparagus also share this characteristic.

Q7   *Answer*: False

Explanation: 'Unpalatable' means unpleasant or foul tasting. It is also a synonym of 'inedible'; however, it has more than one synonym. The author could equally have meant that the berries were, for example, poisonous or indigestible, rather than unpalatable. Inedible is not defined in either the passage or the question.

Q8   *Answer*: False

Explanation: The passage states that wild asparagus grows in Europe, northern Africa and central Asia but it also states that cultivated asparagus grows in Canada so we can infer that the statement is false.

Passage 3

Q9   *Answer*: False

Explanation: It is clear from the passage that a declining population can cause a country economic problems but it does not infer nor does it state that without immigration a country's population will decline.

Q10   *Answer*: Can't tell

Explanation: The passage refers to a period when 500,000 immigrants were present and we can tentatively infer that a change has occurred since then; however, we cannot tell if the statement that 'it is no longer the case that half a million immigrants enter the country' is true or false.

Q11   *Answer*: False

Explanation: The passage states that the indigenous low-paid and low-skilled workers stand to lose out because they face greater competition for work.

Q12   *Answer*: False

Explanation: The passage states that 'Some employers have much to gain from the improved supply of labour and savings made from not having to train young people' and it is reasonable to conclude that such employers are 'winners' in a climate of large-scale inward migration.

Passage 4

Q13   *Answer*: Can't tell

Explanation: Photos were collected and volcanoes were recorded but the passage does not specify that it was the photos that proved the existence of volcanoes. Other evidence may have been collected that proved their existence.

Q14   *Answer*: Can't tell

Explanation: This is another tough question. The passage states that Jupiter has a rocky core but no information is provided regarding the other gaseous planets and this information cannot be inferred from the passage.

Q15   *Answer*: Can't tell

Explanation: The passage does not mention what a telescope might reveal about Jupiter's rings.

Q16   *Answer*: Can't tell

Explanation: Passage 4 is shorter than you might expect in the UKCAT. This is intentional, as we wanted to surprise the reader and provide practice at dealing with questions that seem to have very little direct reference to the passage. We know that Uranus and Neptune both lie beyond Jupiter in terms of being further from the sun. Neptune is stated as taking the longest (165 years) to rotate the sun but we cannot infer from this that it is the furthest from the sun because, for example, it is possible for a slow-moving, narrow-orbit planet to be outpaced by a faster moving, long-orbit planet. It is not possible therefore to say if Neptune is furthest from the sun.

Passage 5

Q17 *Answer*: True

Explanation: It is said that China's economy is projected to grow 6.2 per cent next year, 6.2 per cent this year and grew 7.0 per cent last year. Next year is identified as 2016 so last year can be identified as 2014.

Q18 *Answer*: Can't tell

Explanation: Even though the passage states that the dollar is trading against the Chinese and Indian currencies at a much lower historic rate and this is bound to continue, we cannot speculate from the information given at what level the dollar would trade if the US economy was free of debt. There are too many unknowns to answer true or false.

Q19 *Answer*: False

Explanation: The passage is about the weakness of the US dollar and emergent economies not about the possibility or otherwise of a US recession.

Q20 *Answer*: Can't tell

Explanation: It is clear from the opening sentence that people expected the dollar to weaken and that they expected this to happen sooner than it did, but it is not possible to infer the timeframe for these predictions. We are told that an economy like that of the United States can live beyond its means for years but not that people were predicting the correction for years.

Passage 6

Q21 *Answer*: True

Explanation: To reduce the fuel bills of rural communities and to improve the energy efficiency of rural housing stock are described in the passage as objectives. The three strategies are community partnership working; targeting rural areas with concentrations of low income households and intensive action in clearly defined, specific areas.

Q22 *Answer*: Can't tell

Explanation: Aside from the benefits of saving on infrastructure investment costs and power loss to resistance in transmission wires, the passage does not describe the motive for the investment in the local generation of the community's energy needs.

Q23 *Answer*: Can't tell

Explanation: The energy needs of the community are not quantified and so we are unable to establish whether or even when the wind turbines are turning and the solar panels generating hot water for the hundreds of homes that this amounts to most of the community's energy needs.

Q24 *Answer*: False

Explanation: It is said in the passage that local generation has led to saving on the investment cost of additional transmission lines in the national network. From this it can be concluded that the community has a supply from the national power network that did not need to be expanded due to local generation.

Passage 7

Q25 *Answer*: False

Explanation: Part of the attraction is said to be that in India it is easier to fill highly skilled, English speaking positions. If highly skilled Indian workers did not speak English then filling the positions linked to these business activities would not be easier and so outsourcing them would become less attractive.

Q26 *Answer*: Can't tell

Explanation: the passage states that as many as 30 million skilled jobs are at risk. If more than 30 million were at risk of being moved we are unable to say if these extra jobs would be skilled or unskilled so we can't tell if they would all be skilled.

Q27 *Answer*: True

Explanation: Three reasons why companies are moving jobs to India are identified in the passage: because it is easier to fill highly skilled, English-speaking positions there; because, for the time being, wages for these roles are notably lower there than wages in Europe and the United States; and because companies want to position their businesses where they believe the future lies.

Q28 *Answer*: False

Explanation: This claim is not examined in the passage and none of the passage is relevant in terms of either supporting or contradicting it. It is false therefore that the claim is rebutted in the passage.

Passage 8

Q29 *Answer*: False

Explanation: This question is made more difficult by the statement in the passage that 'the same is sadly true' (this statement links the two parts). But a holiday resort that provides a school for local children is an example of a tour operator who is contributing to the local community. The use of an image of a non-existent farmhouse on the product of a meat factory is cynical, while the employment of local people and the provision of social buildings are not.

Q30 *Answer*: Can't tell

Explanation: The passage only says that tourists want a guilt-free holiday; it does not say anything about those tourists who don't want a guilt-free holiday and whether or not they enjoy themselves more.

Q31 *Answer*: Can't tell

Explanation: The passage states only one motive for why tourists prefer to use the services of a tour operator who is contributing to the local community and ecosystem, and that is that they want a guilt-free holiday. We cannot tell if the tourist has other motives.

Q32 *Answer*: True

Explanation: The passage states that consumers may be misled by location-mimicking breed names, but the use of a location in the name of a tour-operator enhances the local image which is part of what they are claiming.

Passage 9

Q33 *Answer*: False

Explanation: The passage describes beautiful things that we cannot see and if, as instructed, we take the meaning literally then we cannot see all beauty and it is not in the eye of the beholder but in some of the other senses too.

Q34 *Answer*: Can't tell

Explanation: This is a tough question and the answer a close call between false and cannot tell. Cannot tell is the preferred answer because the passage states that an idea can be beautiful and lack physical structure while a smell can be beautiful and lack physical appearance (it still has a physical structure). In the context of the opening sentence the term 'form' could mean either appearance or structure and so we cannot tell if, by saying a thing of beauty can completely lack physical form, it is meant that it lacks physical structure or physical appearance.

Q35 *Answer*: Can't tell

Explanation: The passage states that we cannot see scents and a perfume is the only beauty product that just plays on the emotions. However, from this information we cannot conclude or infer that there are or there are not other beauty products that we cannot see.

Q36 *Answer*: True

Explanation: The passage states that many things contribute to a unique blend of odours, and that specifically each is 'never quite the same', so we can infer from this claim that there is at least a minimal amount of difference in the smell between any two individuals.

Passage 10

Q37 *Answer*: True

Explanation: The opening sentence of the passage states that over $50 billion was spent online last year and it is hardly surprising that criminals want a share of the action, and it is reasonable to rephrase this as online shopping offers the criminal the promise of rich pickings.

Q38 *Answer*: False

Explanation: The passage states that most people do not secure their virtual shops to the same degree as their physical shops, and while the physical shop will be attended and have locks and alarms fitted, their virtual shop will have no more than a firewall, antivirus and anti-spyware software. These virtual securities are therefore not the equivalent of shop assistants, locks and alarms but are inferior in terms of security.

Q39 *Answer*: Can't tell

Explanation: While antivirus and anti-spyware software does update automatically we cannot establish this from the information contained in the passage so the correct answer is cannot tell.

Q40 *Answer*: Can't tell

Explanation: The passage states that virtual locations make criminals hard to trace regardless of success or not, but the reverse is not commented on. Therefore, using virtual locations could make thefts more successful, but we cannot tell from the passage.

Passage 11

Q41 *Answer*: Can't tell

Explanation: The views of the author cannot be established from the passage. The author is reporting findings rather than stating his or her personal opinions and for this reason we cannot tell if he or she is opposed.

Q42 *Answer*: False

Explanation: We are told that 'profits of British pubs have fallen by 20 per cent and many have reported a further worsening of their financial state since the introduction of a new law and a series of tax increases', but it is not possible (or reasonable) to infer from this that some pubs are operating at a loss or not at a profit.

Q43 *Answer*: Can't tell

Explanation: We are told that the smoking ban has led to a marked decrease in pub custom but cannot infer from this that pub customers have been encouraged to drink and smoke less because they may simply be drinking and smoking the same amount but at home instead of in the pub. The decrease in smoking of the general population may or may not apply to this specific demographic, and there is no way of knowing this from the passage.

Q44 *Answer*: Can't tell

Explanation: The passage states that the smoking ban has a strong effect on new smokers and decreasing current smokers, but makes no claim about one of these effects relative to the other.

Passage 12

Q45 *Answer*: True

Explanation: Even though the passage states that millions of law-abiding people have used recreational drugs, it is clear that users, if found in possession of these drugs, are breaking laws as they face penalties of imprisonment or fines. To be a user unavoidably involves being in possession and so someone who has used recreational drugs can only now be law abiding if they are no longer using them. But if they are using recreational drugs then it is not true that they are law abiding.

Q46 *Answer*: True

Explanation: The passage offers the opinion that using these drugs in your own home should be no one else's business but your own and this would include the courts and police.

Q47   *Answer*: Can't tell

Explanation: This question is made more difficult by the intentionally ambiguous passage. However, it is stated in the passage that dealing in these drugs can result in imprisonment for up to 14 years, but the drugs in question are those classified as class C drugs, the lowest classification. We are not informed of the penalties for dealing in the other categories so we cannot know if the statement is true or false.

Q48   *Answer*: Can't tell

Explanation: The passage does not explicitly state what a gateway drug is, nor why cannabis is the most commonly used: this could be due to price, but other reasons such as availability or method of taking could be involved.

Passage 13

Q49   *Answer*: Can't tell

Explanation: We are told that 20 years after the eruption only 4,000 of the original population of 12,000 remain. We cannot infer from this that therefore only 4,000 live on the island because it is possible, for example, that people arrived from elsewhere to live on the island, making the population greater than 4,000.

Q50   *Answer*: False

Explanation: On balance the correct answer is false because the death of 19 people and the irrevocable loss of the way of life that existed before the eruption was a disaster. The evaluation averted an even greater disaster.

Q51   *Answer*: True

Explanation: The eruption occurred in 1997 and we are told that it was 13 years after the eruption that only 4,000 of the original population remain. Thirteen years after 1997 = 2010 so the statement is true.

Q52   *Answer*: True

Explanation: This is a close one, but 'high pressure' is a relative term, and in this case the relative increase in pressure caused the eruption, which means that at the very least, erupting volcanoes have a higher pressure than dormant ones, and as is explained in the passage, this was the cause of its eruption.

Passage 14

Q53 *Answer*: Can't tell

Explanation: We are told that the first manned landing was made in 1969 and that probes made soft landings in the 1960s, but we cannot tell from the information given if any landings (unmanned) occurred before that time.

Q54 *Answer*: Can't tell

Explanation: The passage states that the later missions visited highlands but we cannot tell from this whether or not the landing occurred in a mountainous region.

Q55 *Answer*: True

Explanation: The passage is about the manned lunar landings and the search for suitable sites for those landings. The soft landings performed by probes are described in terms of the search for suitable sites for the manned landings. Given the context, reference to a suitable site in the second sentence can be taken to mean suitable for manned missions.

Q56 *Answer*: False

Explanation: The passage merely states that fuel consumption falls under the category of 'waste of energy', so although no greenhouse gases are emitted into the atmosphere, that is not the contention of the passage, therefore this statement is false.

Passage 15

Q57 *Answer*: False

Explanation: The first sentence of the passage states that we suffer a suspension of judgement only when we spend money that we intended to use for something essential or unintentionally create an unauthorized overdraft. It is false therefore that we suffer a suspension of judgement whenever we hand over a card to purchase something.

Q58 *Answer*: True

Explanation: The passage states that there is a widely held perception that electronic money and credit are somehow not as real or valuable as notes and coins and that retailers play on this emotional weakness. It is reasonable to take this to mean that electronic money and credit have a lower psychological value than cash in your hand.

Q59 *Answer*: Can't tell

Explanation: The passage does not mention a licensing scheme, nor does it indicate if unregulated sites are also unlicensed.

Q60 *Answer*: Can't tell

Explanation: The loss to sellers is described as offset by the benefit of having a more appealing product, but this cannot be quantified, and so there could be a large loss which is offset by an equally large benefit. We cannot be sure from the passage.

Mini-test 1

Passage 1

Q61 *Answer*: False

Explanation: The case for smaller families in the developed world is not dependent on the question of whether or not the population of the developed world is growing or contracting but on the higher carbon-dioxide emission lifestyle of people living in the developed world.

Q62 *Answer*: Can't tell

Explanation: The passage states that having a child in the developed world has a greater environmental impact than having a child in the developing world. Before we can know that a child not born in the developing world will effect a major cut in a family's future carbon-dioxide emissions we would need information about the level of carbon-dioxide output produced by the family. If they produced no or very little carbon dioxide then having fewer children would not result in a major cut in their family's future carbon-dioxide output.

Q63 *Answer*: True

Explanation: The passage indicates that people in developed nations are more likely to take regular flights and drive cars as part of a 'high carbon dioxide emission lifestyle', and given this higher likelihood, its relative impact is greater in developed countries compared to developing ones.

Q64 *Answer*: Can't tell

Explanation: Supporting children is reliant on subsistence agriculture, and fast-food consumption is another of rainforest removal, but we cannot be sure of the relative amounts.

Passage 2

Q65   *Answer*: False

Explanation: You are only likely to get this question wrong if you are sacrificing accuracy too much to speed. The passage states that of the 4 million workers who have paid into a pension scheme for the bulk of their working life, only those who have paid into a final salary scheme will enjoy retirement on two-thirds of their final salary and the rest will have to manage on far less because their pension scheme lacked the final salary guarantee.

Q66   *Answer*: Can't tell

Explanation: We are told that workers need two-thirds of their final salary to be comfortable in their retirement but we are not told the amount needed to be secure. It is reasonable to infer that the amount needed to be secure (safe) is less than the amount needed to be comfortable. But we cannot infer that 40 per cent of final salary is either sufficient or insufficient to be secure in retirement so the correct answer is cannot tell.

Q67   *Answer*: False

Explanation: We are told that the population of workers is 15 million (4 million contributing to a pension scheme and a remaining 11 million who have made no or very little contribution to a scheme other than the compulsory state scheme). We can also establish from the passage that the total population of the country to which the passage refers must be greater than 15 million because it also includes some retired people (see the first sentence which reads 'to enjoy a comfortable retirement, many retired people recommend retiring on two-thirds of final salary'). The correct answer therefore is false.

Q68   *Answer*: Can't tell

Explanation: Social and psychological health have also been shown to make an impact (in addition to physical health), but their relative value is unknown.

Mini-test 2

Passage 1

Q69   *Answer*: False

Explanation: The fact that the French national health service is probably the best in the world is left aside so is not a factor attributed to the lower level of heart disease. The passage therefore attributes three factors to the lower level of death caused by heart disease: remaining active, consuming more fruit and vegetables and enjoying more red wine.

Q70 *Answer*: False

Explanation: It is true that twice as many may still amount to very few but the last sentence of the passage states that 'this allows significant numbers of people to live until their centenary' and just a few people living until their centenary would not be described as a significant number.

Q71 *Answer*: Can't tell

Explanation: As stated above, the pattern of drinking is critical to its effect. She could be drinking in a stable pattern, giving no reduction; equally she could be barely meeting the binge-drinking threshold. We cannot tell.

Q72 *Answer*: True

Explanation: The pattern of binge vs non-binge is a cultural difference, and furthermore the passage states that even if red wine is the alcohol type consumed, the negative effects are the same.

Passage 2

Q73 *Answer*: False

Explanation: The passage states that if extreme weather was occurring more frequently then it is feasible that the forecast might include the prediction that the frequency of these events will continue to be higher than the historic average. It is therefore not a mistake to believe that the exceptional can be forecast in the long term.

Q74 *Answer*: Can't tell

Explanation: Neither the date when the passage was written nor the year of the summer to which the passage refers is indicated, so it is not possible to tell from the passage if the summer of 2007 was very wet and windy.

Q75 *Answer*: Can't tell

Explanation: It is clear from the passage that the frequency of exceptional events can be predicted, but this is not to predict specific weather events such as an incidence of extreme flooding. While the forecast failed to predict these events last summer, it cannot be established from the passage whether or not it is possible to predict such events as a matter of principle.

Q76 *Answer*: True

Explanation: Falling significantly below the level of 'most accurate' can be considered 'inaccurate', especially as the wording of 'in the majority of cases' ties in well with 'generally'.

Mini-test 3

Passage 1

Q77 *Answer*: False

Explanation: The passage states that in almost zero gravity and no wind, very large droplets or, in other words, globules of water can form so it is false to say that the passage disproves this.

Q78 *Answer*: False

Explanation: The passage states that 'in every situation droplets do collide and these combine to form larger droplets that may well survive'.

Q79 *Answer*: False

Explanation: Since static charge rate is inversely proportional to drop size, a low drop size means a high rate, and the highest rate would therefore be in a gale whereby the droplets are smallest.

Q80 Answer: Can't tell

Explanation: There is no way of knowing how small the resultant drops of the 5mm drops breaking up will be as it is not stated, therefore we cannot tell.

Passage 2

Q81 *Answer*: True

Explanation: English is described as a dominant, apparently all-conquering, language and as more and more of the world speak it, it will break up into dialects and then distinct languages.

Q82 *Answer*: True

Explanation: The inability of the scholars to revive the langauge is directly linked to the lack of written material, and as a corollary sufficient material is required to undertake such a revival.

Q83 *Answer*: False

Explanation: The passage does answer the question (although the answer is incomplete). It is stated that in the case of a language spoken by a small linguistic community it becomes extinct when there is no one left in that community and it describes how a dominant language might become extinct if it breaks down into dialects that then evolve into new languages.

Q84   *Answer*: True

Explanation: Ambivalent means in two minds and the passage offers first an account of the theory that English will evolve into dialects and then new languages but also describes this view as controversial because speech is standardized and dialects are prevented from forming.

Mini-test 4

Passage 1

Q85   *Answer*: Can't tell

Explanation: We are only informed that there were a total of 23 student volunteers and cannot infer from this how this number was split between the various roles.

Q86   *Answer*: False

Explanation: Looking for records, and indeed only overt signs of psychological evidence, cannot be concluded as being comprehensive in filtering such volunteers out.

Q87   *Answer*: True

Explanation: All the volunteers were male and the passage provides no indication that women might act differently. For this reason it is true that it is wrong to deduce from the passage that women volunteers would act differently.

Q88   *Answer*: False

Explanation: Three of Philip Zimbardo's factors are identified in the passage: conformity, anonymity and boredom.

Passage 2

Q89   *Answer*: True

Explanation: The passage is about how Japan can maintain its competitiveness given the projected fall in its population and the disproportionately elderly character of that population. The proposed answer is through innovation. Although the passage also considers how Japan can remain innovative, unless it engages in new ways of thinking and changes in worldwide values this is a secondary issue and the 'big' question posed is one of competitiveness.

Q90   *Answer*: False

Explanation: No abilities are attributed to India or China in the passage, nor can you infer from the tone of the passage that the predicted success of these nations is due to their ability to engage in new ways of thinking.

Q91   *Answer*: Can't tell

Explanation: This is quite likely to be true, but since we cannot determine Japan's future spending allocation, it may be that research and development remains a high priority for future governments and spending is maintained or even increased. Without being able to exclude this possibility, we cannot tell.

Q92   *Answer*: True

Explanation: The United States is currently the largest GDP alongside the EU, which we know will be fourth. Since Japan is stated to be fifth, and China is larger than India (being five times that of Japan compared to twice for India), then this order is correct.

Mini-test 5

Passage 1

Q93   *Answer*: False

Explanation: The passage states that one in four of the world's population claims to speak elementary English but you cannot deduce how many people this statement represents.

Q94   *Answer*: True

Explanation: The passage states that the S section of the English dictionary is the largest in terms of the number of entries and that 'the longest section in the Italian dictionary and the section that contains the most entries is the S section'.

Q95   *Answer*: Can't tell

Explanation: The passage states that the S section contains the largest number of entries but we cannot infer from this that the section is also the longest. It is possible that another section has fewer entries but is longer because of the extent of the definitions.

Q96   *Answer*: Can't tell

Explanation: We are told that the Q section of the English dictionary is the shortest but this does not mean that it necessarily has close to the fewest number of entries. The Q section of the Italian dictionary contains close to the shortest number of Italian entries but we are not told how many foreign word entries the J, K, Y and W sections of the Italian dictionary contain (we are told that they are very short as they only contain foreign words used in Italian) and they may be shorter than the Q section.

Passage 2

Q97   *Answer*: False

Explanation: The passage does not state the reason why tropical storms do not form near or at the equator. The water might at times reach these temperatures but some other cause may be at work and prevent tropical storms forming.

Q98   *Answer*: False

Explanation: We are told that each successive storm is given a name beginning with successive letters of the alphabet but we are not told that at the start of each season the tradition is to reset the sequence and start again with the first letter of the alphabet.

Q99   *Answer*: False

Explanation: The list is correct in that the names begin with successive letters of the alphabet and alternate between boy and girl names but there are only eight names and in a typical year nine named storms would occur.

Q100 *Answer*: Can't tell

Explanation: We are told that initially only girls' names were used but later this was changed so that the names alternated from boy to girl names. But we cannot establish when this change took place. The question implies that weather forecasts are no longer broadcast over shortwave radio but if this practice stopped there is nothing in the passage to suggest when or whether it stopped before the change to the naming of storms with both boy and girl names.

Mini-test 6

Passage 1

Q101 *Answer*: Can't tell

> *Explanation*: We can determine that the current flag is rectangular because the passage states that all modern flags except Nepal's are rectangular. The colours of the Ethiopian flag at the time of the pan-African movement are also stated in the passage, however we cannot know if the current national flag of Ethiopia remains these colours.

Q102 *Answer*: False

> *Explanation*: The passage states that their colours hark back to the days when flags were extensively used for identification and communication. So their previous use gave rise to the colours and symbolic designs used today and not the rectangular shape.

Q103 *Answer*: False

> *Explanation*: You are informed in the passage that the flag of the Republic of Ireland was inspired by the tri-colour of the French revolution and that the tri-colour was blue, white and red. It is possible to infer from the passage that the tri-colour design was the inspiration for the flag of the Republic and that they adopted different colours from those adopted by France.

Q104 *Answer*: True

> *Explanation*: We can tell that this statement is true because in the passage the use of the symbolic designs and their meanings is mentioned. For example, the crescent moon and cross are referred to as identifying the official religion of a nation.

Passage 2

Q105 *Answer*: Can't tell

> *Explanation*: Although these protections do exist and are significant, there may be others.

Q106 *Answer*: True

> *Explanation*: The EU Court of Justice ruling gave people the right to be forgotten and by re-publishing these search results they are frustrating this right.

Q107 *Answer*: False

Explanation: The passage states that the new threat to personal liberty is how to prevent complete strangers finding out our personal details. While this is quite the opposite problem of the old issue of secrecy, it does not mean that the old problem of finding out the personal details that organizations are holding on us no longer exists. It could be that we now face two threats and for this reason the statement is false.

Q108 *Answer*: True

Explanation: Penultimate means last but one and the sentence states 'if the person for whom you are searching is active on a social network site or an internet specialist interest forum then you may well be able to identify a database of friends and contacts and by reading recent postings obtain a flavour of their views and preferences'. From this it is clearly the case that the penultimate sentence of the passage illustrates the sort of things that people post on the internet.

More UKCAT-style verbal reasoning

Q1   True: From the text: 'holding views that some racial groups have intrinsically better characteristics than others' is a form of racism, and positive views are covered by this statement.

Q2   True: From the text – it acts as discriminatory against other groups in favour of the favoured group.

Q3   False: This question states it has to be discriminatory against racial groups – those words are sneakily missing from the question!

Q4   Cannot tell: 'The belief that people from certain ethnic backgrounds are worse at some things than other races still continues today' does not allow us to gauge a quantity of many or otherwise.

Q5   True: Whilst it is not a certain breach of the rules, the second bullet point states that you should strive to maintain a professional image online, and it is possible that contravening this will result in a breach of the rules, although this is not certain.

Q6   Cannot tell: 'Main' is difficult to prove in this case, and even though these problems do exist, there is no quantification of them.

Q7   Cannot tell: There is nothing specific in this text as the rules are for social networking, not for generally online!

Q8   Cannot tell: Although this case was effected by a tutor on social network, this is not a

Q9   Cannot tell: Since 'there are those who think' could be 10 people or 10,000, we have no way to equate this to 'many' or not.

Q10   True: Don't be put off by political correctness or what you know! Look at the definition of democracy according to the passage – based on this information, it is true.

Q11   True: The lowering of prices, increases tourism and the added income aids recovery.

Q12   False: 'Usually' means most of the time – but not always therefore no, not always.

Q13   False: first paragraph, second sentence: almost one-quarter.

Q14   True: second paragraph, second sentence.

Q15   Can't tell: last paragraph, fourth sentence: 1.1 only indicates a need to lose weight.

Q16   Can't tell: last paragraph, last sentence: only maximal stated with no reference to obesity.

Q17   True: first paragraph, fifth sentence: family history.

Q18   False: first paragraph, sixth sentence: usually the doctor's surgery.

Q19   Can't tell: true but not stated in the text.

Q20   True: second paragraph, second sentence: psychotherapy encourages a person to talk freely.

Q21   True: first paragraph, sixth sentence: below 18°C remain dormant.

Q22   False: to more than 1,000 at body temperature; not at room temperature.

Q23   True: second paragraph, first sentence: campylobacter is responsible for most of the food poisoning in the United Kingdom.

Q24   True: second paragraph, second and fourth sentences.

Q25   False: first paragraph: four books; fifth and sixth sentences.

Q26   True: compare fifth sentence first paragraph and third sentence second paragraph.

Q27   False: last paragraph, last sentence: float is topped up to original level.

Q28 Can't tell: second paragraph, fifth sentence: there may or may not be discrepancies because there could be differences.

Q29 Can't tell: first paragraph: impossible to say; honey was used for medicinal purposes in ancient times but its use as a foodstuff is not commented on.

Q30 True: second paragraph, third sentence: UKCAT questions do not require specialist knowledge but bactericidal clearly means killing bacteria.

Q31 False: second paragraph, second sentence: states as a key feature but this does not identify it as the main aim.

Q32 True: last paragraph, last sentence: 'no report' does not mean that it has been ruled out.

Q33 True: first paragraph, second sentence: over age 30 (age 29 in the question).

Q34 True: second paragraph, second sentence: for a further 15 years.

Q35 False: second paragraph, third sentence: non-UK EU citizens are disenfranchised where UK general elections are concerned; their position is clarified further in the last sentence.

Q36 Can't tell: second paragraph, first sentence: only if resident in the UK.

Q37 True: first paragraph, fourth sentence: states height restriction is 2 metres although the daily rate is punitive.

Q38 True: second paragraph, first sentence: short stay and long stay (with different tariffs).

Q39 Can't tell: last paragraph, fifth sentence: insufficient information given on the charges.

Q40 Can't tell: first paragraph, last sentence: states on the ground floor of car park 3 with no reference to parking on the roof.

Q41 True: second paragraph: private mint in Birmingham used steam power prior to the Royal Mint.

Q42 False: last paragraph, second sentence: first phase opened in 1968.

Q43 Can't tell: last paragraph: insufficient information to establish whether the Tower could also strike special proof coins as well as Llantrisant.

Q44 True: last paragraph, first sentence: decimalization 1971; last sentence: Tower Hill 1975.

Q45   Can't tell: the type of fungus that causes wet rot is not mentioned.

Q46   False: second paragraph, second sentence: less than 10 per cent moisture.

Q47   True: second paragraph, third sentence: wet rot is more common than dry rot but it cannot spread into brickwork.

Q48   Can't tell: second paragraph, seventh sentence: impossible to tell because an intact paint surface can mask fungal penetration.

Chapter 2: Decision analysis

Test 1: 28 questions in 33 minutes

Q1   *Answer*: B

Explanation: The code states reverse delete, wooden flooring. Notice that the comma is after delete, so we can take this to mean that the code C refers to delete, and the reverse of delete is add.

Q2   *Answer*: D

Explanation: The code reads add pasta, cigarettes parallel delete. A and C could be right but for the modifier E, which means parallel. A parallel is a sort of synonym, and only answer D offers a parallel to delete = remove.

Q3   *Answer*: A

Explanation: The code reads gasoline, similar add, parallel the basket of goods and services. Answer A uses similar add to mean 'on' and parallel basket of goods and services to mean 'list'. Answer C does not include the concept of add. D does not code for similar. B does not offer a word similar to add but states add.

Q4   *Answer*: B

Explanation: The code reads append popular, parallel elevated, pasta. Append means 'add', and the phrases 'all the rage' and 'very popular' are phrases with similar but greater meaning to popular. A parallel to elevated is promote. Only suggested answer B offers both something appended to popular and a parallel to elevated.

Q5   *Answer*: C

Explanation: The code reads reverse commodity, mobile phone contract, landscape gardening. Reverse means the antonym or opposite. A commodity is a useful product that can be bought or sold. Both goods and services can be described as commodities (services are not tangible commodities but they are commodities all the same) so these terms cannot be taken to be the antonym. The reverse of commodity is 'not commodities', and the best explanation of the code is C; mobile phones and landscape gardening are not commodities.

Q6   *Answer*: D

Explanation: The code reads banking, append service, similar temperate, inflation. To append service we must add something, and making it plural, services, can be taken to be adding something. In this context, temperate means mild or moderate but not pleasant.

Q7   *Answer*: A

Explanation: The code reads milk, similar unfashionable, inflation, parallel lessen. Only suggested answer A contains a word or phrase similar to unfashionable (obsolete).
Answers B and D include the words add and increase respectively which are not coded for. Answer C codes cutting out as similar unfashionable which is inaccurate in comparison to obsolete in answer A.

Q8   *Answer*: B

Explanation: The code reads unfashionable, mobile phone contract, pasta, reverse. Of the code words it only makes sense to reverse unfashionable to fashionable or, in other words, popular. Option A can be questioned because the code makes no reference to a decision to delete mobile phones or pasta from the list. Out of favour and out of date are synonyms, not antonyms, of unfashionable.

Q9   *Answer*: C

Explanation: The code reads soft furnishings, lessen delete, popular, parallel elevated, inflation. Lessen delete can be to 'think about or consider deleting' (but it can't be 'don't delete'). Parallel elevated can be high or very high. The code for popular is unmodified, so very popular is not the best suggestion. This leaves only suggested answer C as correct and including all the codes.

Q10   *Answer*: A and D

Explanation: The code reads parallel, add, gasoline; notice the comma, which implies that the modifier parallel could relate to either add or gasoline. Include is a parallel of add, and petrol is a parallel of gasoline, but put on the list is not a parallel of add. B is also questionable, because both gasoline and add have been modified. E is likely to be wrong because neither add nor gasoline has been modified.

Q11   *Answer*: A, B and C

Explanation: The code reads soft furnishings, delete, refrigerator. The code only provides a single instruction, delete. We should only use this operation once and can use it either to delete (both) soft furnishings and refrigerator or to delete one or the other. D and E are questionable because they imply more than one instruction: to delete one item and keep another.

Q12   *Answer*: C

Explanation: The code reads octane, alcohol, gasoline, new, high.
A does not include gasoline, B uses high twice and D fails to use new.

Q13   *Answer*: B

Explanation: The code reads gain, turn around contradiction, may.
Turn around contradiction means the antonym of contradiction, which is agreement. We can favour suggested answers A and B over C and D because A and B use terms that are either an antonym of contradiction (agreement) or a term related to its antonym (permission). We can favour B over A because it uses the antonym of contradiction (rather than a related term) and because it introduces fewer clauses unsupported by the sequence of codes (in A we have the suggestion that permission may be denied but try). While it is not incorrect to use additional terms not in the sequence of codes, we can favour the suggested answer that does not introduce them over one that does.

Q14   *Answer*: D

Explanation: The code reads diesel, more green, enlarge alternative, similar new. Enlarge alternative can be alternatives, and similar new can be innovative or recent. Only D uses all the codes and correctly applies the transformers. A does not include similar new, B fails to enlarge alternative and C fails to include more.

Q15   *Answer*: D

Explanation: The code reads investment, new, bio, similar know, fuel turn around gain. We can reject A because it does not include a concept of turn around gain. B and C use know rather than similar know and can be rejected. D is the favoured answer as it codes remember as similar know and risky as turn around gain.

Q16   *Answer*: A

Explanation: The code reads tell, turn around could. The antonym of 'could' is 'could not' or its abbreviation 'couldn't'. Only suggested answer A offers a correct antonym of could.

Q17   *Answer*: C

Explanation: The code reads green, turn around may, ethanol. If you turn around may you get may not. Only suggested answer C offers a correct antonym of may.

Q18   *Answer*: B

Explanation: The code reads enlarge alternative, enlarge more, investment, more. Note that the code C(more) occurs twice in this sequence and so we can use it twice (once transformed). D is less favourable because it uses a synonym of more (extra) as well as its enlargement (most). A and C can be eliminated because they do not include an enlargement of more.

Q19   *Answer*: D

Explanation: The code reads gain, similar high, turn around can, tell, new, oil. Soar and gain are similar to high but gains is not. Turn around can is can't. Only D makes use of all the codes and correctly applies the transformations.

Q20   *Answer*: B and C

Explanation: The code reads similar contradiction, similar investment, bio, fuel. Words or phrases that occur in the suggested answers that are similar to contradiction are inconsistent, disagreement and conflicting evidence. Terms similar to investment include venture, speculation and arguably capital. Suggested answers A and D can be eliminated because they do not make use of the code for similar contradiction. Both B and C make full use of the code.

Q21   *Answer*: A, B and C

Explanation: The code reads similar few, ethanol, investment, alternative. Answers A, B and C all include terms similar to few: minority, hardly any, small amount. D includes the antonym: many. Suggested answers A, B and C therefore correctly utilize the sequence of code.

Q22   *Answer*: D

Explanation: The code reads turn around gain, diesel, fuel, gasoline, turn around new. If we turn around gain we get decrease, dwindle, decline and fall. If we turn around new we get old, traditional or conventional. Only suggested answer D includes the meaning of all the codes. Answers A and B both fail to include an antonym of new. (B also uses the term bio, which is in the matrix but does not appear in the question sequence.) Answer C does not include the term fuel.

Q23   *Answer*: B and D

Explanation: The code reads ethanol, gasoline, fuel, octane, high. Suggested answers B and D both use all parts of the sequence; however, suggested answer A does not include gasoline, while answer C fails to utilize the term fuel.

Q24   *Answer*: D

Explanation: The code reads information, expand try, he or S, online. Tries and trying are both examples of expanded try. Suggested answers A, B and C fail to use the code for online. B and C do not include an expanded try.

Q25   *Answer*: A

Explanation: The code reads works, he or S, seems, reverse week. The reverse of week could be many things, including arguably weekend, days and hourly, but it cannot be weekly, which means we can reject suggested answer C. We can also eliminate B and D because the code for seems is not used.

Q26   *Answer*: C

Explanation: The code reads we, same as ready, online, he or S. Words or phrases the same as ready include, for example, all set and standing by. Suggested answers A and B do not use the code for he so can be rejected. Suggested answer D does not use a term the same as ready.

Q27   *Answer*: B and C

Explanation: The code reads he or S, proves, works. Only answers B and C correctly utilize the three components of the sequence.

Q28   *Answer*: A and C

Explanation: The code reads we, know, expound no, similar he or S, similar steal. Answer A codes not as expand no and similar he or S as she, and makes correct use of all the codes. Answer B does not include a code for we. Answer C makes correct use of all the codes and transformations. Answer D does not make adequate use for similar steal.

Test 2: 28 questions in 33 minutes

Q1 *Answer*: C. We eat breakfast quickly.

The code reads: HE, B7(108), 15(6) = personal plural, opposite large (meal), short time.

Explanation: Eliminate answers A and D straight away as they have no concept of *We* (I plural); translate short time as *quickly* (answer C) noting that *breakfast* could be a small meal (opposite large) and that B has no concept of *small*, and E only a weak concept of *short time* (morning).

Q2 *Answer*: D. Equations are hard for many people.

The code reads: (106,10) 14, B16(E1) = (number work) problem, opposite few (plural person).

Explanation: Eliminate answers C and E straight away as they have no concept of *people* (plural person); translate opposite few as *many* (answer D) noting that A and B have no concept of many.

Q3 *Answer*: D. We should work less and play more.

The code reads: HE, 10(BA), B10(A) = Personal plural, work (opposite increase), opposite work (increase).

Explanation: Eliminate A, B and C, taking plural personal to mean *We*; translate opposite work to mean *play* in answers C and D, noting that only answer D includes the concepts of less (opposite increase = decrease).

Q4 *Answer*: B. Hard work never hurt anyone.

The code reads: 14(10), BF, A110, 1 = problem (work), opposite always, increase pain, person.

Explanation: Only answer B correctly translates opposite always as *never*.

Q5 *Answer*: A. Others are not as fit as me.

The code reads: B(HE), B(C105)H = opposite (personal plural), opposite (similar health) personal.

Explanation: Eliminate B and D because the code does not include concepts of Most or Many; translate similar health as *fit* and its opposite as *not as fit* (answer A) or less healthy (answer C), noting that opposite (personal plural) is opposite (we) which translates better as *others* rather than *no people*.

Q6 *Answer*: C. There is no room in my father's house.

The code reads: BD(7 17), H(7G), 12 = opposite positive (large space), personal (large male), house.
Explanation: Choose B and E as the most likely, translate personal large male to mean husband or father and (opposite positive) large space as negative large space or no large space, meaning *no room* (Answer C).

Q7 *Answer*: B. I never break the law.

The code reads: H(BF), B201, C102 = personal (opposite always), opposite fix, similar rules.

Explanation: Eliminate A, C and E which do not code *never* (opposite always); choose B which codes for *I* (personal) noting that *break* is coded as opposite fix and *law* as similar rules.

Q8 *Answer*: C. It is hard to stay on a healthy diet.

The code reads: 105, 2(B7),14, A6 = health, eat (opposite large), problem, increase time.

Explanation: All concepts must be coded for; eliminate A, B and E because *hard* (problem) is not coded, noting that C codes for *stay* (increase time).

Q9 *Answer*: D. I was off work due to illness.

The code reads: H, B10, B105 = personal, opposite work, opposite health.

Explanation: Eliminate A, C and E because *I* is coded for once and not twice; eliminate B because seldom take is not coded.

Q10 *Answer*: C. There are many buildings and a few open spaces.

The code reads: B16, C(E12), 16(7E17) = opposite few, similar (plural house), few (large plural space).

Explanation: Opposite few codes *many*, and similar (plural house) codes buildings, ie Answer C, noting that few (large plural space) codes *few open spaces*.

Q11 *Answer*: B. My colleagues and I hold the same view.

The code reads: H(10J), A(3C) = personal (work together), increase (think similar).

Explanation: Eliminate D and E because personal codes *My*; eliminate C because increase similar think translates as *same* thoughts or same view and work together codes as *colleagues*.

Q12 *Answer*: E. We never consume unhealthy food.

The code reads: EH, BF, 2, B(105), C2 = plural personal, opposite always, eat, opposite health, similar eat.

Explanation: Eliminate C and D which do not translate opposite always (*never or don't*); eliminate B which does not translate similar eat (*food*); and eliminate A which translates as healthy instead of *unhealthy*, noting that in E, eat codes for *consume*.

Q13 *Answer*: A. We seldom drink hot tea.

The code reads: EH, BA(BF), C(11 8) = plural person, opposite increase (opposite always), similar (fire water).

Explanation: There is no concept of drink in the code so you have to insert it; plural personal translates as *We*, so B and D can be ruled out; opposite increase is reduce and opposite always is never and reduce never translates as seldom, ie A or E; reject E because there is no code for juice whereas C(11 8) means similar to fire water which could code *hot tea*.

Q14 *Answer*: E. Unemployment will rise.

The code reads: B10, A(B13M) = opposite work, increase (opposite fall future).

Explanation: Opposite work translates as jobless or unemployment, ie B, C or E; opposite fall is rise, or will rise in the future.

Q15 *Answer*: C. People take a ferry across the sea.

The code reads: E1, 4K, 18(7 8) = plural person, vehicle specific, travel (large water).

Explanation: Eliminate answers A and D which have no concept of *people* (plural person); eliminate E because Most is not coded; B mentions no vehicle whereas C codes ferry as vehicle specific noting that travel large water means as across the sea.

Q16 *Answer*: B. We are employed at a hotel.

The code reads: EH, 10(101), C(7 12) = plural personal, work (money), similar (large house).

Explanation: Translate work money as paid work or employed and similar large house as hotel.

Q17 *Answer*: B. Scotland.

Explanation: There is no concept of *Scotland* in the table of code words, whereas the remaining words can be translated from the table's codes: *sold* codes as money increase (101A); *We* codes as plural personal (EH); *home* codes as house personal (12H) and *moved away* codes as travel increase (18A).

Q18 *Answer*: A. exercise.

Explanation: There is no concept of *exercise* in the table; *weight* can code as light opposite (202B); *diet* can code as eat opposite increase (2, BA) or eat meal opposite increase (2, 108, BA); *lose* can code as opposite increase (BA); *Most* can code as opposite few (B16).

Q19 *Answer*: E. Pollution is bad for my breathing.

The code reads: (107,14), BD(H107) = (air, problem), opposite positive (personal air).

Explanation: Eliminate A, C and D taking *personal* air to refer to I or my, which are only found in answers B or E; eliminate answer B because the concept of air is only translated once when it should appear twice; opposite positive (personal air) codes for *bad for my breathing* in answer C, noting that pollution codes as *air problem*.

Q20 *Answer*: B. People sleep on train journeys.

The code reads: E1, B10, B15(4), 18 = plural person, opposite work, opposite short (vehicle), travel.

Explanation: Eliminate D which contains no concept of plural person and the word period is not coded; eliminate E which contains no concept of opposite work nor any strong concept of vehicle; eliminate C which includes Many and the concept of people twice, which are not coded; A and B are the most obvious choices; reject A because it includes no concept of travel, ie choose answer B where *journey* codes as travel.

Q21 *Answer*: D Fresh food should be eaten soon.

The code reads: 2, 15(6), B204(108) = eat, short (time), opposite old (meal).

Explanation: Eliminate B which fails to translate opposite in relation to old meal; similarly A and C; both D and E translate opposite old meal as *fresh food* but only D translates the concept of short time (*soon*), noting that the order of the words in the answer is discounted.

Q22 *Answer*: A Many young people do voluntary work.

The code reads: B16, B7(E1), 10(BD 101) = opposite few, opposite large (plural person), work (opposite positive money).

Explanation: Eliminate C and E which do not translate opposite few; eliminate D which has no concept of work; eliminate B which has no concept of money, noting that work (opposite positive money) is work negative money or work for free, ie voluntary work, answer A.

Q23 *Answer*: D. Eating barbecued food made them ill.

The code reads: BD(105,A), E1, (2,11,108) = opposite positive (health, increase), plural person, (eat, fire, meal).

Explanation: Answer A looks plausible but it includes the concept of me rather than people so eliminate it; of the remaining answers only D includes a translation for eat, fire, meals, ie *barbecued food*, noting that opposite positive (health, increase) or negative healthier can mean ill, and that *them* has been coded as plural person, so D is the correct answer discounting the order of the words.

Q24 *Answer*: D. Obese people risk diabetes.

The code reads: (108, K, 105,14), B(?02), E1, C(104) = (meal, specific, health, problem), opposite (light), plural person, similar (danger).

Explanation: Eliminate E which has no concept of plural person; eliminate A and C which have no concept of health; eliminate B which has no concept of large; answer D correctly translates *diabetes* as meal, specific, health, problem, noting that *obese* is coded as opposite light.

Q25 *Answer*: A. After a night out I felt generally unwell.

The code reads: C(BK), B105, M, H, B103, 17, = similar (opposite specific), opposite health, future, personal, opposite day, space.

Explanation: Eliminate B which does not translate personal or health; eliminate E which does not translate opposite day; eliminate C because diabetes is a specific health problem which is not coded for; eliminate D which contains no concept of future; answer A reflects the code, noting that opposite day, space, translates as *night out*, similar (opposite specific), opposite health, future translates as *After* and similar (opposite specific), opposite health, translates as *generally unwell*.

Q26   *Answer*: E. Doctors diagnose illness.

The code reads: BD(105), C(BD,14), E1 = opposite positive (health), similar (opposite positive, problem), plural person.

Explanation: Eliminate A, B and C which contain no concept of opposite positive health; eliminate answer D which has no concept of plural person, noting that similar (opposite problem) could translate as similar (solution) or diagnose as in answer E.

Q27   *Answer*: B. Diets are easy for poor eaters.

The code reads: E108, 202, BD(14), E(1,2)BA = plural meal, light, opposite positive (problem), plural (person, eat), opposite increase.

Explanation: Eliminate A, D and E which contain no concept of plural (person, eat); C has no concept of opposite positive (problem), ie negative problem or no problem, whereas B translates no problem as *easy,* plural meal light as *diets,* noting that plural (person, eat), opposite increase can be translated as eaters decrease, ie poor eaters.

Q28   *Answer*: E. People find maths confusing.

The code reads: 3, 14, 10, 106, 205, E1 = think, problem, work, number, seek, plural person.

Explanation: Eliminate A, C and D which contain no concept of plural person; eliminate B which contains no concept of seek, which is translated as *find* in answer E, noting that *maths confusing* codes as think, problem, work, numbers.

Test 3: 28 questions in 33 minutes

Q1   *Answer*: A.

Code ●E1, BD (B●) = happy person plural, opposite positive (opposite happy) or happy people, negative sad.
Explanation: There is no need to translate every code; look for common elements between the answer choices as these are strong contenders and anticipate what code you would expect to see, for example: E1 rather than 1, *not* coding as negative (BD), and depressed as the *opposite* of happy (B●). The remaining answer choices range from close matches to contradictory.

Q2   *Answer*: D. failed and E. test.

Explanation: There is no concept of *test* in the table; there is no concept of *passed* test in the table but it can code as opposite (B) failed; *My* can code as personal (H); *old* (204) is in the table; *car* can code as personal vehicle (H4).

Q3   *Answer*: B. city and E. live.

Explanation: There is no concept of *city* or *live* in the table of code words; countryside can code as large space (7,17). Sell can code as money increase.

Q4   *Answer*: B. appetising and C. neither.

Explanation: The word *appetising* is difficult to code from the table, with eat (2) and meal (108) not sufficient; *neither* is difficult to code from the table, with together (J) more akin to both than to *neither*; *restaurant* can code as similar meal house C(108, 12).

Q5   *Answer*: C.

Code 1(BM3), BD(205), 104L = person (opposite future think), opposite positive (seek), danger situation, where opposite future think is taken as the past tense of think or thought and opposite positive seek is avoid.

Explanation: Code BM3 is at the front of three codes so translate it first; BD(205) is the second code in three codes so translate it second; answer C with both of these codes is the strongest candidate; eliminate the remaining answers if time allows.

Q6   *Answer*: E.

Code B(G E1), 10, BA(101), G E1 = opposite (male plural person), work, opposite increase (money), male plural person; ie women, work, reduce money, men.

Explanation: answers A, C and D code for females and males rather than women and men; answer B is less appropriate than answer E because B fails to include the concept of work, which in conjunction with reduce money translates as earn less, rather than less money.

Q7   *Answer*: B.

Code B204(E1), D(C20), BD109 = opposite old people, negative heard, positive similar vision.

Explanation: Answers B and C use opposite old people to convey the word children, which is preferable to opposite large people (A,D) or small people (E). Answers B and C are very similar; however, answer C fails to convey the notion of *should be*, merely stating similar vision rather than positive similar vision, contrasting with negative heard.

Q8   *Answer*: E.

Code B204, 202(207), BA(K10) = opposite old, light (object), opposite increase specific work.

Explanation: Answers B and E use opposite old to mean new, which is preferable to specific future or similar future (A, C, D). Answer B conveys positive increase instead of opposite increase which conveys *less*.

Q9   *Answer*: E. Prescriptions are free for unemployed people.

The code reads: BD(10)E1, BD(203), 105 206 = opposite positive (work) plural person, opposite positive (expensive), health notes.

Explanation: Eliminate A, C and D which have no concept of plural person; eliminate B which concludes the concept of *time* which is not coded, noting that *prescriptions* are health notes, opposite positive (expense) translates as *free* and opposite positive (work) as unemployed.

Q10   *Answer*: A. Carrying a weapon is a crime.

The code reads: (18, 6) (207, 110) C(B102) = (travel, time), (object, pain), similar (opposite rules).

Explanation: Eliminate E because criminals (ie people) are not coded; eliminate C which contains no concept of time; eliminate B which contains no concept of opposite rules; eliminate D because heavy is not coded noting that in A, *weapon* codes as object pain and *Carrying* codes as travel time.

Q11   *Answer*: C. Showers are forecast for tomorrow.

The code reads: M, B7(8), 7(106), M(103) = future, opposite large (water), large (number), future (day).

Explanation: Eliminate B and D because us and we are not coded; eliminate E because it has no concept of future; eliminate A because future and future day are not expressed, noting that in C, *tomorrow* codes as future day, *forecast* codes as future, and opposite large water, large number as showers.

Q12   *Answer*: C. Friendly people make satisfactory neighbours.

The code reads: ◆E1, ◆(BA), 12J = friendly plural person, friendly (opposite increase), house together.

Explanation: Eliminate D and E because I and My are not coded; eliminate B because unfriendly should code as friendly (opposite); eliminate A because excellent is not coded, noting that in C, friendly (opposite increase) means friendly reduce or *satisfactory* and *neighbours* codes as house together.

Q13 *Answer*: E. I can't breathe without oxygen.

The code reads: BD(107A), H, BD(H107) = opposite positive (air increase), personal, opposite positive (personal air).

Explanation: Eliminate A and C which have no concept of personal; then opposite positive (personal air) translates as either my breathing rate (B), shortness of breath (D) or I can't breathe (E); in which case opposite positive (air increase) means either exercise increases (B), suffer from (D) or without oxygen (E); eliminate B and D which have no concept of air, ie only answer E has two concepts of air, noting that *oxygen* codes as air increase and opposite positive as *without* (ie without oxygen I can't breathe).

Q14 *Answer*: D. We walked across the bridge yesterday.

The code reads: 17(18), 18E1, H18, BM(103) = space (travel), travel plural person, personal travel, opposite future (day).

Explanation: Eliminate B and E which have no concept of plural person; eliminate A, which has no concept of day; eliminate C which has only two concepts of travel (ie travelled and train), noting that in D *walked* codes as personal travel, *We crossed* codes as travel plural person, *bridge* codes as space travel and opposite future (day) codes as *yesterday*.

Q15 *Answer*: A. I envisaged numerous problems.

The code reads: H(E14), 20M, 7, 106 = personal (plural problem), vision future, large, number.

Explanation: Eliminate E which has no concept of personal; eliminate B and D taking personal (plural problem) to mean I problems, ie answers A or C; eliminate C which has no concept of vision future which translates as envisaged in answer A.

Q16 *Answer*: C. Nobody had considered it risky.

The code reads: 104, BM(3), BD1 = danger, opposite future (think), opposite positive person.

Explanation: Eliminate answer E which contains no concept of person; opposite positive person means negative person or no person so eliminate B and D which do not include the concept; both A and C look plausible; however, opposite future (think) translates as past think so eliminate answer A, taking *had considered* as past think, noting that *nobody* codes as opposite positive person.

Q17   *Answer*: A. source and D. town.

Explanation: *Source* (A) cannot be coded from any word in the table and *town* (D) only indirectly as large number people, space; water (C) is already in the table; *reservoir* (B) codes as large water vessel (7(8, 21)); *fresh* (E) codes as new or opposite old (B204).

Q18   *Answer*: A. possibility and C. deterioration.

Explanation: *Possibility* (A) cannot be coded from any word in the table; *complications* (B) can code as plural problem (E14); *unconcerned* can code as opposite anxious (B♥); deterioration (C) cannot code accurately and is the second choice.

Q19   *Answer*: B. client and D. store.

Explanation: *Store* (D) codes for filed away and is the first choice; clients' might code indirectly as specific plural person (KE1), however, *client* is the second choice because health (C) is already in the table, *separate* codes as opposite together (BJ) and records codes as similar notes (C206).

Q20   *Answer*: C. good and E. won.

Explanation: C codes for *better*, ie good increase; *won* cannot code from the table; *nobody* codes as negative plural person (BD, E1); *protest* is a synonym of object (207); *player* codes as person opposite work (1 B10).

Q21   *Answer*: B.

Code B(G E1), 20A, 202D = opposite(male plural person); vision increase, light positive, ie women, see more, light on.

Explanation: Answers A and E translate as opposite positive man and opposite positive men respectively, ie negative man and negative men, instead of opposite men; answers C and D translate large light and light situation respectively, rather than light on.

Q22   *Answer*: C.

Code 11(110), 19, B(15,6), 201(105) = fire (pain), take, opposite (short time), fix (health).

Explanation: Answer A fails to include the concept of health when referring to *heal*, stating only fix which is too general; answers D and E also fail to translate heal as fix health, stating only health; B is wrong because it codes *long time* as opposite few time instead of opposite short time.

Q23 *Answer*: A.

Explanation: The code reads B204(B G1), 205(BM), L◆, B105, H(7, BG) = opposite old (opposite male person), seek (opposite future), situation friendly, opposite health, personal (large opposite male), ie young female person, sought, situation friendly, sick, personal large female. Answer B lacks the concept of opposite future, ie seeks rather than sought, meaning solicits instead of *solicited*; C translates opposite plural females, ie women rather than *woman*; in the last set of codes, D translates personal large male rather than female and E translates opposite large male instead of personal large female.

Q24 *Answer*: D.

Explanation: The code reads E1, BM(2), L(C11, 202) = plural person, opposite future (eat), situation (similar fire, light), which is a good fit for *We ate by candlelight*. Answers A and C express eat as *take meal* when *eat* is already coded for. Answer B lacks the concept of *We* and answer E lacks the concept of fire combined with the light.

Q25 *Answer*: B. I feel lonely on my own in the evening.

The code reads: H■, BJ, B103 6 = personal lonely, opposite together, opposite day time.

Explanation: Personal translates as *I* so eliminate C, E and also D because it contains we; opposite daytime is night-time or evening, ie B which also codes on my own as opposite together.

Q26 *Answer*: A. Many ill people are depressed.

The code reads: B(16), E1, BD(105), 14(B●) = opposite (few), plural person, opposite positive (health), problem (opposite happy).

Explanation: Translate opposite few, plural person as *many people*, which occurs in A, B or C, but not in E nor D which state Some and all. Eliminate C because there is only enough coding to support two health concepts not all three (depression, illness, sad). Finally, (opposite happy) is the coding for sad (B); however, the inclusion of problem modifies this to depression, ie A.

Q27 *Answer*: E. Married people are the happiest.

The code reads: E1, J, A(A●) = plural person, together, increase (increase happy).

Explanation: Take increase happy to be happier and increase (increase happier) to be happiest, ie answers C or E; the concept of people is coded only once so eliminate C.

Q28   *Answer*: D. My neighbours are unfriendly people.

The code reads: H, J(E1), B♦(E1) = personal, together (plural person), opposite friendly (plural person).

Explanation: Personal refers to I or My; together (plural person) refers to neighbours in the context of the *Answer* options; the final plural person at the end of the code could refer to people (D) or friends (E) but not me (eliminate A) nor my (eliminate B); C is eliminated as it fails to translate plural person; E is eliminated as it includes the concept of not, noting that not friendly people would be coded as opposite (friendly plural person).

Chapter 3: Quantitative reasoning

Q1   *Answer*: D. 29,900. Skill set: Table reading, addition

6,450 + 7,600 + 8,450 + 7,400 = 29,900.

Q2   *Answer*: D. 25%. Skill set: Table reading, addition, percentages

6,450 + 7,600 + 8,450 + 7,400 + 5,550 = 35,450, (35,450/131,250) = 0.270, therefore approximately 25%.

Q3   *Answer*: C. 1/7. Skill set: Table reading, additional fractions

9,600 + 7,950 = 17,550, (17,550/131,250) = 0.134, therefore approximately 1/7.

Q4   *Answer*: A. 4 : 5. Skill set: Table reading, addition, ratios

Schoolchildren: 7,600 + 8,450 + 7,400 = 23,450, retired: 7,450 + 7,100 + 6,450 + 4,500 + 2,750 = 28,250. The ratio 23,450 : 28,250 is about 4 : 5.

Q5   *Answer*: D. Black £20. Skill set: Table reading, multiplication, addition

Green £10 = 10 + (10 × 0.4) = 14p
Green £20 = 10 + (10 × 0.35) = 13.5p
Black £10 = 8 + (10 × 0.5) = 13p
Black £20 = 6 + (10 × 0.4) = 10p.

Q6   *Answer*: B. 60%. Skill set: Table reading, multiplication, addition, percentage

The total cost of calls would be £3.90 (see question 5 above), leaving £6.10 unused. (6.10/10.00) = 0.61, or approximately 60% wasted.

Q7   *Answer*: B. 10. Skill set: Table reading, mean

You do not need to find the average time for each month, just take the total calls and the total duration to find the average.
The total number of calls was 325 and the total duration 3,243 minutes; therefore the average was (3,243/325) = 10.0.

Q8 *Answer*: D. Black £20. Skill set: Table reading, percentages

The price per minute for the Black £20 is now 0.4p + (0.4p × (70/100)) = 0.68p. The cost for 10 minutes is now 6 + (10 × 0.68) = 12.8p. Still the cheapest (see question 5 above).

Q9 *Answer*: B. 4. Skill set: Chart reading, percentages

19,000 people in a population of 200,000 as a percentage, (19,000/200,000) = 0.095, 9.5%. Anything bigger than 9.5% will therefore employ more than 19,000 people, ie 12%, 18%, 10% and 14%.

Q10 *Answer*: A. 8 times. Skill set: Chart reading, ratio/proportion

If 12% work in manufacturing and 2% in agriculture, there are six times as many in manufacturing and they produce a third more per person, so in total they generate 6 × 1.33 times more, ie 8.

Q11 *Answer*: E. 62.5m. Skill set: Fractions, multiplication

Half of £100m is £50m. 50m × 1.25 = 62.5m.

Q12 *Answer*: A. 1,000. Skill set: Chart reading, percentage, division

Number of people in hotels and catering = 10% of 200,000 = 20,000. Number of employers = 20,000/20 = 1,000.

Q13 *Answer*: D. 0.64. Skill set: Table reading, percentage

7 out of 11 products have at least 1.5 g of salt; 7/11 = 0.636, equivalent to 64%.

Q14 *Answer*: B. 117%. Skill set: Table reading, fractions decimals

Each 100 g contains 2 g of salt so 350 g contains 3.5 × 2g = 7g
Dividing by the recommended maximum allowance of 6g gives 7/6 = 116.67 (117%).

Q15 *Answer*: D. £3.30. Skill set: Percentage, ratio

The price of Paella is 1.1 × 1.50 = £1.65. The fish curry costs twice as much = £3.30.

Q16 *Answer*: C. 6.6 cents. Skill set: Decimal currency

2.65 × (115.0 − 112.5) = 2.65 × 2.50 = 6.6 cents.

Q17 *Answer*: D. 53%. Skill set: Addition/subtraction, percentage

106 − 50 = 56 people 1.6m or under; therefore 56/106 = 0.53, ie 53%.

Q18 *Answer*: D. 89. Skill set: Venn diagram, addition/subtraction

There are 62 people born in this country, 50 taller than 1.6m and 14 left-handed, making a total of 126. As there are only 106 people in the survey there are an 'extra' 20 people. As three people are in all three groups they have been counted twice more, accounting for six of these 'extra' people. This leaves 14 extra who have been counted twice. $14 + 3 = 17$ from an original group of 106, leaving 89.

Q19 *Answer*: E. Can't tell. Skill set: Venn diagram

There is no information about how many in the groups overlap.

Q20 *Answer*: A. 6. Skill set: Simultaneous equations

This is really a question of simultaneous equations. Let BL equal the number born in this country and left-handed, L = number just left-handed. $L + BL + 3 + 2 = 14$; therefore, $BL + L = 9$. Also $L = 2 \times BL$; therefore $L = 6$ and $BL = 3$.

Q21 *Answer*: E. $3X + 2Y = 1285$, $2X + 3Y = 1040$. Skill set: Simultaneous equations

X is cod, Y is chips and the price is in pence.

Q22 *Answer*: B. 20%. Skill set: Simultaneous equations, percentage

Multiply the first equation by three and the second equation by two to give 6Y (6 portions of chips) in both equations, then subtract the two equations to eliminate Y (chips) and leave X (cod)
$3(3X + 2Y = 1285)$, $2(2X + 3Y = 1040)$
$9X + 6Y = 3855$, $4X + 6Y = 2080$; so $5X + 0Y = 1775$, giving $X = 355$
New price is £4.26 which is 71p higher or 20% higher ($71(/)355 \times 100 = 20\%$).

Q23 *Answer*: A. 1 : 1.15. Skill set: Simultaneous equation, ratio

We have the old and new prices of cod so we need the price of chips. Substitute $X = 355$ into $2X + 3Y = 1040$ to find $X = 110$
The old price of cod and chips is £3.55 + £1.10 = £4.65 and the new price is £4.26 + £1.10 = £5.36. The ratio of old to new is 4.65/5.36 = 0.87, (0.87 to 1) and reciprocal of this is 1.15, ie 1 to 1.15.

Q24 *Answer*: C. 15.42. Skill set: Money, proportion

Cost in euros of one cod is $1.20 \times 3.55 = 4.26$; a portion of chips is $1.20 \times 1.10 = 1.32$. Therefore the total cost is $(3 \times 4.26) + (2 \times 1.32) = 15.42$.

Q25 *Answer*: E. (95 × 87.5 × 4.55)/30. Skill set: Formulae, table reading

The number of gallons required would be 95/30 and the price per gallon would be 87.5 × 4.55. This can be rearranged to give (95 × 87.5 × 4.55)/30.

Q26 *Answer*: C. Belgium, Finland, United Kingdom, Italy. Skill set: Chart reading.

Q27 *Answer*: D. 22.5%. Skill set: Compound interest

The information about the car and distance is a red herring. The increase is $1.07^3 = 1.225$, ie 22.5%.

Q28 *Answer*: B. 328.1. Skill set: Addition/subtraction, multiplication/division

Cost in the Netherlands is (210/30) × 4.55 × 100.3 = 3,194.555. In Germany it is (210/30) × 4.55 × 90 = 2,866.5. 3,194.555 − 2,866.5 = 328.055.

Q29 *Answer*: E. Can't tell. Skill set: Table reading

As the number with the substance present in the 780 samples is unknown, it is impossible to tell.

Q30 *Answer*: C. About 46. Skill set: Addition, percentage, table reading

500 were identified as having the substance present; 8% of these would be wrong, ie 40. The remaining 280 were identified as having no substance present; of these 2% would be wrong, ie 5.6. 40 + 5.6 is about 46.

Q31 *Answer*: D. About 20 more. Skill set: Table reading, percentages

Allcheck: of the 390 positive, 5% would be wrong, giving 19.5; of the 390 negative about 10% would be wrong, giving 39. This makes a total of around 60 wrong. Truespot: of the 390 positive, 8% would be wrong, giving 31.2; of the 390 negative about 2% would be wrong, giving 7.8. This makes a total of around 40 wrong. Therefore there are about 20 more wrong for Allcheck. Hopefully, no one sues.

Q32 *Answer*: B. About 465. Skill set: Formulae, table reading, percentage

Let P be the number that actually have the substance present; then 0.95P would be the number identified by Allcheck as positive. Because the result can be only positive or negative, 800 − P are negative, but Allcheck would identify 10% of these as positive, 0.1(800 − P). The total number identified as positive would be 0.95P + 0.1(800 − P) = 475. Rearranging gives 0.85P = 395; therefore P = 395/0.85 = 464.71, about 465.

Q33   *Answer*: A. 30. Skill set: Table reading, mean, estimation

The average can be estimated reasonably accurately by saying that, for example, the group of students who play between 10 and 14 hours are 2 students who play 12 hours each (halfway between 10 and 14). This then equates to 2 × 12 = 24 'student hours'. The total number of student hours can then be summed and divided by the number of students to give the average = 6,560/220 = 29.8 or about 30. Or you can just estimate, which is much quicker.

Q34   *Answer*: C. 14. Skill set: Table reading, addition

2 + 12 = 14.

Q35   *Answer*: E. 5/9. Skill set: Addition, division, proportion

The average, as seen in question 33, is 30. There are 77 + 38 + 8 = 123 students who play more than this. 123 divided by the total number of students gives 123/220 = 0.559. 5/9 = 0.555, which is near enough.

Q36   *Answer*: D. 27. Skill set: Percentage, proportion

The heaviest users will have the largest effect on the number of student hours and they reduce their playing by 10%. A large proportion remains unchanged, so a reasonable guess would be about a 10% reduction in average time, ie 30 − 3 = 27. If you choose to calculate, it should come out to 27.2.

Q37   *Answer*. C. C. Skill set: multiplication/division

BMI = weight (kg) divided by height^2 (m^2) i.e kg $\div m \div m$
$A = 21.4; B = 22.2; C = 22.9; D = 20.8; E = 21.6.$

Q38   *Answer*: D. Minus 9%. Skill set: percentages, multiplication/division

100% × 1.1 ÷ 1.1 ÷ 1.1 = 100 ÷ 1.1 = 90.9 = 9.1%.

Q39   *Answer*. A. 9 kg. Skill set: transposition, multiplication/division

BMI = kg ÷ m^2 so m^2 = BMI ÷ kg = 80/28 = 2.86
To have a BMI just within the 'normal' range a value of 24.9 is needed.
BMI = kg ÷ m^2 so kg = BMI × m^2 = 24.9 × 2.86 = 71.2 kg
Person A needs to lose just under 9kg.

Q40   *Answer*: C. 1/5. Skill set: Transposition, fractions

Kg = BMI × m^2 (or BMI × m × m) so original weight is 24.9 × 1.8 × 1.8 = 80.7 kg. Weight at a BMI of 30 is 97.2kg. The difference is 16.5, which is 16.5/80.7 or 1/5 of the original.

Q41 *Answer*: E. Region 2, year 1. Skill set: Table reading

Around 3%.

Q42 *Answer*: A. Year 1. Skill set: Percentages, table reading

A 4.4% difference compared to year 3 with 3.5%, for example.

Q43 *Answer*: B. £7,000. Skill set: Percentages, table reading

Difference in percentage in year 3 = 3.5%. 3.5% of £200,000 = £7,000.

Q44 *Answer*: C. 1.015 × 1.03 × 1.075 × 1.023 × 0.99. Skill set: Compound interest

Compound interest and reducing by 0.1% is equivalent to multiplying by 0.99.

Q45 *Answer*: D. 200 × 1.2 × 0.97 − 1.20 (1.2) Skill set: Formulae

×1.20€ 3% commission and £1.20 fee
200 × 1.20€ (1.00 − 0.03) − 1.20 (1.20€).

Q46 *Answer*: E. Concurrency. Skill set: Multiplication, table reading

For a large enough sum, the fee is irrelevant. You can then calculate the number of euros by subtracting the commission from the exchange rate; thus HH: 1.20 × 0.97 − 1.164; BB: 1.18; XC: 1.22 × 0.98 = 1.1956; FEC: 1.22 × 0.97 = 1.1834; CON: 1.20. Therefore Concurrency will buy you the most euros.

Q47 *Answer*: A. 2.5%. Skill set: Table reading, subtraction, money

The biggest is £177.60 and the smallest £173.20; the difference between percentages is 173.20/177.60 = 0.975 = 2.5%.

Q48 *Answer*: B. 1/10. Skill set: Table reading, money, percentage

With no losses, £20 becomes €24.40, but from the table you would receive only €22.00, ie €2.40 less. 2.40/24.40 = 0.098, or about 0.1 or 1/10.

Q49 *Answer*: E. 5/9. Skill set: Fractions, percentage, chart reading

The total is 32% + 23% = 55%, which is approximately equivalent to 5/9 = 0.555 recurring.

Q50 *Answer*: B 1.67 : 1. Skill set: Chart reading, percentage

PP increases to 20% and 3A decreases to 12%. This is now a ratio of 20 : 12, or 1.67 : 1.

Q51   *Answer*: E. 95%. Skill set: Proportion, ratio, chart reading, percentage

It would be theoretically possible for the major brands to have market shares of 0.0032%, 0.0017%, 0.0015% and 0.0023% respectively, thus maintaining the ratios, but for the own brands to have captured the part of the market, 5%, not occupied by the newcomer. This may seem unlikely, but likelihood wasn't the question.

Q52   *Answer*: C. 17%. Skill set: Addition, proportion, chart reading, percentage

If the current total sales represent a value of 100, then the current sales of 3 Across are 15. Increasing this by 15% gives new sales of 17.25, 2.25 bigger, and new total sales of 102.25. Therefore the new market share of 3 Across is (17.25/102.25) × 100 = 16.9%.

Q53   *Answer*: B. Havanaisday. Skill set: Multiplication, table reading

Multiplying the number of claims by the cost of claim gives the lowest figure for Havanaisday.

Q54   *Answer*: E. £163. Skill set: Division/multiplication, table reading

There are 37.7 claims per 100, but this is divided over the 100 cars, so the cost per car is (37.7/100) × 433 = 163.

Q55   *Answer*: A. 2/5. Skill set: Multiplication, division, fractions

Original cost = 36.4 × 223 = 8,117. New cost = 25 × 200 = 5,000. Fractional saving = (8,117 − 5,000)/8,117 = 0.384, nearly 0.4 or 2/5.

Q56   *Answer*: A. £25. Skill set: Proportion, table reading

1 in 12 cars breaks down at a cost of £250, so the cost per car is 250/12. The company wants to make 20% more than the cost, ie a factor of 1.2, so the premium would be (250/12) × 1.2 = 25.

Q57   *Answer*: B. 4.429. Skill set: Table reading, division, money

To get from Robbers to Yangs you have to multiply by 4.429 (104.93/23.69).

Q58   *Answer*: A. 56%. Skill set: Percentages, table reading

The first exchange rate drops by 20%, ie 0.8 times the original value; the other increases by 25%, ie 1.25 times the original. Therefore going from one that has dropped to one that has increased the difference is 1.25/0.8 = 1.5625, or 56%.

Q59   *Answer*: A. Up 1/4. Skill set: Fractions, proportions

The value of the denominator (the bottom of the fraction) compared to the numerator (top) has dropped to a factor of 0.8. The relative value is therefore 1/0.8 = 1.25, ie up a quarter.

Q60   *Answer*: C. 3.09 Dollally. Skill set: Money, division

In the first transaction the tourist loses 3 Dollally (3%). In the second he or she loses 3 Barts or 3/33.15 = 0.09 Dollally.

Mini-test 1

Q61   *Answer*: C. 1/30. Skill set: Fractions, Graph reading

The maximum sales were 33,000, the minimum 1,000. 1,000/33,000 =1/33, so the fraction is about 1/30.

Q62   *Answer*: A. 500%. Skill set: Proportion, percentage, graph reading

In the same way that a 100% increase is equivalent to doubling, the sales have gone from 1,100 to 6,600, ie 5,500 or a 500% increase.

Q63   *Answer*: E. £45m. Skill set: Addition/subtraction

The total sales over the year add up to £104.7m. The total costs = 12 × £5m = 60m, so the total profits are 104.7 − 60 = 44.7.

Q64   *Answer*: A. 1.001^{12}. Skill set: Formulae, compound interest

A 0.1% increase is the same as multiplying by 1.001; do this 12 times (once for each of the 12 months) and you have 1.001^{12}. Compound interest in action.

Q65   *Answer*: B. A and E. Skill set: Speed, division

As you are not required to give any units, the quickest way to determine speed is probably to calculate in miles per minute. A and E both then give the highest values of 1.0.

Q66   *Answer*: C. s = 65 / (1 + (11/60)). Skill set: Formulae

There are 60 minutes in one hour, so 11/60 represents the fraction of the hour for 11 minutes, so the total time taken is 1 + (11/60). Speed is distance divided by time, as suggested by the units, miles per hour. Be careful of the right number and position of the brackets.

Q67   *Answer*: C. +25%, −17%. Skill set: Percentage, proportion

If you reduce the time by 20% it is now 0.8 times the original value, but because you need to divide by the time to calculate the velocity you get 1/0.8 = 1.25, ie a 25% increase. Similarly, when you increase the time by 20% you get 1/1.2 = 0.8333, a 17% decrease.

Q68   *Answer*: A. 26.82 m/s. Skill set: Multiplication, division, speed

There are 95 minutes, 95 × 60 = 5,700 seconds. 95 miles = 95 × 1,609 = 152,855 metres. Speed = 152,855/5,700 = 26.82 m/s.

Mini-test 2

Q69 *Answer*: B. 360 TeraBytes. Skill set: Mean, graph reading, estimation

From the graph the average can be seen to be about 15. $15 \times 24 = 360$.

Q70 *Answer*: E. 9/24. Skill set: Fractions, graph reading

Nine of the hours *exceed* 15 TeraBytes.

Q71 *Answer*: B. 5 and 6 or 8 and 9. Skill set: Graph reading, proportion

Tricky question. The largest absolute increase was between 8 and 9, going from 10 to 29, but the largest *relative* increase was between 5 and 6, from 2 to 6, a factor of 3 times.

Q72 *Answer*: A. 14. Skill set: Graph reading, multiplication, division

To change GigaBytes per second to TeraBytes per hour you need to multiply by 3,600 (to change from seconds to hours) and then divide by 1,000 (to change GigaBytes to TeraBytes). So, 3 GigaBytes per second = $3 \times 3,600/1,000 = 10.8$ TeraBytes per hour. From the graph, you can see there are 14 values higher than this.

Q73 *Answer*: B. 4/3. Skill set: Proportion

If the pressure changes by 3/4, in order to give the same constant result the volume must correspondingly change by 4/3.

Q74 *Answer*: C. +1/5. Skill set: Proportion

To compensate the pressure must increase to 6/5 the original volume or increase by 1/5.

Q75 *Answer*: D. The volume 0.133 should read 0.013. Skill set: Formulae, table reading

All the others when multiplied together (PV = constant) give a value of 2.

Q76 *Answer*: A. 10%. Skill set: Proportion, formulae

The answer should be 0.0022222, but the experimenter will only read 0.002. This gives a percentage error of $((0.0022222 - 0.002)/0.0022222) \times 100 = 10\%$.

Mini-test 3

Q77 *Answer*: D. 3/20. Skill set: Table reading, proportion

A total of 85% (55 + 30) made some pronouncement, so 15% were undecided. 15/100 = 3/20.

Q78 *Answer*: C. 65%. Skill set: Proportion, formulae

Population Y represents two-thirds of the total population and X, 1/3 (2/3 is twice as big as 1/3 and 2/3 + 1/3 = the entire population). The average value, therefore, is (1/3 × 85) + (2/3 × 55) = 65.

Q79 *Answer*: A. Population X for juice A. Skill set: Table reading

This has shown a 20 per cent drop.

Q80 *Answer*: C. Around 7% more. Skill set: Table reading, percentage change

Original revenue, with Y = 2X, price P: (0.85(X) + 0.55(2X)) × 100%P
New revenue: (0.65(X) + 0.62(2X)) × 110%P
Percentage change = (0.65 + 1.24)/(0.85 + 1.1) × 1.1
= 1.89/1.95 × 1.1 = 1.066 (around 7% more).

Q81 *Answer*: E. 5. Skill set: Simultaneous equations, table reading

If you look at team A and team E you can create simultaneous equations:
2W + 2D = 26 and 2W + 1D = 21; therefore D = 5.
(W = 8 and L = 1 by substitution methods)

Q82 *Answer*: A. 9. Skill set: Table reading, multiplication, addition, subtraction

Each of the five teams plays the four others twice, 5 × 4 × 2 = 40, but each match involves two teams, so there are 20 matches; 11 have been played already (there are 22 'results' in the table), so there are 9 to play.

Q83 *Answer*: B. 61. Skill set: Multiplication, addition, table reading

Each of the five teams plays the four others twice so the maximum points available to any team is 8 wins × 8 points = 64.
Team E has played 3 matches for a total of 21 points and could win the remaining 5 matches for an additional 40 points, ie 61.

Q84 *Answer*: A. 1/5. Skill set: Table reading, proportion

Team C will have 28 points (18 + 2 draws = 18 + 10 = 28)
(A – 46, B – 36, C – 28, D – 39, E – 46).

Mini-test 4

Q85   *Answer*: C. 88 Skill set: Table reading, percentage

Two students (10% of the sample) obtained this score or more.

Q86   *Answer*: E. 50. Skill set: Table reading, percentage

If we follow the same procedure as above then the failure mark would be 38 (the score of the second lowest candidate) giving a range of 50 (88–38).

Q87   *Answer*: C. 75%. Skill set: Table reading, percentages

15 out of 20 (75%) have achieved more than half marks (>50%).

Q88   *Answer*: B. 3. Skill set: Table reading, percentage

The top four marks, rounded to the nearest integer, are now 85, 90, 91, 94, three of which exceed the key, 87.5.

Q89   *Answer*: C. March, April, May, June. Skill set: Graph reading

The four highest points.

Q90   *Answer*: A. 11/20. Skill set: Graph reading, division

2.75/5 = 0.55 or 11/20.

Q91   *Answer*: D. £8,500. Skill set: Graph reading, mean, multiplication

The average is 3.4. This gives 0.034 × 250,000 × £8,500.

Q92   *Answer*: B. $C = 50,000 \times 1.05^{(1/12)}$. Skill set: Compound interest, indices, multiplication

At the end of the year the amount paid with 5% interest will be 1.05 times the loan amount. The interest for each month multiplied together, ie multiplied by itself 12 times, will give this factor. So the factor for the month must be the 12th root of this factor, ie $1.05^{(1/12)}$. Multiply this by the loan amount to give the total due after one month.

Mini-test 5

Q93   *Answer*: A. 100%. Skill set: Chart reading, percentages

The key is how much *more*. The leisure time is twice the travel time, so with the 100% you have already you need the same amount again to give the 200% (2 times).

Q94   *Answer*: E. 1 : 2. Skill set: Chart reading, proportion

The number of hours spent travelling is now twice the number of hours' leisure, so the ratio is 1:2.

Q95   *Answer*: D. 11 minutes. Skill set: Chart reading, multiplication, division

$(1.20/6.50) \times 60 = 11.07$ minutes.

Q96   *Answer*: E. 30p/hour. Skill set: Subtraction, division

Travel costs are now $3.00 - 1.20 = £1.80$ more expensive. So the student must earn at least £1.80/6 hours, 30p/hour, more than before.

Q97   *Answer*: A. 2751. Skill set: Chart reading, proportion

$(5,241$ divided by $0.52) \times 0.273 = 2,751$.

Q98   *Answer*: B. 2935. Skill set: Chart comparison, proportion, percentage

$(5,241 \times 0.8)$ divided by $0.39 \times 0.273 = 2,935$.

Q99   *Answer*: B. 137 kg. Skill set: Chart reading, proportion

$(0.5 \times 1000) \times 0.273 = 136.5$.

Q100 *Answer*: E. 48%. Skill set: Chart reading, weighting, percentage

carbon-dioxide $= 0.8 \times 1 = 0.8$
methane $= 0.12 \times 22 = 2.64$
nitrous oxide $= 0.06 \times 300 = 18$
fluorocarbons $= 0.02 \times 1000 = 20$
total $= 0.8 + 2.64 + 18 + 20 = 41.44$
then for fluorocarbons 20 divided by $41.44 \times 100\% = 48\%$.

Chapter 4: Abstract reasoning warm-up questions

Exercise 1

Q1   Set A – Shapes drawn with straight lines

Set B – Shapes drawn with curved lines

1. A
2. A
3. C
4. B
5. C

Q2   Set A – Triangles

Set B – Squares and rectangles

6. A
7. B
8. C
9. A
10. A

Q3   Set A – At least one line of symmetry

Set B – No lines of symmetry

11. A
12. A
13. B
14. B
15. A

Q4   Set A – Straight lines and curves

Set B – Straight lines or curved lines

16. B
17. B
18. A
19. A
20. A

Q5   Set A – At least one internal right angle

Set B – No internal right angles

21. B
22. B
23. A
24. B
25. A

Q6   Set A – Reflection symmetry

Set B – No reflection symmetry

26. B
27. B
28. A
29. B
30. A

Q7   Set A – Circle, shaded square, shaded triangle, left to right

Set B – Shaded square, circle, shaded triangle, left to right

31. C
32. A
33. B
34. C
35. C

Q8   Set A – Three simple shapes in a diagonal row

Set B – Three similar shapes in a horizontal or vertical row

36. B
37. A
38. B
39. C
40. B

Q9   Set A – One shaded square in a corner

Set B – One unshaded square in a corner

41. C
42. B
43. A
44. B
45. C

Q10   Set A – At least one shaded circle

Set B – At least one unshaded rectangle

46. A
47. B
48. C
49. B
50. C

Q11   Set A – The square and rectangle are along one side of the square and orientated in line

Set B – The square and rectangle are on adjacent sides

51. B
52. C
53. C
54. A
55. A

Exercise 2

Q1   Set A – Even number of shapes

Set B – Odd number of shapes

1. B
2. A
3. B
4. A
5. B

Q2   Set A – Eleven straight lines

Set B – Twelve straight lines

6. C
7. B
8. A
9. C
10. C

Q3   Set A – One line of symmetry

Set B – Four lines of symmetry

11. B
12. C
13. A
14. A
15. C

Q4   Set A – Two shaded areas

Set B – Three shaded areas

16. B
17. A
18. C
19. B
20. C

Q5   Set A – Number of circles equals number of triangles

Set B – Number of circles is twice the number of triangles

21. C
22. B
23. A
24. A
25. C

Q6   Set A – One shaded area

Set B – Two shaded areas

26. A
27. B
28. A
29. C
30. C

Q7   Set A – Odd number of sides

Set B – Even number of sides

31. B
32. A
33. A
34. A
35. B

Q8   Set A – Reflection symmetry in the vertical axis

Set B – No reflection symmetry in the vertical axis

36. B
37. A
38. B
39. A
40. B

Q9   Set A – Biggest shape is the same as the smallest (respective of shading)

Set B – Same shapes are the same size (irrespective of shading)

41. A
42. A
43. C
44. B
45. C

Q10   Set A – Three shapes are the same

Set B – Two shapes are the same

46. A
47. B
48. A
49. C
50. B

Q11   Set A – Four cross-over points (intersections)

Set B – Six cross-over points

51. A
52. C
53. A
54. C
55. B

Chapter 5: Situational judgement analysis

Scenario 1

Q1   *Answer*: D. The response is very inappropriate.

Explanation: Phillip has dismissed Aisha's explanation without any consideration. He does not know for certain that she has breached the policy.

Q2   *Answer*: D. The response is very inappropriate.

Explanation: Phillip needs to follow up the matter if he believes that there has been a breach of policy that might put patients' health at risk. The fact that there is a lack of scientific evidence to support the policy does not mitigate this.

Q3   *Answer*: A. The response is a very appropriate thing to do.

Explanation: Acting in a way that ensures that colleagues comply with hospital policies and guidelines is entirely correct.

Q4   *Answer*: B. The response is appropriate but not ideal.

Explanation: Phillip has correctly identified that it is a matter for the Ward Manager, but not that there are equality and diversity issues.

Q5   *Answer*: A. The response is very appropriate.

Explanation: Phillip should do this as a first step to check how the infection control policy caters for equality and diversity issues.

Scenario 2

Q6   *Answer*: B. The response is appropriate.

Explanation: The response is appropriate in that it may offer a solution to the problem, but this is by no means certain.

Q7   *Answer*: A. The response is very appropriate.

Explanation: The response would resolve the issue in the best way.

Q8   *Answer*: C. The response is inappropriate, but not awful.

Explanation: It may be possible to give out generalized information without breaching hospital guidelines but it may not satisfy the caller.

Q9   *Answer*: D. The response is inappropriate.

Explanation: The response is materially incorrect; patient information can be given once the identity of the caller has been confirmed.

Scenario 3

Q10   *Answer*: B. The response is appropriate but not ideal.

Explanation: Carl has already stated what the problem is. However, it does afford Carl the opportunity to explore the issue in more detail.

Q11   *Answer*: B. The response is appropriate but not ideal.

Explanation: Other members of the team can provide support; however it is not ideal because it fails to tackle the underlying issues with the mentor.

Q12   *Answer*: A. The response is a very appropriate thing to do.

Explanation: It suggests a suitable way forwards for Carl given the circumstances.

Q13   *Answer*: D. The response is very inappropriate.

Explanation: Expressing one's grievances in writing is rarely a satisfactory way forward as a first step.

Q14   *Answer*: A. The response is very appropriate.

Explanation: Carl should speak to his academic supervisor if he has difficulties with his mentor.

Q15   *Answer*: C. The response is inappropriate but not awful.

Explanation: It does identify that communication between the parties has broken down but then goes on to dismiss it as a minor matter without offering any solutions.

Scenario 4

Q16   *Answer*: D. The response is very inappropriate.

Explanation: The doctor must work within his own clinical knowledge, skills and expertise.

Q17   *Answer*: D. The response is very inappropriate.

Explanation: The doctor's decision to delegate work to a colleague who is not competent to undertake the task puts the patient at risk.

Q18   *Answer*: D. The response is a very inappropriate.

Explanation: The doctor has identified that prompt action is needed so waiting for a colleague to return from lunch break is unacceptable.

Q19   *Answer*: A. The response is very appropriate thing to do.

Explanation: It offers a solution to the problem without compromising patient safety.

Scenario 5

Q20 *Answer*: A. This factor is very important.

Explanation: The needs of the patients are paramount whatever the circumstances and Mike has a duty of care.

Q21 *Answer*: B. This factor is important.

Explanation: It has been exceptionally busy in the Emergency Department, which might explain why Mike has fallen asleep; the impact of this factor cannot be discounted.

Q22 *Answer*: B. This factor is important.

Explanation: It marks a change in Mike's behaviour not seen previously.

Q23 *Answer*: A. This factor is very important.

Explanation: Mike knows the rules yet he is in breach of them.

Q24 *Answer*: B. This factor is important.

Explanation: The possibility that Mike has taken strong painkillers with a sedative effect cannot be discounted at this time.

Scenario 6

Q25 *Answer*: B. This fact is important (though not vital)

Explanation: This suggests that competency with health promotion would be anticipated.

Q26 *Answer*: A. This factor is very important.

Explanation: This is a key part of the doctor's role and must be taken into account.

Q27 *Answer*: B. This factor is important but not overriding.

Explanation: Jasmine's health damaging activities may undermine her credibility with health promotion, but this is not an excuse for avoiding the topic with her patients.

Q28 *Answer*: C. This factor is of minor importance.

Explanation: A family history of obesity is a predictor of obesity and offers an explanation for it but not why the issue has been ignored.

Q29   *Answer*: B. This factor is important.

Explanation: The factor identifies that Jasmine took to 'comfort eating' to deal with her break-up. However, it was three years ago and cannot mitigate her lax attitude today.

Scenario 7

Q30   *Answer*: D. Not important at all

Explanation: It doesn't matter how hard a day he is having, disrespect is inappropriate and unprofessional on every occasion.

Q31   *Answer*: C. Of minor importance

Explanation: Everyone makes mistakes and if this were happening regularly it would be very serious; however, the fact that it is unusual for the senior nurse to be disrespectful doesn't change the fact that on this occasion he acted unprofessionally.

Q32   *Answer*: D. Not important at all

Explanation: All patients have a right to be treated with courtesy irrespective of the circumstances.

Q33   *Answer*: D. Not important at all

Explanation: His status in the department is irrelevant and no excuse for inappropriate behaviour.

Q34   *Answer*: A. Very important

Explanation: Everyone can make mistakes; the important matter is to deal with it quickly and appropriately as was done in this case.

Q35   *Answer*: C or D. Of minor importance or not important at all

Explanation: Racism towards a member of staff is unacceptable, staff should be protected from it and it should be challenged – but always in an appropriate manner. Disrespect is inappropriate; all patients must be treated with professional courtesy irrespective of their challenging behaviour.

Chapter 6: Mock exam

Verbal reasoning

Q1   Can't tell: first paragraph, sixth sentence: we are told that Titan is the second largest satellite and 1.5 times the size of the moon but there could be several satellites ranging in size between the two.

Q2   Can't tell: Jupiter has 60 moons but this is not stated to be the most.

Q3   Can't tell: there is no information in the passage about craters on the surface of Europa so the statement can neither be proved nor disproved and the correct answer is can't tell.

Q4   Can't tell: water on Europa is capable of sustaining life but there is no mention of the atmosphere.

Q5   True: end of last paragraph: cooking oil fires are class F.

Q6   True: three types: water, foam and dry powder.

Q7   Can't tell: foam is suitable for Classes A and B but not Classes E and F; Class D is not mentioned.

Q8   Can't tell: no comparison is drawn between the likelihood of flammable liquids and solids re-igniting.

Q9   True: first paragraph, fourth sentence: more in China than in any other country.

Q10 Can't tell: last paragraph, first sentence: Latin must have been displaced by another language but one is not stated.

Q11 True: last paragraph, fourth sentence: three time as many non-native speakers as native speakers.

Q12 Can't tell: last paragraph, last sentence: India is ranked above the United States, and Nigeria is ranked above the United Kingdom but the ranking of the United States in relation to Nigeria is not indicated.

Q13 True: first paragraph, last sentence: the canal network was doomed and investment was redirected into railways.

Q14 Can't tell: last paragraph, second and third sentences: no direct comparison of leisure and industrial use is made.

Q15 False: first paragraph, fifth sentence: quicker than by canal.

Q16   Can't tell: last paragraph, last sentence: there may be more boats but these are not necessarily all narrowboats.

Q17   True: last paragraph, sixth sentence: failure of a single system will not affect any other workstations.

Q18   False: last paragraph, seventh sentence: direct contradiction; only one computer can send and receive data at any one time.

Q19   True: last paragraph, last but one sentence: it is possible to infer that the network might grind to a halt if too many computers are added because there will be more collisions and each collision slows the system down.

Q20   True: last paragraph, eighth sentence: when joined to a common ring each computer must have another computer connected either side of it so every node on the loop is connected to two other nodes.

Q21   Can't tell: first paragraph, fourth sentence: the 154 includes dispensaries as well as hospitals.

Q22   True: first paragraph, third sentence: Exeter (1741), before Liverpool (1745) but after Bristol (1733) and York (1740).

Q23   False: last paragraph: Louis Pasteur's work is referred to as a theory and not a method of identifying the germ that is responsible for a disease.

Q24   False: second paragraph, last but one sentence, and last paragraph, first sentence: anaesthetics were not used in surgery prior to 1847 but there is nothing to suggest that the opiates and alcohol referred to in the second paragraph were not administered for pain relief.

Q25   True: first paragraph, final sentence: 8 hours with breaks at 2, 4 and 6 hours.

Q26   False: first paragraph, sixth sentence: temporary measure only.

Q27   True: last paragraph, fourth sentence: at a time normally spent sleeping, for example in the early hours of the morning.

Q28   Can't tell: there is no information given on reaction times.

Q29   True: second paragraph, third sentence states: covers old ground.

Q30   False: second paragraph, fifth sentence: patients are asked to tick boxes that request information about their sexuality; there is no compulsion to reveal information as suggested by the words 'must declare'.

Q31   Can't tell: third paragraph: the passage states only that the NHS suspended a nurse for offering to pray for an elderly patient. The information is insufficient to tell whether or not the NHS equality and diversity policy was breached so the answer should be can't tell.

Q32   False: first paragraph, first sentence: freedom of expression not of thought.

Q33   False: first paragraph, fourth sentence: about 65% (approximately two-thirds) of those that fail to meet the highest standards go on to be sold as Cripps Pink; the percentage of apples not meeting the Pink Lady™ standard is not specified.

Q34   Can't tell: no information is provided on the relative prices of Pink Lady™ and Sundowner™.

Q35   False: second paragraph, first sentence: the Cripps Red is stated to be equally popular to the Pink Lady™ in which case sales of its premium grade, the Sundowner™, would be less so.

Q36   True: first paragraph, fifth sentence and second paragraph, sixth sentence: colour intensity for Pink Lady™ and colour ratio for Sundowner™.

Q37   True: British Isles = all land masses (first paragraph); whereas the British Islands = UK + CI + IOM.

Q38   False: last paragraph, first and second sentences: Wales is part of Great Britain, so the Isle of Anglesey (Ynys Mon in Welsh) must also be part of Great Britain.

Q39   True: last paragraph, first sentence.

Q40   True: British Isles = all land masses (first paragraph); second paragraph. fourth sentence, CI and IOM are not part of the UK.

Q41   False: second paragraph, third sentence: carbon dioxide is the greenhouse gas not carbon monoxide.

Q42   Can't tell: third paragraph: not stated either way.

Q43   False: second paragraph, third sentence: nitrogen oxides also contribute to acid rain.

Q44   False: last paragraph: methane is not indicated to be a precursor chemical for ozone and acid rain; methane contributes to global warming.

Decision analysis

Q1   *Answer*: A. He was evicted from the house.

The code reads: HG, A(C18), 12 = personal male, increase (similar travel), house.

Explanation: Personal male translates as *He*, as per answers A and D; increase similar travel translates as *evicted*.

Q2   *Answer*: B. There are fines for illegally parking your car.

The code reads: 101(BA), 102(BD), 18B, K4 = money (opposite increase), rules (opposite positive), travel opposite, specific vehicle.

Explanation: Specific vehicle must refer to car so rule out answer D and E; money opposite increase could be pay, fines or fined so this does not help nor does travel opposite which indicates parking; rules opposite positive suggests negative rules or illegally, ie B.

Q3   *Answer*: D. The rising tide caused water damage.

The code reads: 8(B13), 8(14A) = water (opposite fall), water (problem increase).

Explanation: Water opposite fall translates as *rising* water and water problem increase could mean *water damage* or *flooding* but not great damage or increased the damage so eliminate A and C; eliminate B because More is not coded. E looks plausible but is rejected on the basis that tide is plural, which is not coded.

Q4   *Answer*: E. Passive smoking is a health risk.

The code reads: EH17(11 107), 104 105 = plural personal space (fire air), danger health.

Explanation: Answer C looks plausible because it translates plural personal as We; fire air as smoke, space as inhalation and danger health as unhealthy; however, C the concept of not (smoke) is not coded so C is eliminated; A does not make use of health, only danger, so A is eliminated; B introduces the concept of many, which is not coded, and D introduces the term cigarettes which is not coded. E combines all the concepts successfully if plural personal space (We space) refers to environment.

Q5   *Answer*: E. The son stole his father's fortune.

The code reads: B7(G), 19(5), H(G7), 7(101) = opposite large (male), take (wrong), personal (male large), large (money).

Explanation: Eliminate B and D since take (wrong) codes as *stole* rather than inherited; personal male codes for *his* so eliminate A; eliminate C because large is not coded, noting that *fortune* codes as large (money), ie answer E.

Q6   *Answer*: B. The e-mail was sent from an internet café.

The code reads: C(9),18(MB), BA(12 2) = similar (speak), travel (future opposite), opposite increase (house eat).

Explanation: Eliminate E as He is not coded; eliminate A and C which fail to include any concept of house eat, which in conjunction with opposite increase (reduce), is coded from internet café; both B and D correctly identify the past tense *was* coded by future opposite, but only B correctly codes *sent* as travel.

Q7   *Answer*: A. The court found him not guilty of the crime.

The code reads: C(102 12), H(BD5), (14 102) = similar (rules, house) personal (opposite positive, wrong), (problem, rules).

Explanation: Eliminate B and C which fail to code *court* as similar (rules, house); eliminate D and E which fail to code *crime* as problem rules, noting that personal (opposite positive, wrong) translates as *him not guilty*, ie answer A.

Q8   *Answer*: C. Men take home more pay than women.

The code reads: G(E1), 19(C12), A(C101), BG(E1) = male (plural person), take (similar house), increase (similar money), opposite male (plural person).

Explanation: The code supports all five answers for men, males, women and females; increase (similar money) is not same money or similar money so eliminate E and D, and also B because increase is linked with money not house; earn more (A) and more pay (C) could both code as increase (similar money) but A lacks the concept of take (similar house).

Q9   *Answer*: D. A mortgage is a loan paid back over many years.

The code reads: 7(12 101), (14 101), A16(7 6) = large (house money), (problem money), increase few (large time).

Explanation: Identify straight away that increase few (large time) codes *many years*, as stated in answer D, noting that large (house money) codes for mortgage and problem money for *paid back*; A is the second best interpretation of the code but an instalment is a payment which should incorporate the concept of money; B is wrong because it does not link the concept of money with house; C is wrong because expensive house would code as house (large money); E fails to include a concept of time.

Q10   *Answer*: E. Outpatients receive hospital care except at night.

The code reads: 1E(B105), C19, C(105 12), BD(B103) = person plural (opposite health), similar take, similar (health house), opposite positive (opposite day).

Explanation: Translate similar (health house) as hospital and eliminate answer B; translate opposite positive (opposite day) as not night and eliminate answer C, noting that E (*except at night*) is preferred to answers A and D (during the day).

Q11   *Answer*: C. Children receive weekly pocket money.

The code reads: E1(B7), C19, B(7 101), (15 6) = plural person (opposite large), similar take, opposite (large money), short time.

Explanation: Eliminate A and E because there is no coding for school meals or parents, respectively. Eliminate D because it conveys the concept of money but not opposite (large money); eliminate B because the concept of money has been introduced twice, as paid and wage, which leaves answer C, ignoring the word order.

Q12   *Answer*: C. Some people ride a motorcycle to work.

The code reads: A16(E1), 18(10), B(E)1, 4 = increase few (plural person), travel (work), opposite (plural) person, vehicle.

Explanation: Translate increased few to mean *some* so eliminate B and D; opposite (plural) person translates as single person; E contains no concept of vehicle, so eliminate it, noting that a motorcycle rather than a car is a single person vehicle, ie answer C.

Q13   *Answer*: E. The management stopped the strike.

The code reads: 10J, BD(18), B10 = work together, opposite positive (travel), opposite work.

Explanation: Work together is conceptualized in all five answers so ignore this initially; eliminate C and D which has no concept of travel and eliminate B which has no concept of work, noting that *stopped* (E) can code as negative travel but not *went* (A); stopped could code as opposite work but this is tenuous; ie answer E not A.

Q14   *Answer*: C. A child walks before it talks.

The code reads: B(7 1) H18, C(MB), 9 = opposite (large person), personal travel, similar (future opposite), speak.

Explanation: Eliminate A, B and D as these refer to people (plural person) not person; similar (future opposite) is similar (past) which translates as *before* in answer C, noting that personal travel is the code for *walks* and a *child* is opposite (large person).

Q15 *Answer*: B. business and E. successful.

Explanation: *Future* (C) is already coded in the table and *people* (D) is plural person; *optimistic* (A) can code as positive or happy; *business* and *successful* are very difficult to code from the table codes.

Q16 *Answer*: C. three and D. points.

Explanation: *Three* (C) and *points* (D) cannot be translated from any code in the table; *on* (B) is not needed to convey the message; *your* (E) can be coded using personal person (H1); *penalty* is difficult to code but problem rules 14(102), pain rules 110(102), or negative money rules BD101(102) could give a notion of it.

Q17 *Answer*: A. test and D. study.

Explanation: *Time* (B) is already coded (6); *well* (C) can code indirectly from positive health (D105); there is little concept of *test* (A) in the table, with situation rules (L102) being a very tenuous link, so *test* is one choice; *studying* could code as similar (work notes); however this is also tenuous, and as two answers are needed, *study* is the second choice, noting that spend can code from money (reduce) or expense (increase).

Q18 *Answer*: A. growth and E. parent.

Explanation: Child's *development* could code as child's increase; however, this does not indicate the notion of development as well as *growth* (A), which becomes the first choice; child can code as opposite old person (B204(1)) and *harm* as similar danger C(104) so hinder can be discounted; *parents* can code as together male, female, J(G, BG) however, this is convoluted, so parent is the second choice.

Q19 *Answer* A.

The code reads E1, 12, B(19,7)101 = we, house, opposite (take, large) money; ie we, house, (give small) money, or we paid a *small deposit* on the house. Answer B includes the concept of *deposit* (small money) but not of payment (opposite take); C is erroneous, stating large money; D and E fail to include *house*.

Q20 *Answer* C.

The code reads H, 2, BE, 11, 108, B(103) = personal, eat, opposite plural, fire, meal, opposite (day); ie I eat singular hot meal at night; A and D code for day not *night*; E fails to code *meal*; B is a close match but does not include opposite plural which codes for *one* in Answer C.

Q21   *Answer* B.

The code reads E1(J), BM19, L(B7,17) = plural person (together), opposite future take, situation (opposite large, space); ie people together taken small space situation. A and E fail to code the concept of *meeting* (people together); C has no notion of *conditions* only of *cramped* (small space); D is contrary to the sentence.

Q22   *Answer* C.

The code reads ΩK(Σ3),π,C11,16 = Improve miss, (opposite drink), better, plural (issue), other. Eliminate A and D which make reference to meals/eating rather than drink, noting that B, C and E all include a word that indicates a lack of fluid/drink. Eliminate B which uses the word drink twice but coded for only once. E looks plausible but erroneously codes 'higher' as 'better'; in addition the word 'people' is not coded for. C codes 'preferable' as 'better' and 'other issues' as 'plural issue other' which are clearly correct; 'missing' is coded as 'improve miss' and 'drought' as 'opposite drink'.

Q23   *Answer* D.

The code reads π17,◊4,C8 = Better future, communication computer, plural person. 'Plural person' can be picked out quickly to be either A(people), B(we) or D(generation) but not C or E which have no concept of it. Answer A contains no concept of 'better' and is also eliminated. Answer B fails to code 'communications'. Answer D correctly codes 'communication computer' as 'internet' and 'plural person' as 'generation'; 'better future' becomes 'bright futures'.

Q24   *Answer* E.

The code reads C8,(◊10 A 7), 17, (ΣN) = Plural person, (communicate technology behaviour increase), future(opposite solution). Rule out answer A which does not include the concept of 'Plural person' (people). Rule out B because 'more' (or increase) is associated with 'people' instead of 'communication technology'. Rule out C because it contains no concept of technology. Rule out D because it includes no concept of 'opposite solution' (problem).

Q25   *Answer* A.

The code reads λ3(Ω¥8) m Ω 11 = Special drink (improve function person), towards improve issue. All the answers look plausible at first sight, though 'water' in Answer C is unlikely to be the 'Special drink'. Answer D does not include any concept of person and can be ruled out. Answer C states 'improve themselves' rather than 'improve issue' and is ruled out.

Answer E does not include the concept of 'function person' merely stating 'helps me'; Answer B has the same deficit, whereas answer 'A' correctly expresses 'function' as 'think'.

Q26 *Answer* E.

The code reads AH, λ, 15, C8, π1 = Increase travel, special vehicle, plural person, better money. Every answer codes for 'plural person' so this is not helpful; the same applies to 'special vehicle'. We can see that answer A does not make any reference to 'money' and can be ruled out. Answers B and D do not contain the concept of 'travel' and can be ruled out. Answer C starts with 'I' which is not coded for, so C is ruled out. Answer E expresses all the concepts without introducing new ones.

Q27 *Answers* A and D. The message reads 'Men and women can solve problems with counselling and medication'. Looking at the table of codes we can see that 'Men' can be coded as 'opposite female' (Σ12), with women coded as 12 already. 'Solve problems' can be coded as 'improve opposite solution' (Ω(ΣN)). This means that we can eliminate 'Men' and 'Fix' as answer choices. Counselling is difficult to code from the existing table, so we can use 'Counsellor' (Answer A) linked to 'increase'. 'Medication' is also difficult to code and Drug (Answer D) is a direct alternative.

Q28 *Answers* A and C. The message reads 'Vans are better than cars for travelling in the country'. The table includes codes for 'better' and 'travel' so the answers 'Best' and 'Distance' are unlikely to be helpful. The answer choice 'People' can already be coded for using 'plural person' making it superfluous. There is no concept of 'country' in the table so 'Wilderness' (Answer A) is an answer choice when combined with 'reduce'. 'Cars' can be coded for as 'personal vehicle plural' (L15C), in which case 'High' (Answer C) 'personal vehicle plural' can be used to code Vans.

Quantitative reasoning

Q1 C. 10 out of 12 pupils = 83.3%.

Q2 E. 9 out of 10 pupils = 90.0%.

Q3 A. 7 out of 12 pupils = 58.3%.

Q4 D. 5 out of 7 pupils = 71.4%.

Q5 D. 1,701 = (100 − 83) = 17%; 1,701 ÷ 0.17 = 10,006.

Q6   B. 10,006 × (10 + 2)% = 1201; or 12/17 × 1701 = 1,201.

Q7   C. 0.83 × (3 ÷ 7) × 100 = 35.57%.

Q8   A. 35.57% × 10,006 = 3,559; 3,559 × (55 + 5)% = 2,136.

Q9   D. (20 × £3,500) + (40 × £4,000) = £70,000 +£160,000 = £230,000.

Q10   B. Bar at age 35–44 = 15 staff, of which two-thirds are men (given) = 10 men and 5 women. Sales by females = (5 × £3,000) + (10 × £3,000) + (5 × £3,500) = £62,500.

Q11   D. male total = £230,000 (question 9) + two-thirds × 15 × 3,500 = 265,000; female total = £62,500 (question 10); male + female = 327,500; percentage male = 80.9%.

Q12   C. male total = 265,000; female total = 62,500 × 1.1 = 68,750; male + female = 333,750; × 52 weeks = 17.36 million.

Q13   B. 90 ml/100 ml × 50 g × 9 kcal/g = 405 kcal.

Q14   E. 405 kcal from Calogen (question 13) and from Twocal per bottle: 21 × 2 × 4 = 168 carb; 8.4 × 2 × 4 = 67.2 protein; 8.9 × 2 × 9 = 160.2 fat; total per Twocal = 395.4; for 6 Bottles: 6 × 395.4 = 2,372.4; plus 405 = 2,777.4; 2,777.4 ÷ 2,550 = 1.09 = 109%.

Q15   A. Per Twocal: fat is 160.2; total per Twocal = 395.4 (from previous answer). Proportion: 160.2/395.4 = 0.405 × 100 = 41%.

Q16   D. Calogen: 30 ml/100 ml × 50 × 9 = 135; 1,940 − 135 = 1,805; total calories per 100 ml Twocal = 197.7 (Question 14); 1,805 ÷ 197.7 × 100 ml = 913 ml.

Q17   E. Valu = 2 × 8 × 2 × £10,000 = £320,000

Wilat = 3.5 × 6 × 3 × £10,000 = £630,000
Xsels = 1.5 × 10 × 1 × £10,000 = £150,000
Yamit = 2.5 × 5 × 4 × £10,000 = £500,000
Zonika = 3 × 5 × 6 × £10,000 = £900,000.

Q18   A. Cost per copy = 3.5p (Wilats) of which 1p = paper (given); therefore 2.5 p = toner; 2.5 ÷ 3.5 × 100% = 71%.

Q19   B. Cost per copy = 1.5p (Xsels) of which 1p = paper (given); double-sided copies cuts the paper costs in half = 0.5 p per copy saving ie 0.5 p × 10,000 × 1,000 = £50,000.

Q20 E. Cost per copy = 2.5 p (Yamit) of which 1p = paper (given)

At the normal A4 size: total cost = 2.5p × 4,000 × 5,000 = £500,000 = £200,000 paper + £300,000 toner. At the reduced A5 size, toner consumption = 50% = £150,000.

Q21 B. $\sqrt{\dfrac{cm \times kg}{3,600}} = \sqrt{\dfrac{180 \times 80}{3,600}} = \sqrt{4} = 2$

Q22 D. $2 = 1/60 \times \sqrt{170 \times h}$; $120 = \sqrt{170 \times h}$; squaring both sides: 14,400 = 170 h, giving h = 84.7 kg.

Q23 E. $\sqrt{\dfrac{cm \times kg}{3,600}} = \sqrt{\dfrac{160 \times 60}{3,600}} = \sqrt{\dfrac{16}{6}} = 4 \div \sqrt{6}$.

Q24 D. $BSA^2 \times 3,600 = cm \times kg$; 1.73 × 1.73 × 3,600 = 160 × kg giving new kg = 67.5; increase = 7.5 kg.

Q25 A. 3 across × (1,100 ÷ 80) = 3 × 13.75 ie 3 × 13 = 39.

Q26 D. 2 across × (1,100 ÷ 120) = 2 × 9.2 ie 2 × 9 = 18; 18 × £30 = £540.

Q27 C. small = 3 × 13 × £10 = £390; medium = 3 × 18 × £12 = £648; conventional = 3 × 18 × £20 = £1,080; large cube = 2 × 11 × 22 = £484; circular = £540.

Q28 E. most efficient stacking = 3 across × 18 along = 54 bales; least efficient stacking = 1 across × 13 along = 13 bales. Loss of stacking efficiency = (54 – 13)/54 × 100% = 75.9%.

Q29 B. 35 ml × 0.4% = 14 ml; 14 ml ÷ 10 ml × 8 g = 11.2 g.

Q30 D. max safe limit = 3 units = 3 × 10 ml = 30 ml pure alcohol; 30 ÷ 0.17 = 176 ml; 176 ÷ 35 = 5.03.

Q31 C. Vodka = 1.5 × 40% = 0.6; Tia Maria = 0.5 × 26.5% = 0.1325; Bailey's = 0.5 × 17%. = 0.085. Total = 0.6 + 0.1325 + 0.085 = 0.8175 measures of alcohol in 2.5 measures of drink = 32.7% ABV.

Q32 A. Maximum sensible limit is 4 units = 40 ml of pure alcohol; John consumes 150 ml × 1/3 × 0.17 = 8.5 ml + 50 ml × 0.4 = 20 ml; total = 28.5 ml = 71.3%.

Q33 E. Clearly not B. Phillip (Barbara slower) or D. Luke (Aran slower) so eliminate these two from the calculations.

Distance = speed × time and time = distance ÷ speed;
Barbara: time = 2/3 hr = 40 minutes (arrives 08.55 hrs);
Aran: time = 2/10 hr = 12 minutes (arrives 08.52 hrs);
Katie: time = 2/30 = 4 minutes (arrives 08.59 hrs), ie E Katie.

Q34 A. New average speed = 11; new time = 2 ÷ 11 × 60 = 10.9 minutes. Departs at 08.45 hrs arrives at 08.56 hrs.

Q35 A. Average speed = total distance ÷ total time; first leg: one mile at 3 mph = 0.33 hr; second leg one mile at 20 mph = 0.05 mph; total distance = 2 miles, total time = 0.38 hrs. Average speed = 2 ÷ 0.38 = 5.26 mph.

Q36 E. Barbara leaves at 08.15; Katie at 08.45 hrs, so Barbara has been walking for 30 minutes before Katie sets off, that is a minimum of 3 mph × 30/60 hr = 1.5 miles, so eliminate answers A, B, C and D, leaving only E. The exact solution is as follows: after 1.5 miles the 'extra' distance (d) walked by Barbara for time 't' to the point where they meet is given by d = 3t (distance = speed × time); so the total distance (D) to the meeting point is: D = 1.5 + 3t; then for Katie we have D = 30t (30 mph × t), so 30t = 1.5 + 3t giving 27t = 1.5 and then t = 1.5/27; substituting t in D = 30t gives D = 30 × 1.5/27 = 45/27 = 5/3 = 1.67 miles.

Another way to look at it is:
Barbara leaves at 08.15 at 3mph, Katie leaves at 08.45 at 30mph, with 1.5 miles travelled before Katie departs. Distance = speed x time. In minutes:
1.5 + 3/60t = 30/60t
1.5 + 0.05t = 0.5t
1.5 = 0.45t
1.5 / 0.45 = t = 3 and 1/3 minutes
At 0.5 miles per minute, this gives a total of 1.67 miles in 3 1/3 minutes

Abstract reasoning

Q1 Set A – Odd number of shapes (shading irrelevant)

Set B – Even number of shapes

1. A
2. A
3. B
4. A
5. B

Q2   Set A – Group of three similar shapes and two similar shapes

Set B – Group of three similar shapes

   6. B
   7. A
   8. C
   9. B
 10. B

Q3   Set A – Fifteen straight lines

Set B – Twelve straight lines

 11. B
 12. A
 13. A
 14. C
 15. B

Q4   Set A – Odd number of shaded overlapping regions

Set B – Even number of shaded overlapping regions

 16. A
 17. B
 18. A
 19. A
 20. B

Q5   Set A – Number of unshaded triangles equals number of shaded circles

Set B – Number of shaded triangles equals number of shaded circles

 21. A
 22. B
 23. C
 24. C
 25. A

Q6   Set A – Number of shapes in top and middle rows equals number of shapes in bottom row

Set B – Number of shapes in middle row minus top row equals number of shapes in bottom row

26. A
27. B
28. C
29. A
30. B

Q7   Set A – Big shape has a shaded diamond in the 0, 90, 180 or 270 degree position

Set B – Big shape has a shaded triangle in the 0, 90, 180 or 270 degree position

31. C
32. B
33. A
34. A
35. B

Q8   Set A – Three similar shapes in a line

Set B – Four similar shapes in a block

36. C
37. A
38. B
39. A
40. C

Q9   Set A – Where there are two similar shapes, only the smaller is shaded

Set B – Where there are two similar shapes, both are shaded

41. C
42. B
43. B
44. A
45. C

Q10   Choose ONE drawing that best completes the statement

    46. 4 (double the number of sides)

    47. 1 (size of shapes switches around and borders touch)

    48. 3 (simple reflection)

    49. 1 (shapes remain in the same position; unshaded shapes become
        shaded and vice versa)

Find the ODD ONE OUT

    50. 2 (one-quarter shaded, not half shaded)

    51. 2 (the triangle has no similar pair)

    52. 3 (there is no triangle on top of the circle)

Q11   Which of the five numbered drawings comes next in the series?

    53. 2 (90° degree rotation; turn the book if unsure)

    54. 2 (thick line is fixed; thin line moves gradually down)

    55. 1 (square, circle, triangle repeat pattern; triangle is the next shaded
        shape)

Situational judgement

Q1   *Answer*: A very inappropriate thing to do.

    Explanation: This is inappropriate because it implies he is sharing
confidential information. It may even be dangerous. The reality could be that
the patient faces serious challenges and his false reassurance could make
matters worse.

Q2   *Answer*: A very inappropriate thing to do.

    Explanation: Discussing the details of a patient without their express
consent, even with a relative, breaches patient confidentiality.

Q3   *Answer*: A very inappropriate thing to do.

    Explanation: Once again, discussing the details of a patient without their
express consent, even with a relative, breaches patient confidentiality.

Q4   *Answer*: Inappropriate but not awful.

    Explanation: The clinician has inadvertently breached patient confidentiality.
If they are not made aware of this it may happen again.

Q5   *Answer*: A very inappropriate thing to do.

Explanation: In speaking about the patient in such an unguarded way, the clinician is breaching patient confidentiality. However, in pointing this out in front of those waiting, the surgery manager may well compound the situation by bringing their attention to what has already been said.

Q6   *Answer*: Very appropriate.

Explanation: This ensures that the clinician becomes aware of their own behaviour and the subtleties of how confidentiality may be compromised, and is given the opportunity to learn from their mistake.

Q7   *Answer*: A very inappropriate thing to do.

Explanation: It is totally inappropriate to discuss a patient in a public place. By continuing the conversation he is inviting further information to be revealed.

Q8   *Answer*: Inappropriate but not awful.

Explanation: The result is important therefore simply to raise the matter at the next meeting is not sufficient a response and is not active enough. This response would become very inappropriate if he forgot to raise the matter at the meeting.

Q9   *Answer*: A very inappropriate thing to do.

Explanation: This response does nothing but seek to attribute blame; it will not serve the interest of the patient because it is not focused on finding their important test result. It will also undermine good team working.

Q10   *Answer*: A very inappropriate thing to do.

Explanation: This is a stressed and passive response that will make a bad situation worse. It is unsustainable and could lead to mistakes or a failure in maintaining the required professionalism.

Q11   *Answer*: Very appropriate.

Explanation: This response is very appropriate because it seeks to understand the reasons for the new form and asks for support to manage a heavy workload.

Q12   *Answer*: Appropriate but not ideal.

Explanation: This response is appropriate as it gets the matter out in the open in a positive manner and allows collaborative and supportive team working. It is not ideal because it fails to inform or involve management.

Q13 *Answer*: Inappropriate but not awful.

Explanation: The consultant has taken the initiative in arranging for more time and time is essential if communication is to be effective, however it fails to address the possibility that additional factors may need considering. For example, the services of an interpreter or advocate may be required.

Q14 *Answer*: Very appropriate.

Explanation: The consultant has taken clear initiative and instigated direct communication to establish the patient's needs. This means she will have the time to make appropriate arrangements in advance of the meeting.

Q15 *Answer*: A very inappropriate thing to do.

Explanation: This response is unlikely to improve the patient's understanding because it does not address the cause of it. The likely outcome is that the patient will again fail to understand.

Q16 *Answer*: Very appropriate.

Explanation: This response is highly proactive. It makes good use of the available support and expertise in the team, is collaborative and helps build good practice.

Q17 *Answer*: A very inappropriate thing to do.

Explanation: The response shows a lack of trust in the ability of colleagues. A clinic depends on collaborative working and the sharing of responsibility.

Q18 *Answer*: Very appropriate.

Explanation: The response is an example of direct communication, responsible collaborative working and sharing of information. It is likely to ensure the patient's complications are addressed and the colleague is properly prepared.

Q19 *Answer*: A very inappropriate thing to do.

Explanation: Effective team working involves mutual trust and respect for one another's professionalism. The response indicates a low expectation in the colleague's clinical abilities and will contribute to a poor working relationship.

Q20 *Answer*: Appropriate but not ideal.

Explanation: the response is trusting of the colleague's clinical abilities but it is not proactive nor supportive so is less than ideal.

Q21   *Answer*: Very important.

Explanation: The point made is very important. Stefan's self-medicating behaviour is contrary to his own profession and potentially dangerous.

Q22   *Answer*: Of minor importance.

Explanation: The point to consider is of minor importance. Whilst ethics are important in medicine, the issues are not necessarily clear-cut and in this case they cloud the problem.

Q23   *Answer*: Important.

Explanation: The point made is important. There are potentially risks to health which need to be addressed.

Q24   *Answer*: Not important at all.

Explanation: The fact that there was nothing in the purse to identify its owner is of no importance as the owner could return to claim their property.

Q25   *Answer*: Not important at all.

Explanation: The passing of a month does not change the fact that it is someone else's property.

Q26   *Answer*: Not important at all.

Explanation: The money does not belong to the receptionist. This is a question of integrity and the sum involved is irrelevant.

Q27   *Answer*: Not important at all.

Explanation: This information informs how the staff member might frame their response or the timing of it but not whether to tell her or not.

Q28   *Answer*: Very important.

Explanation: The wishes of the next of kin must be considered and an action that is not in accordance with their wishes would need to be agreed with them or someone in authority beforehand.

Q29   *Answer*: Important.

Explanation: the patient's past wishes are important and must be taken into account in responding to their current requests.

Q30   *Answer*: Very important.

Explanation: A 14 year old is a dependant and witnessing violence is harmful.

Q31   *Answer*: Important.

Explanation: Before sharing this information the clinician should seek to obtain the patient's consent and explain the importance of sharing it.

Q32   *Answer*: Not important at all.

Explanation: The lack of collaboration from the victim would be irrelevant to how the clinician responded to the disclosure.

Q33   *Answer*: Appropriate but not ideal.

Explanation: Safety does come first, making this an appropriate response. However, in this situation with a doctor potentially contracting blood-borne diseases for herself and her baby, it is important to also be sensitive. The very appropriate response would look more like 'Acknowledge the distress of the doctor and reassure her, before swiftly locating and dispose of the needle'.

Q34   *Answer*: Very appropriate.

Explanation: A sample from the patient is vitally important as it will reveal if they have any current infectious diseases. You may think that the sample from the doctor should not be taken immediately, but actually later when any infection would become apparent. In fact, a sample of the doctor's blood should also be taken as a baseline as they may have diseases which they are currently unaware of, for example. They will also need a sample several weeks or months later, but it may not be necessary if the patient is clear of disease.

Q35   *Answer*: A very inappropriate thing to do.

Explanation: Reporting adverse events in medical practice is not about allocating blame, but preventing future accidents. It is unlikely that the doctor will be penalized in any way, but this could inform the practice of dealing with severely needlephobic patients for example.

Q36   *Answer*: Inappropriate but not awful.

Explanation: Irrational fears and phobias are not necessarily the fault of the patient, and even though the majority of people can cope with a painful situation, it does not mean that he must be able to. Blaming the patient after the event is not helpful or useful. Nevertheless, putting some context on his fear, such as the numbers of patients, may help him to understand his own problem. Note that a very inappropriate response would be to scold or shout at the patient, rather than to remind him of this issue with regards to safety.

Q37   *Answer*: Very appropriate.

Explanation: It is sensible for a student to research whenever they have an application to write: as you will no doubt have done for your university application! It is also important to tread carefully on the thin line that separates plagiarism from learning: it is not acceptable to simply copy an application form that was a previous success. Regardless of whether or not this is successful (for example, if the assessment panel changes, they may not notice that this was very similar to a previous year's application), it is not ethical to simply copy: however, from the wording of the question, adopting style, tone and structure are very general things. For example, a conversational style, humorous tone and five-point structure are not uniquely copyrighted, and so can be sensibly used, particularly if they were successful! Taking whole sentences and very slightly altering them is quite different from this.

Q38   *Answer*: Inappropriate but not awful.

Explanation: Unlike the previous question, the fine-line between cheating and learning have been crossed, so this is inappropriate. However, the degree of falsehood is mild: the student was a co-founder of the project and was involved in it, which is less awful than simply making up the whole enterprise.

Q39   *Answer*: Appropriate but not ideal.

Explanation: I expect that most of you expected this to be inappropriate: however consider the following. What constitutes making up a learning point? The student may not have seen first-hand a team approach to research, but they may have reflected on the negative sides of a lone scientist approach to solving problems, and concluded that approaches they have seen elsewhere are superior. In the context of a short application letter, they may present this as 'learned about the role of teamwork'. It is not ideal, however, as they have slightly misrepresented the issue, and a very appropriate response might frame it as 'learning about the problems of solitary research'.

Q40   *Answer*: Very appropriate.

Explanation: In the case of work distribution where there is not a single specified leader, agreement of the group can be helpful to the student. If all persons share the opinion she is lazy, this will be informative. However, if others do not feel she is being lazy, this can prompt further discussion. Either way, the information is of key importance to decision making.

Q41 *Answer*: Appropriate but not ideal.

Explanation: Discussion regarding work distribution can be helpful, and is more personable than e-mail which can diffuse the tension. However, it is not ideal as there is a delay in surmounting this issue by waiting until the next session.

Q42 *Answer*: A very inappropriate thing to do.

Explanation: A mature response to a criticism would be to try and assess its truth or falsehood, which the previous answers have indicated. Working in a group also demands some compromise. Therefore, immediately rushing to a higher authority without exploring other steps first is a very poor choice of action.

Q43 *Answer*: A very inappropriate thing to do.

Explanation: Patients are free to choose their treatment and determine their movement, except under special circumstances such as posing a risk to the public or themselves through a mental health issue or disease requiring quarantine. Physically restraining a patient in these circumstances is not ethical and may result in legal charges also.

Q44 *Answer*: Inappropriate but not awful.

Explanation: Medical investigations are usually undertaken with the express purpose of helping patients, and so repeatedly missing such an opportunity is unhelpful. However, presenting the facts in a threatening manner, given the scenario, could well inflame the situation.

Q45 *Answer*: Very appropriate.

Explanation: Reasoning with patients should be the first line of action for diffusing tense hospital situations. Offering some proactive form of help may aid in this regard, and could also prompt more rapid action on behalf of the patient.

Q46 *Answer*: Very important.

Explanation: The GP must explain serious and common risks to the patient, as failure to do so might result in manifest harm to him, even if this is an unlikely scenario.

Q47 *Answer*: Very important.

Explanation: Pain management should be undertaken as a cooperative exercise between doctor and patient, and trying new medications is the first step which could solve the problem at hand.

Q48   *Answer*: Important.

Explanation: Doctors should have a comprehensive understanding of the effects and side effects of the range of treatments available to patients. These data are important, but may be difficult to read up on in the context of this active consultation. All doctors should be engaged in lifelong learning, so this is important.

Q49   *Answer*: Not important at all.

Explanation: In the case of a vomiting patient, giving them oral medications may simply result in them being thrown back up and not being absorbed. Intravenous medication and rehydration would be far more suitable in this case.

Q50   *Answer*: Very important.

Explanation: Severe outbreaks of disease such as Ebola, swine flu and H5N7 flu tend to have geographical boundaries: therefore this is a critical question in establishing whether or not this patient may need quarantining, and the doctor may need to use protective clothing when treating him. Compare this to the question which follows.

Q51   *Answer*: Of minor importance.

Explanation: Compared to having a highly infectious disease from abroad, the eating of a dodgy or unusual food is not of high importance, and may be a red herring. Therefore, this question has minor usefulness in the next steps to be undertaken by the doctor.

Q52   *Answer*: Important.

Explanation: A dehydrated patient who looks severely unwell can warrant senior input, once the junior doctor has stabilized him and established some key information. This is important, but not immediately necessary.

Q53   *Answer*: Very important.

Explanation: Looking up injuries which were suffered in the past gives insight into a pattern: for example, repeated trauma, unusual or unexplained injuries, which may indicate child abuse. This must not be overlooked.

Q54   *Answer*: Of minor importance.

Explanation: This information is not critical, but could shed some light onto the family environment, how busy the parents are. However, it is not of direct importance.

Q55   *Answer*: Very important.

Explanation: Multiple or hidden injuries, patterns such as burn-marks, cigarette marks or bite wounds are more indicative of child abuse. A full examination is very important in this case.

Q56   *Answer*: Inappropriate but not awful.

Explanation: The student refuses to cheat himself, which is an appropriate thing to do, but by taking no further action, exposes the public to doctors who have not been properly assessed in their knowledge.

Q57   *Answer*: A very inappropriate thing to do.

Explanation: This involves not only personal cheating but also encouraging dishonest academic behaviour in his peers. Terrible!

Q58   *Answer*: Appropriate but not ideal.

Explanation: Cheating in a vocational examination is dangerous for the public and also displays unethical behaviour, and therefore should be dealt with. In this case, the student will be handled by higher authority, but an opportunity has been missed for the student to come clean, and also for any effort to save the friendship.

Q59   *Answer*: Very appropriate.

Explanation: In the first instance, appealing to the better nature of the student may allow him to redeem himself by reporting the situation, and also be in the better position to tackle the problem lecturer who is also at fault. Regardless of the outcome, the discussion is very appropriate.

Q60   *Answer*: Very appropriate.

Explanation: The doctor acts in a professional manner to dissuade the patient, without needing to damage the therapeutic relationship which is built.

Q61   *Answer*: A very inappropriate thing to do.

Explanation: The doctor lies to the patient, which could later harm their clinical relationship, and acts in a dishonest way which is not necessary to diffuse the situation.

Q62   *Answer*: Appropriate but not ideal.

Explanation: The refusal of a patient's advances is appropriate when they are unwanted: however the manner in which it is done is harmful to their clinical relationship.

Q63   *Answer*: Appropriate but not ideal.

Explanation: This is a close one: The action does not deal with the issue at hand, and could therefore be seen as technically inappropriate. However, avoiding the topic may allow the question to be bypassed and the session to be concluded, and therefore this is an appropriate, but not ideal response as the patient may 'get the hint' and not raise the issue again, thereby completing the criteria for 'appropriate' as it tackles the situation.

Q64   *Answer*: Important.

Explanation: This information is important to the situation and other helpers: however given that no one else has medical experience, it is not the most important thing as he must just cope to the best of his abilities.

Q65   *Answer*: Very important.

Explanation: In the event of a collapsed person, having people nearby to consult with and ask for assistance is of high importance in managing the situation and dividing labour.

Q66   *Answer*: Very important.

Explanation: Obtaining information regarding a collapsed person is vital to their treatment: information could include causes for collapse such as a heart arrhythmia or insulin-dependent diabetes, and they may have witnessed other causes such as alcohol intoxication or head trauma.

Q67   *Answer*: Of minor importance.

Explanation: The inconvenience caused to others is of minor importance, as the student must weigh up the risks of the patient's life and health compared to a delay in transport for a large number of people. Given his inexperience, his threshold for recommending such a descent may be lower than a confident, experienced clinician who may be able to manage the situation.